TRADITION AND RENEWAL

CENTER FOR LATIN AMERICAN
AND CARIBBEAN STUDIES

Number 2

Published in conjunction with the

OFFICE OF INTERNATIONAL
PROGRAMS AND STUDIES

TRADITION AND RENEWAL

Essays on Twentieth-Century
Latin American Literature and Culture

Edited by

Merlin H. Forster

UNIVERSITY OF ILLINOIS PRESS
Urbana   Chicago   London

LIBRARY OF CONGRESS CATALOGING IN PUBLICATION DATA

Main entry under title:

Tradition and renewal: essays on twentieth-century
Latin American literature and culture

"Center for Latin American and Caribbean Studies,
Number 2."
Includes bibliographical references and index.
1. Latin American literature—20th century—History
and criticism—Addresses, essays, lectures. I. Forster,
Merlin H., ed.
PQ7081.T78   860'.9   74–31179
ISBN 0-252-00440-X

El cosmopolitismo, que hemos de aca-
tar como una irresistible necesidad de
nuestra formación, no excluye, ni ese
sentimiento de fidelidad a lo pasado,
ni la fuerza directriz y plasmante con
que debe el genio de la raza imponerse
en la refundición de los elementos que
constituirán al americano definitivo
del futuro.

Rodó, *Ariel*

Contents

Preface   ix
Robert E. Scott

Introduction   1
Merlin H. Forster

Latin American *Vanguardismo*: Chronology and Terminology   12
Merlin H. Forster

Graça Aranha and Brazilian Modernism   51
Anoar Aiex

Notes on Regional and National Trends in Afro-Brazilian
Cult Music   68
Gerard H. Béhague

The Black Presence and Two Brazilian Modernists: Jorge
de Lima and José Lins do Rêgo   81
Richard A. Preto-Rodas

Native and Foreign Influences in Contemporary Mexican
Fiction: A Search for Identity   102
Luis Leal

The Function of Myth in Fernando del Paso's *José Trigo*   129
Dagoberto Orrantia

Four Contemporary Mexican Poets: Marco Antonio Montes
de Oca, Gabriel Zaid, José Emilio Pacheco, Homero Aridjis   139
Merlin H. Forster

Jenaro Prieto: The Man and His Work   157
Thomas C. Meehan

From *Criollismo* to the Grotesque: Approaches to José Donoso   208
    Kristen F. Nigro

Contributors   233

Index   235

Preface

This volume is the result of a collaborative program of humanities field studies on twentieth-century Latin America carried out over several years by members of the University of Illinois Center for Latin American Studies. In April, 1970, five faculty participants, together with Professor Aníbal Sánchez-Reulet (University of California at Los Angeles), held an introductory colloquium attended by a large group of Illinois staff members and students interested in Latin America. At that time they discussed the program's general goals and suggested ways of integrating individual research projects into the collective operation.

During the summer of 1970 and the following academic year, eight projects were carried out in various countries, with particular emphasis on Mexico, Argentina, Brazil, and Chile. After preparation of preliminary research findings, a three-session colloquium met in May, 1972, to discuss "Native versus Foreign Influences in Twentieth-Century Latin American Culture and Literature." Five faculty members and three doctoral candidates presented papers in English, Spanish, and Portuguese for discussion by the staff and students of social science and humanities departments. This volume includes revised and expanded versions of the colloquium offerings together with two studies based on program-supported investigation which were presented orally elsewhere.

The introduction places each essay within the context of a single general theme: the effects of rapid change on traditional humanistic norms in Latin America. It can do so because cooperation in planning the humanities program and close interaction among the participants in discussing preliminary versions of their individual contributions produced a nucleus of shared insights into the nature of cultural and literary change. One important consequence of this relationship is that every study reinforces the others, enhancing their collective impact considerably.

The Latin American humanities program was given financial assistance from the Center for International Comparative Studies and the Office of International Programs and Studies at the University of Illinois, and that support is acknowledged with appreciation. In the same spirit, the university's Department of Spanish, Italian, and Portuguese has generously released time from teaching responsibilities and provided funds for research assistants. Administrative and editorial responsibility for the program was assumed by Professor Merlin H. Forster, and Dorothy Osborne handled the typing and reproduction of several successive versions of these materials with her usual skill and dispatch.

This humanities research program is another result of a vigorous Center for Latin American and Caribbean Studies at the University of Illinois. The administrative help provided by its director and its director of research and the opportunity for cross-disciplinary contact it has given its associates make this sort of collective investigation practical and significant.

ROBERT E. SCOTT
Associate Director
Center for International
Comparative Studies

Introduction

Merlin H. Forster

In an essay on the intellectual and artistic currents of the nineteenth and twentieth centuries, Eugen Weber describes the common interpretative technique of seeing movements, centuries, and
generations as discrete and limited wholes,[1] with each unit following closely upon its predecessor in disciplined and easily identifiable
ranks like a military parade. The seventeenth century, for example,
is perceived as classical, and it in turn is followed by the rationality
of the eighteenth century. The nineteenth century is both romantic
and scientific, and in the same processional sequence the twentieth
century will pass on, leaving one or two key words which will characterize it.

Several fundamental problems arise in connection with this view.
In the first place, the flow of time is constant ("La inconsútil tela
de nuestros males," as Rubén Darío suggests), and the theoretical
limits used by scholars for easier interpretation at times impose
artificial seams or boundaries in that flow. Classicism and romanticism, for example, have persisted far beyond the bounds of the
period in which they were considered to be in full flower. At the
same time, that temporal flow seems confused to a viewer from
within and might lead him to describe his own age with the often-
quoted opening words from Dickens' *A Tale of Two Cities* on the
moment of the French Revolution: "It was the best of times, it was
the worst of times...." It is only from the perspective of a later time

[1] Eugen Weber, *Paths to the Present: Aspects of European Thought from Romanticism to Existentialism* (New York: Dade, 1960), p. 4.

that the confused welter of actual reality becomes in any way clear.

In spite of such problems, however, it is possible to make a case for the uniqueness of what we might term the "twentieth century," at least as it extends from about 1910 to the present. In many areas of human activity the magnitude of change during those few decades is probably unequaled by any other period of comparable length. To begin with, the scientific and technical developments of the nineteenth century produced an incredibly complex flowering. The impact of Darwin, Freud, and Einstein on scientific thought can be seen throughout the current century, and the development of several technical and industrial processes revolutionized transportation and communications. For example, the refinement of the internal combustion engine and its wide use in the automobile and the airplane brought about profound alterations in individual and collective transportation, and the use of radio and ultimately of television has caused the same kind of change in communications. In a few short years man has gone from the beginnings of heavier-than-air flight to the intricate techniques of lunar travel and interplanetary explorations. At the same time, the massive industrialization which has made these things possible has also produced in many people a feeling of depersonalization. The patterns established by the early automobile assembly lines are carried to an extreme degree in increasing mechanization and computerization; the reduction of many things to numbers which can be scanned by computers, by which communication on a personal level is reduced to a minimum, weighs heavily at times.

The twentieth century also has been a period of war on a scale previously unknown. Modern military weaponry, beginning with the aircraft, the poison gases, and the submarines of World War I and developing through the atomic bomb of World War II to the extensive use of napalm and defoliants in the Vietnam war, has brought about death, destruction, and human suffering on an unprecedented scale. Whole societies have been made the objects of genocide. The Spanish Civil War was a prelude to the world-wide conflict which began in 1939, and the Bolshevik Revolution in 1917 is important for its long-term ideological effect and its influence on the balance of world political power. The tensions of a protracted "cold war," with its nuclear possibilities for complete world destruction, form a unique and disquieting characteristic of a bellicose age.

In the years since 1910, the arts have expressed the same sense of violence and rapid change, and through insistent formal and tonal experimentations they have communicated the stresses and the disconnection of the period. For example, the frequently dissonant and fragmented creations of such giants as Igor Stravinsky in music and Pablo Picasso in painting revolutionized artistic expression early in the century and decisively affected that of more recent decades. The Dadaists and the surrealists early probed the absurdity and the complexity of perception and experience, while such thinkers as Jean-Paul Sartre and Albert Camus later evolved an influential view of contemporary man and his circumstance. In literature, the innovations of Marcel Proust, James Joyce, Franz Kafka, T. S. Eliot, and William Faulkner produced a progressively more involved literary form in which linear structures give way to more subtle approaches involving associative patterns—the use of symbol, myth, and contrastive procedures which demand increasingly greater reader participation in the creative act.

The Twentieth Century in Latin America

The Argentine critic Luis Harss entitles the English edition of a series of interviews with Latin American writers *Into the Mainstream*, and it would seem that that phrase might well serve as a synthesis for the entire twentieth century in Latin America. Europe had traditionally been the model for Latin American societies and the mecca for its intellectuals, but in the early years of the century this influence began to wane. The view of a Europe laid to waste by two international conflicts and uprooted from its own traditional cultural values caused Latin Americans to look more assiduously toward their own realities. The United States, which shared with Latin America a past colonial mentality, exercised a much stronger influence after the Spanish-American War of 1898, but it has subsequently intervened in the affairs of a number of Latin American countries, and its industrial and technological production has in turn led to a new kind of economic and cultural dependence. Latin America, progressively more alienated from Europe and pressured by the dominating force of the United States, was obliged to search for unique regional and national definitions.

Although the Spanish-American War was a matter of considerable moment for the Latin American republics, the real opening of a turbulent modern age was the Mexican Revolution, which extended through the entire second decade of the century. This long and violent conflict, which essentially tore Mexico asunder and reconstructed her in a different form, was a radical example for other sister republics. The Cuban Revolution, of almost fifty years later, is the only series of events that can rival the Mexican Revolution of 1910 in political and social significance. Between these two revolutions lie decades of political and social ferment throughout all of Latin America. Strong men rose and fell, military intervention in political affairs was common (particularly in Argentina, Brazil, and Guatemala), and university and labor reforms were pressed on all sides. While the early years were, as Jean Franco points out, a time of hope spurred on by the Mexican Revolution and by the somewhat more distant Bolshevik Revolution in Russia,[2] the more recent decades have been marked by the influence of *caudillos* (Vargas in Brazil, Perón in Argentina, Rojas Pinilla in Colombia, Trujillo in the Dominican Republic, and others) , the establishment of revolutionary military governments such as the current Peruvian junta, the election and overthrow of a Marxist government under Salvador Allende in Chile, and Perón's return to Argentina after a lengthy exile.

In areas outside politics the move toward independence and change has been no less notable. In economic development, for example, Latin America has progressed since the Mexican Revolution from a backwater producer of unprocessed raw materials to an area in the throes of industrialization. Movements toward agrarian reform have occurred in many Latin American countries and have been responsible for fundamental changes in agricultural production, but other countries are still dependent largely on agricultural and mineral exports, and inflationary pressures and changing world markets continue to create serious problems for them. Population

2 Jean Franco, *The Modern Culture of Latin America: Society and the Artist* (Middlesex: Penguin, 1970), p. 83.

in Latin America is increasing more rapidly than in any other region of the world, and many countries are aware, perhaps for the first time, of the ecological and racial pressures of such growth.

In the arts and in architecture the twentieth century has been a particularly fertile period. The influence of Europe and the United States has, of course, continued to be strong, but events occurring closer at hand have had perhaps even more force. For example, the Mexican Revolution produced its own artistic representation in the form of the "revolutionary" novel, which many consider a unique Mexican contribution to world literature. Even more commented on has been the development of the Mexican muralist school of painters. Such figures as Diego Rivera, José Clemente Orozco, and David Alfaro Siqueiros have achieved worldwide renown for their graphic portrayals of the complex and changing face of a revolutionized Mexico. Under their influence, artists such as the Ecuadorian Oswaldo Guayasamín and the Brazilian Cândido Portinari have expanded on the themes of indigenous reality. At the same time, a number of other painters have moved away from the pictorial realism of the muralists; examples are the Mexican Rufino Tamayo, the Venezuelan Alejandro Otero, and the Argentine Emilio Petorutti. Among younger figures, the Mexicans José Luis Cuevas and Alberto Gironella and the Argentine Julio Le Parc stand out in an art which now consistently receives worldwide attention.

Latin American architecture is another area which can boast of a number of figures of international reputation. The Brazilian Oscar Neimeyer, the Mexican Juan O'Gorman, and the Spanish-Mexican Félix Candela enjoy wide acclaim for their work, and the design of such sites as the university campuses of Mexico and Caracas, the anthropological museum of Mexico City, and the new Brazilian capital city Brasília stand as unique architectural achievements. Finally, musical expression in Latin America, which may also be strongly identified with the nationalistic tendencies visible in the other art forms, should be mentioned. In this expressive medium the Brazilians Heitor Villa-Lobos and Camargo Guarnieri, the Argentine Alberto Ginastera, and the Mexicans Carlos Chávez and Silvestre Revueltas are justly considered in the first rank.

In literature the same movement away from previous European and peninsular models is evident. Rubén Darío's modernism (1880–1910) was perhaps the first Hispanic literary movement in which peninsular authors did not play a dominant role, and this pattern was to be repeated many times in succeeding decades. For example, it is significant that three of the last four Nobel awards for literature in the Spanish language have been to Spanish Americans (Gabriela Mistral, 1947; Miguel Angel Asturias, 1967; and Pablo Neruda, 1971), and the vitality of Brazilian poetry and prose fiction makes Brazil the dominant literary force in Portuguese.

Among the various literary genres, poetry underwent the earliest and most significant development. It registers the varied achievements of such poets as the Chileans Vicente Huidobro and Pablo Neruda, the Peruvian César Vallejo, and the Brazilians Carlos Drummond de Andrade and Jorge de Lima during the early years of the century and, more recently, the attainments of such figures as the Mexican Octavio Paz, the Chilean Nicanor Parra, the Nicaraguan Ernesto Cardenal, and the Brazilians João Cabral de Melo Neto and Haroldo de Campos. The development of prose fiction also shows a similar temporal division. The period between the two world wars witnessed the appearance of such "classic" figures as the Uruguayan Horacio Quiroga, the Argentines Eduardo Mallea and Ricardo Güiraldes, the Chilean Eduardo Barrios, the Colombian José Eustasio Rivera, the Venezuelan Rómulo Gallegos, the Mexicans Mariano Azuela and Agustín Yáñez, the Brazilians José Lins do Rêgo and Jorge Amado. Since 1945 a unique "boom" in prose fiction began with such transitional figures as the Guatemalan Miguel Angel Asturias, the Cuban Alejo Carpentier, and the Argentine Jorge Luis Borges. More recent creators of what is now termed the "new novel" are the Argentines Ernesto Sábato and Julio Cortázar, the Uruguayan Juan Carlos Onetti, the Mexicans Juan Rulfo and Carlos Fuentes, the Brazilian João Guimarães Rosa, the Chilean José Donoso, the Cubans José Lezama Lima and Guillermo Cabrera Infante, the Peruvian Mario Vargas Llosa, and the Colombian Gabriel García Márquez. In sum, like the other major art forms in Latin America, literature has come of age during the twentieth century.

Native versus Foreign

A constant problem area in Latin American culture and literature during the more than six decades since 1910 has been the harmonizing of indigenous values with those which have their origins outside the national area or outside Latin America. On the one hand, many artists and critics have insisted on the primacy of indigenous themes and characters and have bent every effort to make those elements functional in their works. A number of terms have been used to designate this insistent attitude, among them *mundonovismo, criollismo, americanismo literario,* or *literary and cultural nationalism.* In accordance with this view, stress is placed on the identity of national areas and on Spanish America or Latin America as a cultural frame. Attention is focused on the local landscape and the people of the native region, especially the rural areas where manners are most different from those of Europe.[3] *Criollismo* seems most securely rooted in prose fiction and the essay; indeed, whole series of novelistic efforts and representational essays depend on assiduous use of American realities.

On the other hand, there are many who have maintained that Latin America is too provincial in its views and that its only salvation is modernization through increased contact with literary and cultural developments in other areas of the world. According to this opinion, the technical revolutions of surrealism and cubism are of infinitely greater importance than the depiction of a backward rural society limited by the Indian, the black, and severe sociopolitical problems. Artists and critics who maintain this position, generally designated as "avant-garde," "universalists," or "vanguardists," see art as individual, international, and experimental, and they stress freedom to innovate and the autonomy of artistic experience.

There is a third and more eclectic view of these matters, particularly among more recent figures. Influence from Europe and the United States is recognized, but at the same time a national or a Latin American frame of reference is considered a necessary part of artistic creation. This position seems to have evolved naturally

3 *Ibid.,* p. 53.

out of the protracted disagreements between Americanists and vanguardists. It not only points up that unique blend of influences which most characterizes America, but it is also, in many ways, a mark of maturity in Latin American art.

Essays on the Theme

Keeping in mind the foregoing discussions of the twentieth century in the western world and in Latin America, as well as the description of the specific problem of local versus cosmopolitan values, we may now appropriately consider the individual studies and place them within this framework. At the outset it should be emphasized that this volume does not attempt to be a complete or panoramic view of Latin American culture and literature during the twentieth century. It is rather a group of research studies focused on various topics and various national areas and organized around a single problematic theme: the relationship between traditional indigenous values and the insistent pressures of a larger world view and modern technical renovations. Certain threads of unity and development do become apparent, however. For example, the studies progress roughly from general to more specific, and they tend to cluster at the same time around several important national areas. In many of the studies there is a careful use of cross-cultural or crossnational frames of reference, while in others chronology is used as a basis for classification and development.

Although the essays are not divided formally into sections, it is possible to discern four interrelated segments in the presentation of the material. My broadly focused study of the chronology and terminology of the vanguardist period in Latin American literature makes up the first segment. I base my comments largely on materials taken from manifestos and literary journals of the 1920's and 1930's, and I show that although futurism, ultraism, creationism, modernism, and surrealism ebb and flow with major and minor groupings in various countries, there is a fundamental unity which transcends national areas, linguistic boundaries, and specific outside influences. The single term which was and is still used to generalize this complicated period is *vanguardist,* and that term serves as the synthesis of unity amidst diversity.

The second subgrouping is made up of three studies on Brazil. The first is Anoar Aiex's description of Graça Aranha as a fundamental figure in early Brazilian modernism, and in that sense his work can be related to my study. Aiex carefully considers the place of Graça Aranha in the noisy modernist renovation and makes it clear that an earlier European philosophical framework must be discerned in order to understand the peculiar Brazilian circumstances of the time. Aiex makes a convincing case for Graça Aranha as the bridge between established philosophical ideas and the socio-intellectual changes which were to come through modernism.

The other two studies on Brazil are concerned with the cross-cultural problems of African elements in Brazilian music and literature. The first is Gerard Béhague's relatively short essay on regional and national elements in Afro-Brazilian cult music. Preliminary in the sense that it is the first portion of a longer examination of repertory and context, the study considers the various transplanted Afro-Brazilian cults in terms of their musical patterns and functions. Typical performers and musicians are characterized, the difficulties of codifying the enormous repertories of religious songs are made clear, and the relative importance of the various musical instruments is also considered. Béhague's hypothesis is that some cults and their musical forms are becoming identity symbols for the majority of Afro-Brazilians and that this music is undergoing obvious stylistic integration with nationally predominant popular music. Further study will be necessary in order to deal fully with this hypothesis.

Richard A. Preto-Rodas' essay on the black presence in the work of two Brazilian modernists, Jorge de Lima and José Lins do Rêgo, is a significant commentary on the literary expression of this cultural phenomenon. Both de Lima and Lins do Rêgo were born and raised in the Brazilian northeast and, surrounded and cared for by black nurses and servants, were products of the waning days of plantation society. Consequently, while both writers contributed to an understanding of traditional Brazilian society, Preto-Rodas concludes that their perspective is both ethnocentric and inadequate and is probably nothing more than a nostalgic view of the Negro as part of a vanishing culture.

A third segment groups three studies which take Mexico as a

primary frame. The first of these, Luis Leal's essay on native and foreign influences in contemporary Mexican fiction, is the most far-ranging of the three. Leal's contention is that Mexican prose fiction is at once traditional and innovative, national and cosmopolitan, Mexican and universal. In order to consider this thesis in contemporary fiction, he goes back to the beginnings of the novel in Mexico and traces the molding of that genre through the synthesis of native and foreign fiction. The content of Fernández de Lizardi's work is Mexican, for example; yet he is strongly influenced by the Spanish picaresque form and by French ideological currents. Leal most carefully examines recent Mexican fiction (the novel and the short story since the 1940's) and asserts that it did not break entirely with Mexican identity but rather incorporated new techniques which at the same time allowed it to be universal. The selection of themes, the creation of backgrounds, and the techniques of characterization were still influenced principally by the older nationalistic writers; however, in the narrative treatment of such themes and in the interplay of points of view the obvious influences are those of North American and European writers.

The second essay in this group, written by Dagoberto Orrantia on the function of myth in Fernando del Paso's *José Trigo*, illustrates Leal's thesis well. Orrantia studies a recent novel by a young Mexican writer who is both Mexican and universal. Through the use of mythology and a complicated interweaving of time and character representation, the ancient and modern site of Nonoalco-Tlatelolco is identified with the ephemeral existence of men and the eternal life of the gods. History becomes myth, and reality is modified accordingly. The theme and setting of the novel are identifiably Mexican, but its formal and technical experimentations make it a part of a universal and international "new novel."

My essay on four contemporary Mexican poets is the third study in this group. I take a brief, retrospective look at the poetic tradition which has molded the present moment and then place Montes de Oca, Zaid, Pacheco, and Aridjis within that tradition. These four poets are strongly individual; they are not slavish imitators of a Mexican past or of a foreign poetic style, but benefit from a rich legacy to express their peculiar circumstances. They are brilliantly rhetorical, aware of social justice, metaphysical, consciously modern, and committed to the careful expression of verbal beauty. Within their country's long poetic tradition they represent both achievement and promise.

The fourth and final segment is made up of two studies which use Chile as a national frame and which deal centrally with individual literary figures. The first of these is Thomas C. Meehan's essay on the life and literary work of Jenaro Prieto. According to Meehan, Prieto was a man of culture, humor, and wide interests whose major achievements were those of a humorist-journalist and a novelist. Meehan first sets up a detailed Spanish American chronology; the experimentations of the years from 1920 to 1940, resisted and at times accepted by transitional writers such as Prieto, created the impetus which produced more recent innovative developments in the prose fiction of Spanish America. Meehan then places Prieto within the particular development of Chilean prose fiction, makes some interesting connections between his work and that of the vanguardists of the period, and, finally, examines the prose style of the Chilean novelist's best-known novel, *El socio*, in order to assert that he not only understood and parodied vanguardist stylistic devices but also applied them consciously and creatively in his best work of fiction.

Kirsten F. Nigro's study of the grotesque world of José Donoso is complementary to Meehan's study. Whereas Prieto belonged essentially to the years before 1945, Donoso is very much a man of the present and a participant in the "new novel" of Latin America. Nigro considers the Chilean polemic on *criollismo* and the generation of 1950 and then comments briefly on the complete novelistic work of Donoso. The central part of Nigro's essay is a detailed study of the grotesque and chaotic *El lugar sin límites*. In Donoso's novel, old traditions disappear with no hope of renewal, order is a false myth, and man possesses no hint of internal symmetry or solidity. Nigro's study brings us face to face with the bitter sense of disintegration which pervades all of Donoso's work.

These, then, are the studies with which we propose to illuminate some aspects of the struggle for meaningful expression. We hope they will lead to increased understanding of the contradictory confluence of Latin American culture and literature in the twentieth century.

Latin American *Vanguardismo:* Chronology and Terminology

Merlin H. Forster

The first fifteen years of the twentieth century marked the decline of the modernist-symbolist period in Latin American literature, and by 1920 there was strong evidence of a fundamental change in literary expression in all of Latin America. The two decades or so that followed, now usually designated by various terms, depending on the area being described, were years of ferment and experimentation during which artistic expression in all media was sharply polarized. On the one hand, many writers received strong influence from such European schools as futurism and surrealism and broke sharply with the representational forms of the past; on the other, many writers vigorously attempted to express what they saw as important national or regional values. These decades of contention developed various groups of first-rate writers in Latin American countries, notably Chile, Brazil, Argentina, Peru, Mexico, and Cuba, and a number of literary journals of primary importance were published. The central focus of this study will be on the experimental and cosmopolitan groups of this period, and a secondary focus will be on the many correspondences between them and the writers concerned with the parallel nativist or *criollista* trend.

Critical work has increased in both quantity and quality, but coverage is still not definitive. Guillermo de Torre's fundamental work *Literaturas europeas de vanguardia* (Madrid, 1925), which has recently been republished in a revised and much enlarged form under the title *Historia de las literaturas de vanguardia* (Madrid,

1965), is indispensable for any study of this period. It attempts to view the important movements and figures in an international framework. However, Torre's treatment is strongly colored by his own participation in many of the events which he chronicles, and the work therefore is often more of documentary than of critical value. Two studies by Octavio Corvalán, *El postmodernismo* (New York, 1961) and *Modernismo y vanguardia* (New York, 1967), present a multinational view of the period; however, neither deals well with the complex problems of chronology and terminology, and both completely ignore the Brazilian centers of activity. A more recent contribution is Frederick S. Stimson's *The New Schools of Spanish American Poetry* (Madrid, 1970). Stimson deals in some detail with major movements and figures, but some of his classifications are questionable (for example, *"jitanjáfora"* as a school), and he makes no attempt to include Brazil.

There are as well a number of studies that concern themselves with a national or regional view. For example, Wilson Martin's *O Modernismo* (São Paulo, 1965) and John Nist's *The Modernist Movement in Brazil* (Austin, 1967) use Brazilian poetry as a main frame of reference, and Fred Ellison's *Brazil's New Novel* (Berkeley, 1954) deals with the novel of this period in the Brazilian northeast. Luis Monguió's *La poesía postmodernista peruana* (Berkeley, 1954) and my own study *Los Contemporáneos: 1920–1932* (Mexico City, 1964) examine certain aspects of this period in Peruvian and Mexican literature. Finally, Boyd G. Carter's recent work *Historia de la literatura hispanoamericana a través de sus revistas* (Mexico City, 1968) is a starting point for coverage of the many important literary journals although Carter does not include Brazilian materials.

This study, then, will be an attempt to suggest, in the light of the considerable criticism now available, an accurate chronology and a survey of the terminology used to delimit and characterize individual movements. The following assumptions are fundamental:

1. It is possible, though at times extremely difficult, to achieve a balanced treatment of both the points of commonality which transcend accepted boundaries and the individuality and uniqueness of each national or regional area.

2. Significant literary activity is concentrated in, though not limited to, a rather small number of major centers in Latin America

and Europe. Mexico City, Havana, Lima, Santiago de Chile, Buenos Aires–Montevideo, and Rio de Janeiro–São Paulo are primary American focal points. Paris and, to a lesser extent, Madrid are major European gathering points for travelers and for writers in exile.

3. Linguistic and geographic boundaries should not separate what is in many ways a unified and organic whole. For example, Huidobro's poems in French are important for this study, and the Portuguese of Brazilian writers should not obscure the fundamental unity between Brazilian literary activities of the period and those of the Spanish-speaking world.

4. Perhaps the most important sources for the history of vanguardism are the manifestos, the anthologies, and, above all, the literary magazines that appeared in great abundance during these years.[1]

Chronology

A first major concern is to suggest an accurate chronology which will in turn serve as a background for more detailed consideration of the various groupings and terms. Such a sketch must take into account an internal chronology as well as a relationship to preceding and following movements.

A fundamental difficulty is discerning a connection to the earlier modernist period in both Spanish America and Brazil. The most general approach is to establish a decade of transition, from 1910 to 1920, more or less, between modernism-symbolism and the newer movements which developed in the early twenties. In Brazilian criticism these years are seen clearly as leading toward modernism and have been called "premodernism" by Tristão de Ataíde.[2] Critics of Spanish American literature are not so much in accord. In general, the modernist movement is considered to be in decline in the

---

[1] I express appreciation to Dr. Sergio D. Provenzano, of Buenos Aires, Dr. Plínio Doyle, of Rio de Janeiro, and Juan Mejía Bacca, of Lima, for allowing me extensive use of their private collections; I am indebted as well to the staffs of public libraries in Santiago de Chile, Montevideo, Rio de Janeiro, São Paulo, Lima, and Mexico City, who made easier the gathering and reproduction of materials. Mrs. Regina Macdonald spent several weeks in the public and private collections of Quito, and I am grateful for the significant additions she has made to my fund of information.

[2] Alceu Amoroso Lima [Tristão de Ataíde], *Quadro Sintético da Literatura Brasileira* (Rio de Janeiro: Agir, 1959), p. 61.

early years of the second decade of the century, and the term *post-modernism* is often used to designate the following ten years or so.[3] Jiménez and Florit, for example, write about the "postmodernist reaction" and mention such exemplary figures as López Velarde, Eguren, Reyes, and Gabriela Mistral.[4]

Several important commentators on modernism, however, have taken exception to this generally accepted chronology. Juan Ramón Jiménez has recommended viewing the entire twentieth century as modernist,[5] and Ricardo Gullón and Ivan Schulman follow much the same line of argument.[6] Gullón would end the period in 1940 and Schulman in 1932, both of them operating on the theory of a "half-century" of modernism. In a recent prologue to an anthology of contemporary Spanish American poetry, José Olivio Jiménez has argued cogently against this view. The postmodernist transition is very clear, he points out, and while certain effects of modernism can certainly be seen in writers of the following decades, there is essential disparity between modernism and the literature of the twenties and thirties: "Para nosotros, en suma, la década de 1920 a 1930 (y contando algunos antecedentes naturales—Huidobro, el más importante—desde 1914) asiste a la aparición de una expresi-vidad poética lo suficientemente dispar a la del modernismo como para que pueda seo cubierta de modo cómodo bajo su rótulo."[7]

The second decade of the twentieth century was a moment of political and cultural turbulence, and the new generation which came to a state of awareness in the early 1920's was strongly affected and in a sense formed by these forces. Manuel Picón Salas comments on these events retrospectively in a 1930 essay:

[3] The term is used also to designate contemporary literary expression beyond the end of modernism. See, for example, Luis Monguió's work on contemporary Peruvian poetry, *La poesía postmodernista peruana* (Berkeley: University of California Press, 1954), or the book by Octavio Corvalán entitled *El postmodernismo* (New York: Las Américas, 1961).

[4] Eugenio Florit and José Olivio Jiménez, *La poesía hispanoamericana desde el modernismo* (New York: Appleton-Century Crofts, 1968), pp. 8–11.

[5] Juan Ramón Jiménez, *El modernismo* (Madrid: Aguilar, 1962).

[6] See Ricardo Gullón, "Juan Ramón Jiménez y el modernismo," in *ibid.*, and Ivan A. Schulman, "En torno a la definición del modernismo," in *Estudios críticos sobre el modernismo* (Madrid: Gredos, 1968); *El modernismo hispanoamericano* (Buenos Aires: Centro Editor, 1969).

[7] José Olivio Jiménez, *Antología de la poesía hispanoamericana contemporánea* (Madrid: Alianza, 1971), p. 14.

En 1920 teníamos diez y ocho, diez y nueve, veinte años. En 1920 nos alumbró la primera intuición de nuestro tiempo. Después de esos cinco años de error universal, en que por otra parte, como lo dice muy bien el alemán Glaeser (el camarada Glaeser, como lo hubiéramos llamado en 1920), lo más importante fué nuestra propia transformación, la etapa crítica de nuestra adolescencia, los dorados días de angustia o plenitud física, el largo clamor sensual de las noches de verano, eso que cosquillea o se encandila en las hermosas páginas del novelista alemán: advertíamos la hora turbia y dudosa de la post-guerra. Cuando cesaron los cañones de Verdun, empezó una guerra más concluyente de principios, clases sociales y órdenes establecidos. Grandes movimientos de multitudes humanas: revolución rusa, agitación islámica, china o india. En nuestra propia América asistíamos a la transformación de Méjico. Las instituciones del siglo XIX que naufragaban en el remolino de nuestro tiempo, el liberalismo de nuestros padres, la sagaz ciencia política, los noventa años de moderada burguesía. Todo constituyó para nosotros un panorama de muchos frentes, exaltó nuestra conciencia inpresionable y sentimos, porque éramos jóvenes y no estábamos amarrados a nada, la embriaguez y la responsabilidad de lo que venía. Tuvimos los primeros conflictos de ideas.[8]

The sense of new generation on which Picón Salas comments here extends from the early twenties into the mid-forties and can be subdivided again into two segments. The first, from 1920 to about 1930, can best be characterized as an iconoclastic period in which conventionality was questioned on all sides and accepted form was attacked with gusto and violence.

This first decade was the period of a multiplicity of groups, of innumerable manifestos, of combative and exclusivist anthologies. A number of important journals appeared: *Proa* (1922–23; 1924–26) and *Martín Fierro* (1924–27) in Argentina, *Klaxon* (1922–23) and *Revista de Antropofagia* (1928–29) in Brazil, *Amauta* (1926–30) in Peru, *Contemporáneos* (1928–31) in Mexico, and *Revista de Avance* (1927–30) in Cuba. There is a proliferation of terms, all of which seek to identify the sense of novelty and exuberance which characterized those years. Curiously, however, there are few definitive works. Mário de Andrade's *Paulicéia Desvairada* (1922) is typi-

[8] Manuel Picón Salas. "Sitio de una generación," *Presente*, 1 (no. 1, July 1930), 3.

cal of the Brazilian modernist attack on traditional prosody and at the same time is powerful and moving poetry. *La casa de cartón* (1928), by the Peruvian Martín Adán, exemplifies experimentation in prose, and some of Huidobro's early calligramistic poems are comparable experimentation in verse form.

The years from 1930 to the early 1940's can be seen as a time of relative maturity and impatience with some of the recent loudly proclaimed solutions. These sharp words from José Carlos Mariátegui, set down in 1930, reflect both an awareness of what had gone before and a hope for a future yet unrealized:

> "Nueva generación," "nuevo espiritu," "nueva sensibilidad," todos estos términos han envejecido. Lo mismo hay que decir de estos otros rótulos: "vanguardia," "izquierda," "renovación." Fueron nuevos y buenos en su hora. Nos hemos servido de ellos para establecer demarcaciones provisionales, por razones contingentes de topografía y orientación. Hoy resultan ya demasiado genéricos y anfibológicos. Bajo estos rótulos empiezan a pasar gruesos contrabandos. La nueva generación no será efectivamente nueva sino en la medida en que sepa ser, al fin, adulta, creadora.[9]

Mariátegui's words express the idea that mere experimentation and novelty are not sufficient for true creation. Technical virtuosity does not replace maturity and profundity of thought, and it is this problem that the young writers, suddenly grown a little older, began to face during these years. There was no longer a pressing need for manifestos, and the number of significant works increased sharply. The works of Carlos Drummond de Andrade in Brazil, *Altazor* (1931) by Vicente Huidobro, *Residencia en la tierra* (1933, 1935) by Pablo Neruda, and *Muerte sin fin* (1939) by José Gorostiza are all examples of this maturity grown from the noisy beginnings of the 1920's.

The last chronological problem is the relationship of the period under study to the one that follows. The most usual pattern is to place the close of vanguardism at the end of World War II and to use terms that would suggest a continuation of, as well as a reaction against, the preceding period. For example, the term *postmodernism*

9 José Carlos Mariátegui, *Presente*, 1 (no. 1, July 1930), 12.

is widely used in Brazilian criticism, and the most frequent term in Spanish America is *postvanguardism*. Again, the reactions and uncertainties of a postwar period would seem to make this relationship a proper one, especially when coupled with the flowering in all centers of literary activity of a new and articulate generation. This postvanguardist grouping, then, would be characterized by such figures as Octavio Paz, José Lezama Lima, Nicanor Parra, Julio Cortázar, João Guimarães Rosa, and João Cabral de Melo Neto.

Some critics have taken exception to this chronology. For example, Florit and Jiménez begin postvanguardism in 1930 and include such important figures as Neruda, Vallejo, and Borges in the first of two successive groupings and Paz and Parra in the second.[10] This is a very debatable formulation, and I much prefer to view the years from 1930 to 1945 as a period of deepening and consolidation within vanguardism proper and to suggest that postvanguardism began in the mid-forties.

There is an *estribillo* couplet from a poem by José Gorostiza which goes as follows: "No es agua ni arena / la orilla del mar."[11] These lines represent in large part what I have attempted to describe up to this point. The lines of demarcation between modernism and vanguardism in the early 1920's and between vanguardism and postvanguardism in the mid-1940's are problematic, and I must conclude that it is difficult to say at all times whether they are "water or sand." What is more important, however, is the general outline of the intervening twenty-five years, because it is this sketch which will now be the basis for a survey of major movements and figures.

Terminology

In his article in *Anales de la Universidad de Chile*, Cedomil Goić comments on the motion and variety of the vanguardist period:

> Todas las literaturas, todos los *ismos* fueron atentamente considerados, leídos y practicados por la nueva generación. El nuevo sistema de preferencias que se organizaba no aceptó limitaciones regionalistas y afirmó por encima de toda alusión a la realidad histórico inmediata, el valor universal de la obra creada, despegada

[10] Florit and Jiménez, *La poesía hispanoamericana*, p. 15.
[11] José Gorostiza, *Poesía* (Mexico City: Fondo de Cultura Económica, 1964), p. 33.

de la imitación servil del propio medio y de sus manifestaciones aparentes....

Pocas veces una generación se vio abocada a una tarea creadora tan inquieta, variada y variable; volicitada por tan cambiantes formas, tan novedosas y audaces, como ofrecía la literatura europea y la norteamericana. A la experiencia histórica de esta generación pertenece la activísima moción de los *ismos*. La incitación es originalmente europea, pero—por primera vez—participaron en los momentos mismos de su gestación varios escritores hispanoamericanos, entre ellos Vicente Huidobro.[12]

Goić's mention of the *ismos* suggests the multiplicity of terms which were used to characterize the various groupings and aesthetic directions, and he sees as well both the European and the native American dimensions. I shall now turn my attention to the terms themselves, not with the intention of providing a complete study of each movement represented, but rather to trace principal patterns within a geographic and temporal extension.

There are a number of designations which appear over and over again in the journals and manifestos of the period which are obviously taken from European movements and are often a measure against which any American production is to be judged. For example, in a 1929 article in an obscure journal published in Puno, Peru, Miguel Angel León uses several of these terms as the basis for his argument in favor of new American literary values:

Pasada la labor negativa del saltimbanquismo i humor clownesco de los poetas "Da-da," que supieron hacer atambores fantásticos de los vientres adiposos de los burgueses, pasado el super-realismo con sus acordes wagnerianos de la subconciencia freudiana, cuya expresión ectoplasmática reventaba las escleróticas miopes, pasado el simun del futurismo acrobático i patriotero. Pasadas todas estas escuelas de vandalismo civilizador que maceraron con las pepsinas de la carcajada la mortecina clásico; evacuada, luego, por el torrente del espíritu moderno en excrescencias viscosas hacia los acantilados higiénicos del olvido; urge la labor constructora de nuevos valores literarios i esto nos toca primarimente a los poetas de América que no tenemos aún las manos rojas de tanto asesinar héroes, que aún no hemos luchado, porque nuestro pretérito no

12 Cedomil Goić, "La novela chilena actual: Tendencias y generaciones," *Anales de la Universidad de Chile*, 107 (no. 119, 3rd semester 1960), 251.

es más que un pretérito de guiñol, con unos cuantos alaridos escarlata, que hemos dramatizado en la historia para darles una enfocación pragmáticamente cursi.[13]

There are other terms which appear with varying frequency. For example, the intuition and subjectivity of *expressionism* attracted some attention, and the term was one which appeared occasionally in the journals of the period.[14] *Cubism* was a term taken from the plastic arts which represented experimentation in form and was occasionally used to express a sense of change during these years. *Futurism, ultraism,* and *surrealism* had their beginnings in Europe but were of fundamental importance for writers in Latin America. In addition there are other terms, such as *creationism* and *modernism,* which had no direct European counterparts and must be considered in an essentially American framework.

Futurism

Futurism in Europe was founded before the First World War by Filippo Tommaso Marinetti, who was Italian but who had studied in Paris. His manifesto appeared in *Le Figaro* in February, 1909, and announced in eleven separate statements an aesthetic of speed, machine power, and industrial revolution. Futurism came to represent a glorification of aggressive and warlike sentiments, and in the period following World War I Marinetti and others allied themselves with the rising tide of fascism in Italy.

The impact of futurism on Latin American literature was early and of considerable geographic and temporal extent. Probably the first to come in contact with Marinetti's manifesto was Oswald de Andrade, who returned from Paris in 1912 already aware of these rebellious and energetic ideas. By 1915 the word *futurist* was to be seen in the pages of the conservative newspaper *O Estado de São Paulo,* and from that time until the Semana de Arte Moderna in 1922 the term was used frequently. In May of 1921 Oswald de Andrade characterized Mário de Andrade as "O meu poeta futurista," and the young writers themselves began to use the term more fre-

[13] Miguel Angel León, "Acotaciones vanguardistas," *Editorial Titikaka,* no. 28 (February 1929), 1.
[14] See, for example, the article by Jorge Luis Borges, "Acerca del expresionismo," *Inicial,* 1 (no. 3, December 1923), 15–17.

quently. Many things about futurism were attractive, as Mário da Silva Brito points out, but at the same time those writers did not want to be slavish imitators:

> Durante longo tempo, hesitaram os escritores novos em perfilhar o futurismo. Se, de um lado, aceitavam as inovações de Marinetti que lhes proporcionavam um reteiro para combater a literatura e artes praticadas então no Brasil, de outro desejavam preservar a própria personalidade para a construção polêmica dos instrumentos de trabalho fornecidos pelo iconoclasta italiano e na obediência aos impulsos do próprio temperamento. A doutrina futurista era sedutora, facilitava enormemente a tarefa de renovação e, sobretudo, adequava-se à saciedade à paisagem paulista, à mentalidade urbana que S. Paulo criara em seus filhos. Aceitassem ou não o futurismo, para o consenso geral eram futuristas.[15]

After the Semana de Arte Moderna, futurism declined sharply in its appeal, and *modernism* became the term which was most used to designate the new wave of literary expression. In 1924, for example, Ronald de Carvalho could proclaim loudly: "Morra o futurismo! O futurismo é passadismo!"[16]

In Spanish America the impact and effect of futurism were a good deal less concentrated. In the first place, it is more difficult to determine a point of contact with the early pronouncements. Luis Leal points out that Ramón Gómez de la Serna translated and published the futurist manifesto in 1910 in his journal *Prometeo*, and it is quite possible that this may have been the first contact for many Hispanic readers.[17] The eleven points of Marinetti's manifesto appear in Vicente Huidobro's *Pasando y pasando* (1914) together with strong arguments against the novelty of the futurist aesthetic. He continues his attack, it might be noted, in a 1925 essay "Futurismo y maquinismo": "Los futuristas pretenden haber aportado todos los materiales para el arte y la poesía que hacemos y que hacen en todas

---

15 Mário da Silva Brito, "A Revolução Modernísta," in *A Literatura no Brasil*, vol. 5 (Rio de Janeiro: Sul Americana, 1970), p. 12.

16 *Ibid.*, p. 23.

17 Luis Leal, "El movimiento estridentista," in *Los vanguardismos en la América Latina* (Havana: Las Américas, 1970), p. 158. Luis Mario Schneider documents an article by Amado Nervo on futurism which appeared in 1909 in the Mexican publication *Boletín de instrucción pública*; see *El estridentismo* (Mexico City: Bellas Artes, 1970), pp. 16–19.

partes los poetas modernos. Esto es absolutamente falso; no es más que un sueño imperialista en frío. Ellos nada han aportado; salvo algo de ruído y mucha confusión. Un arte de nuevo aspecto, pero nada fundamentalmente nuevo. Un arte nuevo para las once mil vírgenes, pero no para quienes lo conocen algo."[18]

Marinetti himself visited South America in 1926, but by this time his theories were largely outmoded and his political stance in favor of the Italian fascists had discredited him in the eyes of the Latin American writers and intellectuals. Nonetheless, there are continuing traces of futurist techniques and aesthetic ideas in a number of Latin American countries. For example, one of the assertions in the manifesto of *Martín Fierro* is in part an obvious restatement of the fourth point in the futurist manifesto: " 'Martín Fierro,' se encuentra, por eso, más a gusto, en un transatlántico moderno que en un placio renacentista, y sostiene que un buen Hispano-Suiza es una OBRA DE ARTE muchísimo más perfecta que una silla de manos de la época de Luis XV."[19] Another example is the curious collection of poems by Juan Marín entitled *Looping* (Santiago, 1929). Marín is enchanted by motion and power, and his poems have an obvious connection to the postulates of futurism. Even the cover of the collection is suggestive, with the motif being a radial aircraft engine with whirling propeller. The poems of the Ecuadorian Manuel Agustín Aguirre also show influence of futurism, as can be seen in this composition:

> el aeroplano
> hunde su aguijón
> en la flor redonda del ocaso
> y el aviador entre sus manos
> hace girar el horizonte
> como un ventilador
>
> mira como se llena de avispas
> el inmenso panal del sol
>
> las señales caídas de un avión
> se rompieron la espiña dorsal
>
> torbellino de curvas

---

[18] Vicente Huidobro, *Obras completas*, vol. 1 (Santiago, Zig-Zag, 1964), p. 684.
[19] *Martín Fierro*, 1 (no. 4, 15 May 1924), 1–2.

he cogido a la tierra por los brazos
y me he puesto a danzar

nada hay mejor
que pilotear el vértigo
o cortar amápolas
sobre un campo incendiado[20]

Perhaps the most extensive use of Marinetti's theories in all of Latin America is to be seen in the work of the Mexican *"estridentistas,"* who were active in Mexico City and in some of the provincial cities during the years 1922–27. Luis Leal considers this group to be the first vanguardist movement in Mexico and mentions as principal participants Manuel Maples Arce, Luis Quintilla, Germán List Arzubide, Arqueles Vela, and Salvador Gallardo.[21] Marinetti and futurism are mentioned often in the manifestos and journals of the group, and even the noisy title used throughout the active years of production suggests the motion and violence of the European school.

Luis Mario Schneider considers in some detail the principal influences on the Mexican movement.[22] Dadaism, creationism, and ultraism were commented on in the pages of Mexican journals and presumably were important for the writers of this group. However, Schneider documents an early and fundamental discussion of the futurist ideology.

The sense of violent iconoclastic force is apparent in the stridentist pronouncements and manifestos. The following comment, for example, is taken from the second issue of *Actual* and is signed by Manuel Maples Arce. The tasks of *estridentismo* in 1922, he proclaims, were the following:

1º Hacer un aporte de fuerza espiritual a nuestra lírica, del que antes carecía; 2º Improvisar un público; 3º Urbanizar espiritualmente algunos gallineros literarios; 4º Desbandar a los totoles académicos; 5º Cambiar la marcha de los horarios; 6º Exaltar el furor agudo de los rotativos; 7º Libertar el aullido sentimental de

---

[20] Manuel Agustín Aguirre, *Poemas automáticos* (Guayaquil: Gutenberg, 1931), pp. 57–58.
[21] Leal, "El movimiento estridentista," p. 157.
[22] Schneider, *El estridentismo*, pp. 15–29.

las locomotoras estatizado en los manicomios tarahumaras; y 9°
Provocar la la erupción del Popocatépetl. . . .

El estridentismo no es una escuela, ni una tendencia ni una mafia
intelectual, como las que aquí se estilan; el estridentismo es una
razón de estrategia. Un gesto. Una irrupción.[23]

The literary works of the stridentists also showed this same tension
and combativeness. *Urbe* of Maples Arce is an ideological and
mechanized poem to the worker in his new cities:

> He aquí mi poema
> brutal
> y multánime
> a la nueva ciudad.
>   Oh ciudad toda tensa
>   de cables y de esfuerzos
>   sonora toda
>   de motores y de alas.
>   Explosión simultánea
>   de las nuevas teorías. . . .[24]

One more point must be made here in considering stridentism in
connection with futurism in Latin America. My intention is to take
note of a fundamental affinity and frequent use of Marinetti's ideas,
but not to suggest that *estridentismo* is nothing more than an at-
tenuated reflection of the European movement. Maples Arce and
his companions gave considerable thought to innovation and
change, both in literary and social terms, and began a transformation of Mexican literature and culture which is still in progress:
"El espíritu mesiánico del arte unido a un principio de originalidad
y renovación continua trajo como consecuencia una transformación
en la actitud creativa del escritor y, por supuesto, del contexto general de la literatura mexicana."[25]

One final dimension of futurism in Latin America is not connected necessarily to the manifestos of Marinetti. In many countries
the term *futurist* became a popular way to refer, usually in derision,
to anything which smacked of experimentation or modernity. Mário
da Silva Brito comments in the following way on its use in Brazilian

23 Quoted by Schneider in *ibid.*, p. 60.
24 Manuel Maples Arce, *Urbe* (Mexico City: Botas, 1924).
25 Schneider, *El estridentismo*, p. 208.

newspapers: "Os jornais, a partir dêsse momento até o fim de 1922—
e especialmente durante a Semana de Arte Moderna—estão repletos
dessas palavras, que são usadas caricaturalmente e inspiram quad-
rinhas, sátiras, sonetos humorísticos, zombarias de tôda a sorte. Palavras que são aplicadas a torte e a direito e a tudo quanto destrilhe
da normalidade."[26] He also records as an example the final two lines
of an unnamed sonnet, published in 1921, which recognizes novelty
but questions the lasting value of an anonymous young poet: "Em-
bora seja um poeta futurista / Não é, por certo, um poeta futur-
oso."[27] The words of the Peruvian Clemente Palma, written in 1916,
serve as another example of the use of the term *futurismo* to paint all
young writers with the same wide brush: "Nos hemos convencido,
repito, de que todos estos visajes y aspavientos líricos de los modernistas de hoy, que ya no se llaman modernistas, como decíamos
nosotros, sino futuristas, son mentirjillas sinceras, son cachiporrazos
de gong escandalosos, histerismos de arte juvenil desaforado, alaridos de la inofensiva infatuación de quienes tienen un caudal de años
que derrochar en prodigalidades de lirismo ruidoso, búsquedas
afanosas de la senda en la natural desorientación de los pocos
años."[28]

Surrealism / Superrealism

The surrealist movement was founded in France in the early 1920's
by André Breton, Jean Cocteau, Louis Aragon, and Paul Eluard,
and it attempted, following upon the destructiveness of the dadaists,
to find in the subconscious a true reality which is beyond the logical
processes of the mind. Freudian psychoanalysis was applied to literary creation, principally by the use of automatic writing or sketching, and it was supposed by the surrealists that these productions
were more authentic than those set in order by a conscious process.

Surrealism in Europe had three principal developmental periods.
The first was defined by Breton's 1924 surrealist manifesto, which
intended to liberate man through the mechanisms of hypnosis and
dreams. The second was built around Breton's manifesto of 1930
and the emphasis placed on a fusion of artistic and political inten-

[26] Silva Brito, "A Revolução Modernista," p. 12.
[27] *Ibid.*, p. 11, quoting "O Futuro Condicional," *Journal de Comercio*, 26 June
1921.
[28] Clemente Palma, *Variedades*, no. 454 (11 November 1916), 1499.

tions, a combination which was intended to reduce life's essential contradictions. In the third stage, surrealism continued beyond the end of World War II and was fused with existentialism and other political and cultural groups.

The impact of surrealism in its various developmental stages on Latin American literature is widespread and of fundamental importance. However, its effect can be seen much more clearly in the work of individual figures than in generational groupings. In this regard, it is of interest to take note of some observations by the French poet Benjamin Peret, who participated in the French movement and lived during the war years in Brazil and Mexico. These comments were recorded by Stefan Baciu after Peret's death and are, in part, as follows:

> Apesar de que, através de vários caminhos, o surrealismo teve marcada influência sôbre alguns poetas do Brasil e da América Espanhola, não se pode falar em nosso Continente de uma corrente coerentemente surrealista, mas sim de manifestações esporádicas. Pederia, talvez, haver uma só exceção, isto é, o que poderiamos chamar de núcleo surrealista peruano, cuja mais destacada figura foi o poeta e pintor César Moro, autor, entre outros trabalhos raríssimos hoje, do livro de poemas "La tortuga ecuestre" (Lima, 1942), de franca tendência surrealista, guardando, todavía, uma frescura e singeleza tipicamente peruanas.
>
> Em vários outros países, pode ser anotada a presença de poetas isolados, tanto entre os autores renomados, como entre aquêles que trabalharam em um ambiente local, em cuja obra a leitura de Breton, Eluard e Aragon deixára traços profundos. Assim mesmo, a maioria déstes poetas não assimilara completamente as essências do surrealismo.[29]

Peret's observations are borne out in the manifestos and periodical materials which I have seen. First, the only country where the term *surrealist* is used consistently to designate any kind of grouping is Peru, and figures such as Emilio Westphalen and César Moro are the principal names to be mentioned. Interestingly enough, César Vallejo maintained a rather hostile position toward surrealism and

[29] Stefan Baciu, "O Surrealismo, a 'Semana de Arte Moderna' no Brasil e a 'Vanguardia' Hispano-Americana," in *Movimientos literarios de vanguardia en Iberoamérica* (Mexico City: Cultura, 1965), p. 129.

in 1930 wrote from Paris a rather sardonic article entitled "Autopsia del superrealismo."[30]

There are sporadic uses of the term in other countries, and there are writers who can be associated at least for a time with some of the techniques or intentions of surrealism. For example, Cedomil Goić uses the term *superrealismo* to categorize those Chilean novelists who were born between 1890 and 1904 and whose main production came between the years 1920 and 1935.[31] Also within Chilean literature one should remember Huidobro's 1925 manifesto article against the theories of surrealism, and it is possible to attribute some of Neruda's middle works to a surrealistic orientation. *Tentativa del hombre infinito* (1925) and the two volumes of *Residencia en la tierra* (1933, 1935) clearly show surrealistic structures and techniques.

The term was mentioned from time to time in Mexican manifestos and journals, and the works of a poet such as Xavier Villaurrutia are strongly colored by surrealistic disconnection and introspection. In Argentina the appearance of the curious journal *Que* in two numbers (1928 and 1930) underlined a kind of psychoanalytic approach to the self and its expression. The following is an excerpt from the editorial which appears in the first number and is entitled "Pequeño esfuerzo de justificación colectiva":

> Definidos exteriormente como inestables (igual y alternativa repulsión por el movimiento y por la inmovilidad, por la acción y por la inacción) nosotros hemos acudido a la única manera de existir en densidad (es decir sin disolvernos) que es la introspección. Este vocablo no lo entendemos como planteamiento de problemas estériles, sino como una manera de dejarse poseer por uno mismo, estando lo consciente puramente dedicado a revelar por el signo de cada palabra una profunda realidad constitutiva.
>
> En esta actitude se distinguen dos partes:
> 1° placer de una ilimitada libertad expansiva.
> 2° posibilidad de conocernos (especie de método psico-analítico, pero en el cual no partimos de ningún prejuicio sobre nuestra propia estructura).[32]

[30] César Vallejo, "Autopsia del superrealismo," *Letras* (Santiago), 3 (no. 22, July 1930), 27–28.

[31] Goić, "La novela chilena actual," 250–53.

[32] *Que*, no. 1 (November 1928), 1.

Ultraism

Ultraísmo is a completely Hispanic movement which began shortly after the end of the First World War and which in many ways combined several vanguardist positions already established in France. Ultraism lasted only until 1922 or so in Spain, and it is generally considered to have ended with the cessation of publication of the journal *Ultra* (1921–22). This period coincided more or less with Huidobro's visit to Madrid in 1918 and with the guiding presence of Rafael Cansinos-Asséns and later of Guillermo de Torre. Other important periodicals were *Grecia* (1918–20) and *Cosmópolis* (1919–20).

The movement sought to reject modernism, which was seen as completely outmoded, and to reach the uttermost point of newness; hence the use of the term *ultra*. The first manifesto, which is moderate in its call for new horizons, appeared in *Grecia* in 1919:

> Los que suscriben, jóvenes que comienzan a realizar su obra . . . necesitan declarar su voluntad de un arte nuevo que supla la última revolución literaria: el novecentismo.
>
> Respetando la obra realizada por las grandes figuras de este movimiento, se sienten con anhelos de rebasar la meta alcanzada por estos primogénitos, y proclaman la necesidad de un *ultraísmo* para el que invocan la colaboración de toda la juventud literaria española. . . .
>
> Nuestra literatura debe renovarse, debe lograr su *ultra*, como hoy pretenden lograrlo nuestro pensamiento científico y político. Nuestra lema será *ultra*, y en nuestro credo cabrán todas las tendencias sin distinción, con tal que expresen un anhelo nuevo. Más tarde, estas tendencias lograrán su núcleo y se definirán. [33]

More important for the scope of this paper, however, is the extension of *ultraísmo* to Argentina. Jorge Luis Borges was in Madrid during the formative years of the movement, and when he returned to Buenos Aires in 1921 he became a standard bearer for the new literary style. He published almost immediately an article from which the following theoretical points are extracted:

1. Reducción de la lírica a su elemento primordial: la metáfora.

---

[33] Quoted from Gloria Videla, *Ultraísmo* (Madrid, 1963), p. 33.

2. Tachadura de las frases medianeras, los nexos, y los adjetivos inútiles.

3. Abolición de los trebejos ornamentales, el confesionalismo, la circunstanciación, las prédicas y la nebulosidad rebuscada.

4. Síntesis de dos o más imágenes en una, que ensancha de ese modo su facultad de sugerencia.

Los poemas ultraicos constan pues de una serie de metáforas, cada una de las cuales tiene sugestividad propia y comprendiza una visión inédita de algún fragmento de la vida.[34]

Ultraísmo caught hold rapidly. The muralistic journal *Prisma* appeared in 1921 and the more important *Proa* in two successive periods, the first in 1922–23 and the second in 1924. In February of 1924 Evar Méndez founded the journal *Martín Fierro*, which, according to Fernández Moreno, centralized and made concrete the Argentine *ultraísta* movement.[35] The journal appeared in forty-two numbers from 1924 through 1927, and it is an interesting combination of polemic, irreverence, humor, and, above all, a new and engaging sensibility.

Number 4 of the journal includes a manifesto which expresses in characteristic terms the intentions of the journal:

Frente a la impermeabilidad hipopotámica del honorable público. Frente a la funeraria solemnidad del historiador y del catedrático, que momifica cuanto toca.

Frente al recetario que inspira las elucubraciones de nuestros más bellos espíritus y a la afición al ANACRONISMO y al MIMETISMO que demuestran.

Frente a la ridícula necesidad de fundamentar nuestro nacionalismo intelectual, hinchando valores falsos que al primer pinchazo se desinflan como chanchitos.

Frente a la incapacidad de contemplar la vida sin escalar las estanterías de las bibliotecas.

Y sobre todo, frente al pavoroso temor de equivocarse que paralize el mismo ímpetu de la juventud, más anquilosada que cualquier burócrata jubilado:

[34] Jorge Luis Borges, "Ultraísmo," *Nosotros*, 39 (1921), 466–71.
[35] Fernández Moreno, "El ultraísmo," in *Los vanguardismos en la América Latina*, p. 34.

MARTÍN FIERRO siente la necesidad imprescindible de definirse y de llamar a cuantos sean capaces de percibir que nos hallamos en presencia de una NUEVA sensibilidad y de una NUEVA comprensión, que al ponernos de acuerdo con nosotros mismos, nos descubre panoramas insospechados y nuevos medios y formas de expresión.[36]

Martín Fierro is also unique among the publications of the Spanish American groups for its humorous poetry, and it can only be compared in this respect to the *"poema piada"* of some of the Brazilian modernists. Here are some examples taken from "Cementerio de Martín Fierro":

> Yace aquí Jorge Max Rhode
> Dejadlo dormir en pax
> que de ese modo no xode
>   Max[37]

> En este nicho reposa
> un poeta arrabalero.
> ¿No habrán tenido otra cosa
> con que llenar este "aujero"?
>   R.A.[38]

> En aqueste panteón
> Yace Leopoldo Lugones,
> Quien, leyendo "La Nación"
> Murió entre las convulsiones
> De una auto-intoxicación.
>   E.G.L.[39]

> Bajo esta lápida fría
> Yace uno que, sin cautela,
> Se puso a leer un día
> La más húmeda novela
> De Martínez Zuviría.
>   R.[40]

The journal *Martín Fierro* gave its name to the entire *ultraísta* group in Argentina, who are yet often referred to as *"Los martin-*

36 *Martín Fierro*, 1 (no. 4, 15 May 1924), 1–2.
37 *Ibid.*, no. 1 (February 1924).
38 *Ibid.*, nos. 12–13 (October–November 1924).
39 *Ibid.*, nos. 14–15 (January 1925).
40 *Ibid.*, no. 22 (September 1925).

fierristas." This term also suggests another important dispute during these years—the Florida-Boedo quarrel. The members of the "Florida" group were seen by themselves and others as rather aristocratic and in touch with the latest happenings outside Argentina, and they customarily gathered in a *confitería* in the fashionable Florida area of downtown Buenos Aires. The members of the "Boedo" group, expressing themselves primarily in the journal *Claridad* as leftists representing the working man and legitimate Argentine problems, took the name of the working man's district of the city in which their *tertulia* met. The arguments raged back and forth in the pages of both journals, as can be seen from this extract from "Ellos y nosotros," which appeared in May, 1927:

I. Provisionalmente, y por razones de espacio y de comodidad explicativa, aceptemos sin discusión las diversas denominaciones o etiquetas de las dos tendencias o escuelas literarias que hoy y aquí, más escándalo fabrican, y que se oponen la una a la otra en actitudes beligerantes:

Florida	Boedo.
Vanguardia	Izquierda.
Ultraísmo	Realismo.

Y como este procedimiento es cómodo y fácil, podríamos continuarlo hasta desfallecer por falta de argumentos:

"Martín Fierro" y "Proa"	"Extrema Izquierda"
	"Los Pensadores" y
	"Claridad".
La greguería	El cuento y la novela.
La metáfora	El asunto y la composición.
Ramón Gómez de la Serna	Fedor Dostoiewski

. . . .

VI. El ultraísmo—o lo que sea—amenaza desterrar de su "arte puro" elementos tan maravillosos como el retrato, el paisaje, los caracteres, las costumbres, los sentimientos, las ideas, etc. Es una desventaja y una limitación.

En tan poco espacio no caben más razones. Y perdóneme la falta de pedantería por las ausentes citas de Croce, Lips, etc.

Roberto Mariani.[41]

Argentine *ultraísmo* continued until approximately 1927. With the death of Ricardo Güiraldes in Paris and the suspension that

41 "Ellos y nosotros," *Claridad*, 6 (no. 131, May 1927).

same year of the publication of *Martín Fierro,* the group began to disperse. As one participant has suggested,[42] the moment of frivolity had passed, and it was time to get down to business.

Ultraísmo, then, is a term which is restricted to currency in Spain and in Argentina and which in its Argentine extension has the additional interchangeable term of *martinfierrismo.*

Creationism

Creacionismo is unique in several ways among the vanguardist movements in Latin America. To begin with, it is probably the earliest American expression of the new aesthetic position and has the most clearly defined theoretical development. It is also inexorably tied to the person and the travels of a single individual, Vicente Huidobro, and is in its American and European extensions the most international of vanguardist groupings in Latin America.

As early as 1914 an argumentative theoretical stance in favor of innovation was apparent in Huidobro's work:

> En literatura me gusta todo lo que es innovación.
> Todo lo que es original.
> Odio la rutina, el cliché y lo retórico.
> Odio las momias y los subterráneos de museo.
> Odio los fósiles literarios.
> Odio todos los ruidos de cadenas que atan.
> Odio a los que todavía sueñan con lo antiguo y piensan
> que nada puede ser superior a lo pasado.[43]

In 1916 the young poet visited Buenos Aires on his way to Europe and presented a lecture on the program of creationism as he at that time envisioned it. There is no written text of the lecture itself, but Huidobro has this comment to make about it in a later work: "Pero donde la teoría se expuso claramente fue en el Ateneo de Buenos Aires, en una conferencia que dicté en junio de 1916. Fue entonces que me bautizaron como creacionista, pues dije en mi conferencia que la primera condición de un poeta era crear; la segunda, crear, y la tercera, crear."[44]

---

[42] Fernández Moreno ("El ultraísmo," p. 46) quotes Ulises Petit de Murat as follows: "Para nosotros había pasado el tiempo del juego y queríamos construir."

[43] Vicente Huidobro, *Pasando y pasando* (Santiago: Imp. Chile, 1914), p. 29.

[44] Vicente Huidobro, *Manifestes* (Paris: Mondiale, 1925), p. 34.

That same year and also in the city of Buenos Aires, Huidobro published *El espejo de agua*,[45] a brief collection of poems in which his artistic theory was quite visible. Of special importance is the composition entitled "Arte Poética":

> Que el verso sea como una llave
> que abra mil puertas.
> Una hoja cae; algo pasa volando;
> cuanto miren los ojos creado sea,
> y el alma del oyente quede temblando.
>
> Inventa nuevos mundos y cuida tu palabra;
> el adjetivo, cuando no da vida, mata.
> Estamos en el ciclo de los nervios.
> El músculo cuelga,
>
> como recuerdo, en los museos;
> mas no por eso tenemos menos fuerza:
> El vigor verdadero
> reside en la cabeza.
>
> Por qué cantáis la rosa, ¡oh Poetas!
> Hacedla florecer en el poema;
> sólo para nosotros
> viven todas las cosas bajo el Sol.
> El Poeta es un pequeño Dios.[46]

This poem is an early and careful statement of the creationist aesthetic. The poet, in a conscious process, takes those elements about him to produce or create. Poetry does not have to be a reflection of nature or the external world; the creationist poet has divine powers which are sufficient to bring his own world into existence.

In late 1916 Huidobro arrived in Paris and quickly associated himself with various figures in the French literary and artistic world. In 1917, in particular, he participated with Pierre Reverdy in the publication of the avant-garde journal *Nord-Sud* and published several collections of poetry in French. In 1918 he visited Madrid,

---

[45] The 1916 publication date has been much disputed, in particular by Guillermo de Torre and more recently by David Bary. In the prologue to the *Obras completas* Braulio Arenas asserts personal knowledge that the date is correct, and recent work by Richard L. Admussen and René de Costa bears out Arenas' claim. See "Huidobro, Reverdy, and the *editio princeps* of *El espejo de agua*," *Comparative Literature*, 24 (1972), 163–75.

[46] Huidobro, *Obras completas*, vol. 1, pp. 255–56.

and during that same year he published collections in Spanish and was one of the moving forces in the beginnings of *ultraísmo*. Rafael Cansinos-Asséns comments on Huidobro's stay in Madrid:

> El paso de Huidobro por entre nuestros jóvenes poetas ha sido una lección de modernidad y un acicate para trasponer las puertas que nunca deben cerrarse. Sea cualquiera la opinión que un temperamento personal pueda tener de las nuevas tendencias, es innegable que en la seriación del eterno progreso ideal, después del simbolismo y del decadentismo, sólo debe venir esta nueva concepción de lo bello que, emancipándose de las interpretaciones sentimentales, concede al mundo exterior una realidad independiente y prueba a expresarlo en una representación más viva, libre y pimentada de sus infinitas posibilidades de existir y de parecer.[47]

This same year Huidobro was interviewed in Chile by Angel Cruchaga, and in response to a question about the aesthetics of *creacionismo* he had this to say:

> Queremos hacer un arte que no imite ni traduzca la realidad; deseamos elaborar un poema que tomando de la vida sólo lo esencial, aquello de que no podemos prescindir, nos presente un conjunto lírico independiente que desprenda como resultado una emoción poética pura.
>
> Nuestra divisa fué un grito de guerra contra la anécdota y la descripción, esos dos elementos extraños a toda poesía pura y que durante tantos siglos han mantenido el poema atado a la tierra.
>
> En mi modo de ver el "creacionismo" es la poesía misma: algo que no tiene por finalidad, ni narrar, ni describir las cosas de la vida, sino hacer una totalidad lírica independiente en absoluto.[48]

In 1925 Huidobro published in Paris a collection of theoretical documents which he called *Manifestes*. One of these can be considered as a mature résumé of creationist theory in which Huidobro reduces his idea to four basic points:

> 1. Humanizar las cosas. Todo lo que pasa a través del organismo del poeta debe tomar la más grande cantidad de su calor. Aquí una cosa vasta, enorme como el horizonte, se humaniza, se con-

---

[47] Quoted from *Cosmópolis* by *La Nación* (Santiago), 19 May 1919.
[48] Angel Cruchaga, "Conversando con Vicente Huidobro," *El Mercurio* (Santiago), 31 August 1919.

vierte en íntima, en filial con el adjetivo cuadrado. El infinito entra en el nido de nuestro corazón.

2. Lo vago se hace precisco. Cerrando las ventanas de nuestra alma, lo que podía escaparse y convertirse en gaseoso, en estropajoso, permanece encerrado y se solidifica.

3. Lo abstracto se hace concreto y lo concreto abstracto. Es decir, el equilibrio perfecto, puesto que si usted estira lo abstracto hacia lo abstracto, se deshará en sus manos o se filtrará por sus dedos. Lo concreto si usted lo hace más concreto, acaso pueda servirle para beber vino o amoblar su salón, pero nunca para amoblar su alma.

4. Lo que es demasiado poético para ser creado se convierte en una creación al cambiar su valor usual, puesto que si el horizonte era poético en sí, si el horizonte era poesía en la vida, con el calificativo cuadrado llega a ser poesía en el arte.

De poesía muerta pasa a poesía viva.[49]

In the late 1920's the nature of Huidobro's own works began to change considerably, and his fervent apostleship of creationism was somewhat diminished. His long poem *Altazor*, which can be seen in some ways as the destruction of the *creacionista* experiment, appeared in 1931, and for some years after that poem Huidobro turned to the writing of prose fiction and to increased political activity.

The impact of the movement in Europe and in America was widespread but not particularly lasting. In France, for example, Huidobro is virtually forgotten as a participant in the postwar avant-garde, in spite of his own strenuous efforts to be recognized as a contributor of importance. His 1919 interview with Cruchaga makes perfectly clear that he saw *creacionismo* as the most serious and profound movement since symbolism and that his contribution to it was a fundamental one.

In Spain, as we have already observed from the comments of Cansinos-Asséns, Huidobro's presence in Madrid was sufficient to shake the literary establishment and to aid in bringing about some movement toward renovation. However, very few Spanish poets or writers continued to identify themselves with the tenets of cre-

[49] Huidobro, *Manifestes*, p. 36.

ationism or even to follow its techniques in more general ways. Gerardo Diego, and perhaps Juan Larrea, are the exceptions to this general rule. Diego acknowledges openly his debt to Huidobro and *creacionismo*, as can be seen in this excerpt from the prologue to his *Manual de espumas*: "Ese libro . . . nace de un conocimiento más directo del verdadero creacionismo y de Vicente Huidobro, todo ligado con mi primera visita a París (1922?). En esos poemas quiero hacer una transposición poética de lo que entonces era el cubismo. Así como en el cubismo, en un mismo cuadro, se fundan formas diversas, así, en mi Manual, dos o tres temas distintos en un mismo poema."[50]

In Latin America the impact of the movement was scattered and inconclusive. As Alberto Hidalgo suggests in his prologue to *Indice de la nueva poesía americana*, Huidobro was recognized as an important early figure in the renovation of literary style, but he really had few followers in America:

> Huidobro, en España, derroca el rubendarismo, y si bien puede afirmarse que su acción es igual a cero en America, algo se filtra aquí, a través de los ultraístas argentinos puesto que el ultraísmo es hechura suya. Así, el poeta chileno se asemeja a Rubén. Ambos aprenden el tono de la hora en Francia y lo trasladan a España. Con ellos Verlaine y Reverdy entran por turno en América. Ahora, bajo el sosiego de los años, empiezan unos a dar voces nuevas, apartándose de las escuelas iniciales, y otros inventan sistemas para uso propio, del mismo modo que cada quien se ajusta los pantalones a la altura que le conviene.[51]

Huidobro and his works were discussed at considerable length in Chile, with strong polarization of opinion.[52] Among Mexican *estridentistas* creationism was an early example of a need for renovation of literary form. In Ecuador, Huidobro's typographical and spatial experiments had some early influence, as can be seen in this 1921 composition by Hugo Mayo:

[50] Quoted by Dámaso Alonso in *Poetas españoles contemporáneos* (Madrid, 1958), p. 248.

[51] Alberto Hidalgo, *Indice de la nueva poesía americana* (Buenos Aires: El Inca, 1926), p. 9.

[52] See, for example, the comments of Julio Nerval in "Vicente Huidobro," *Renovación*, no. 6 (9 September 1926), 3.

Tres
es-
tre-
llas
como broches de camisa
En el océano de Aire
una gran O baña medio cuerpo
dibujando un paréntesis
huérfano
Ancianos que han lanzado
sus
bar-
bas
al vacío
como geroglíficos pretéritos.
Desde los laboratorios desconocidos
ruedan disolventes
dejando negra la placa
27' – 3"
Una lección de demarcación de fronteras.[53]

In spite of its sporadic effect on contemporary or subsequent writers, creationism has an important place in the development of Latin American literature in the twentieth century. Raúl Gustavo Aguirre observed in 1950: "El surrealismo, el creacionismo y su derivación en el invencionismo, significan la culminación de un proceso histórico por el cual el lenguaje poético alcanza el punto máximo de separación con el lenguaje lógico convencional."[54]

Modernism

Brazilian modernism took four important directions, each represented by major figures and publications. The first revolves around Mário de Andrade, whose experimental poem *Paulicéia Desvairada* epitomizes in its form the belligerent modernist attacks on traditional prosody and at the same time is a strongly Brazilian portrayal of the city of São Paulo in the 1920's. Oswald de Andrade and a

---

[53] Hugo Mayo, "Nocturno celeste," *Singulus*, 1 (no. 1, October 1921), 46–47.
[54] Quoted in "Realismo versus vanguardismo," *El Mundo*, 3 July 1966, 44.

number of other young writers from São Paulo and Rio participated
with Mário de Andrade in what he has called "a maior orgia intelectual que a história artística do país registra."[55] The journal
Klaxon is perhaps the most characteristic publication of this movement and contains manifestos and pronouncements which give a
strong sense of direction. The following excerpts from the *Klaxon*
manifesto provide some flavor of this combativeness and desire for
contemporaneousness:

Significação

A luta começou de verdade em princípios de 1921 pelas colunas
do "Jornal do Comércio" e do "Correio Paulistano." Primeiro Resultado: "Semana de Arte Moderna"—espécie de Conselho Inter-
nactional de Versalhes. Como êste, a semana teve sua razão de ser.
Como êle: nem desastre, nem triunfo. Como êle: deu frutos verdes.
Houve êrros proclamados em voz alta. Pregaram-se idéias inadimis-
síveis. É preciso refletir. É preciso esclarecer. É preciso construir.
Daí, KLAXON.

E KLAXON não se queixará jamais de ser incompreendido pelo
Brasil. O Brasil é que deverá se esforçar para compreender KLA-
XON.

ESTÉTICA

KLAXON sabe que o cinematografo existe. Pérola White é pre-
ferível a Sarah Bernhardt. Sarah é tragédia, romantismo sentimental e técnico. Pérola é raciocínio, instrução, esporte, rapidez,
alegria, vida. Sarah Bernhardt = século 19. Pérola White = século
20. A cinematografia é a criação artística mais representativa da
nossa época. É preciso observar-lhe a lição.

KLAXON não é exclusivista. Apesar disso jamais publicará inéditos maus de bons escritores já mortos.

KLAXON não é futurista.

KLAXON é klaxista.

. . . .

Problema

Século 19—Romantismo, Tôrre de Marfim, Simbolismo. Em
seguida o fogo de artifício internacional de 1914. Há perto de 130
anos que a humanidade está fazendo manha. A revolta é justíssima.
Queremos construir a alegria. A própria farsa, o burlesco não nos

55 Mário de Andrade, *O Movimento Modernista* (Rio de Janeiro: Casa do Estudante,
1942), p. 34.

repugna, como não repugnou a Dante, a Shakespeare, a Cervantes. Molhados, resfriados, reumatizados por uma tradição de lágrimas artísticas, decidimonos. Operação cirúrgica. Extirpação das glândulas lacrimais. Era dos 8 Batutas, do Jazz-Band, de Cricharrao, de Carlito, de Mutt & Jeff. Era do riso e da sinceridade. Era de construção. Era de KLAXON.[56]

A second dimension is one which accentuates the native Brazilian Indian and Negro way of life, as opposed to modern technology, as the basis for artistic renovation. Oswald de Andrade took the lead in the search for Brazilian primitivism by announcing in 1924 a manifesto which he called "Pau-Brasil." This pronouncement is a strong stand in favor of the originality of Brazilian culture, but one which must still be expressed in modern forms, as these excerpts from the manifesto make plain:

> O trabalho da geração futurista foi ciclópico. Acertar o relógio império da literatura nacional.
> Realizada essa etapa, o problema é outro. Ser regional e puro em sua época. . . .
> O estado de inocência substituindo o estado de graça que pode ser uma atitude do espírito. . . .
> O contrapêso da originalidade nativa para inutilizar a desão académica. . . .
> A reação contra tôdas as indigestões de sabedoria. O melhor de nossa tradição lírica. O melhor de nossa demonstração moderna. . . .
> Apenas brasileiros de nossa época. O necessário de química, de mecânica, de economia e de balística. Todo digerido. Sem meeting cultural. Práticos. Experimentais. Poetas. Sem reminiscência livrescas. Sem comparações de apoio. Sem pesquisa etimológia. Sem ontologia. . . .
> Bárbaro crédulos, pitorescos e meigos. Leitores de jornais. Pau Brasil. A floresta e a escola. O Museu Nacional. A cozinha, o minério e a dansa. A vegetação. Pau Brasil.
>
> Oswald de Andrade.[57]

"Pau-Brasil" was continued in the *antropofagia* movement, which was also begun by Oswald de Andrade in his 1928 journal

---

[56] *Klaxon*, no. 1 (15 May 1922).
[57] Oswald de Andrade, "Pau-Brasil," *Correio de Manhã*, 18 March 1924.

Revista de Antropofagia. This cannibalistic stance was at times intentionally humorous, but it nonetheless represented a desire for a primitive culture which would consume European influence. Jorge de Lima also made an important contribution to this primitivist dimension in his *negrista* poems.

Still a different trend in Brazilian modernism is one which disputed futurism and foreign influences and attempted to find essential value in the expression of Brazilian social and political realities. Menotti de Pichia, Plínio Salgado, and Cassiano Ricardo were the important figures in the Anta and Verde-Amarelo groups, which found their essence in the colors of the Brazilian flag:

> O estudo do Brasil já não será o estudo do índio. Do mesmo modo que o estudo da humanidade, que produziu o budismo, o cristianismo, a Grécia, a Idade Média, o romantismo e a eletricidade, não será apenas a pesquisa freudeana do homem da pedra lascada. Se Freud nos dá um algarismo, a História da Civilização nos ofereceu uma equação em que esse algarismo entra tao só como um dos muitíssimos fatores.
>
> Assim, também, o índio é um têrmo constante na progressão étnica e social brasileira; mas um têrmo não é tudo. Êle já foi dominado, quando se agitou entre nós a bandeira nacionalista,— o denominador comum das raças adventícias. Colocá-lo como numerador seria diminuí-lo. Sobrepô-lo será fadá-lo ao desaparecimento. Porque êle ainda vive, subjetivamente, e viverá sempre como um elemento de harmonia entre todos os que, antes de desembarcar em Santos, atiraram ao mar, como o cadáver de Zaratusta, os preconceitos e filosofias de origem.
>
> Estávamos e estamos fartos da Europa e proclamamos sem cessar a liberdade de ação brasileira.[58]

A final development within modernism is a slightly later reaction to the national and primitive dimensions already discussed, and it can best be described as an atempt to achieve a deeper philosophical and spiritual expression. Augusto Frederico Schmidt helped to define this reaction in these lines:

> Não quero mais o amor,
> Nem mais quero cantar a minha terra.
> Me perco neste mundo.
> Não quero mais o Brasil

[58] *Correio Paulistano,* 17 May 1929.

Não quero mais geografia
Nem pitoresco.[59]

Carlos Drummond de Andrade was probably the most important single figure in this more profound modernism. His poetry is simple and introspective and reaches out toward an understanding of himself and the world about him. The journal *Festa*, which was published in 1928 in Rio, was an important contribution in this direction and brought together such figures as Murilo Mendes and Cecília Meireles.

Modernism's most important accomplishment was probably its questioning of self-satisfied traditional values through its insistence upon new ways of looking at things. In aesthetic terms, beauty was not to be perceived only as it had been in the past but to be found as well in the unusual and often disconnected forms suggested by modern life. In literature, in particular, this break with tradition meant the destruction of accepted rhetorical and prosodic patterns and the insistent use of convoluted experimental forms, an ethnic and popular lexicon, and technical virtuosity.

The second major accomplishment of modernism was undoubtedly its contradictory insistence on Brazilian values as opposed to European ones. In spite of a large debt to European artistic and literary experimentations, such as futurism and surrealism, modernism insisted on adapting to a Brazilian setting. Even in the most mocking satires, African and native Indian values were seen as more important than those of Europe. Oswald de Andrade's well-known pun, "tupi or not tupi," is an example.

As can be plainly seen, Brazilian modernism was by no means monolithic in nature, but rather diverse and at times fragmented. Nonetheless, after the Semana de Arte Moderna in 1922, modernism quickly became a term used to refer to all the disparate facets together.

Minor Groups

In addition to the major groupings and terms that I have already examined, there are a number of others which are of even more limited currency or significance. I shall not attempt to deal exhaus-

59 Augusto Frederico Schmidt, *Canto do Brasileiro Augusto Frederico Schmidt* (Rio de Janeiro, 1928).

tively with all of these, but rather try to consider three of them, in three different countries, in a rather brief way.

Alberto Hidalgo was born in Arequipa, Peru, but spent most of his productive years in Buenos Aires. He had an early infatuation with Marinetti and futurism, and his first collections of poetry were in praise of war, speed, and machines. He soon went beyond these things, however, and with his book *Simplismo, poemas inventados por Alberto Hidalgo* (Buenos Aires, 1925) he created a separate vanguardist term. His prologue to this collection, "Invitación a la vida poética," is perhaps the most important pronouncement in regard to *simplismo*. Hidalgo deals with the problems of imagery and talks about the relationship of music to poetry, the abolition of traditional poetic devices, and the liberation of contemporary art forms from the past. Hidalgo's most original contribution is probably experimentation with typography. In the same prologue he made an interesting commentary on the character of individual letters, and much of his simplistic poetry uses that focus. "Jaqueca" (*Química del espíritu*, p. 75), for example, is composed of capital and lowercase letters scattered over a page:

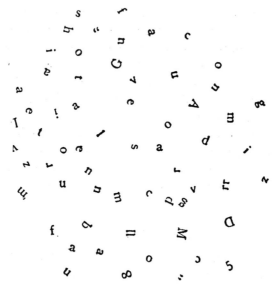

Another of Hidalgo's interesting experiments was the Revista Oral, in which various contributors read aloud their materials as if they together were articles in a journal.

In Mexico the *agoristas* went several steps beyond the stridentists in subordinating aesthetic considerations to a socialization of art: "Mientras existan problemas colectivos, ya sean emocionales, ideológicos o económicos, es indigna una actitud pasiva. Precisada esta situación fundamental, consideramos cuestiones secundarias las de técnica y teorización estética: lo que importa es responder categóricamente al ritmo de nuestro tiempo. Agorismo: arte en movimiento, velocidad creadora, socialización del arte."[60]

In 1928 four young Chilean writers published the "Cartel runrúnico" and the "Manifiesto runrunista," which suggested whispered rumors or false reports. One is tempted to see these pronouncements as not entirely serious, but they show nonetheless a youthful combination of attack and playfulness. These "cablegrams," from the collection *S.O.S.* by Lara, are examples:

> México 7.—Un general mexicano
>   murió de muerte natural   (u.p.)

> londres 15—mientras jugaba
>   una partida
> el príncipe de gales
> se cayó de un caballo
> de ajedrez   (u.p.)

> new york 19—rumbo a nicaragua
> 23 blindados yanquis
>   zarparon
> en misión dé paz   (u.p.)[61]

Vanguardism as a General Term

Among the several designations that I have examined thus far, there are few which can be used in a general sense to describe an entire period or even an attitude within a chronological span. *Postmodernism*, for example, has at times been used as an all-encompassing term although it is insufficient to deal with the substantive changes of the 1920's and 1930's. In the same way, *surrealism* has been used to correlate and schematize the literary development of the period.

---

[60] Quoted by Carlos Monsivais in "Los estridentistas y los agoristas," in *Los vanguardismos en la América Latina*, pp. 171–72.
[61] Poem no. 19 in Lara, *S.O.S.* (n.p.: Ed. Run-run, 1929).

However, it is perhaps too strongly identified with its European origins to be entirely useful as a general American term. *Futurism* had a rather widespread early effect, but it was too soon discarded to be useful in dealing with the large number of movements which developed during the twenties and thirties. *Modernism* has a rather precise meaning in Brazil, but it is useless as a general term in Spanish America because of confusion with the preceding terminology. *Ultraism* is too limited in its geographical extension to be universally useful, and *creationism* is perhaps too individual and too highly theoretical. In short, there seems to be but one term which can in any way be generalized and which at the same time has some considerable basis in contemporary usage. I refer, as must be obvious at this point, to *vanguardism*, which is used almost exclusively in a general sense by commentators of the period as well as by most recent critics.

The term, both in its Anglicized and Hispanicized forms, comes from the French *avant-garde*, which in its fundamental meaning refers to those troops located in the most forward positions of a military or battle formation. The term is certainly not restricted to the period under discussion here, but it is limited in current usage, in the literary sense at least, to refer to something which goes beyond conventional limits. In the historical framework I am considering, however, it was much used and was undoubtedly attractive for several reasons. To begin with, it was a term in vogue in the French groups, and from the point of view of the Latin Americans it expressed in a very real sense a desire for commonality. At the same time it represented the combativeness of at least the early years of the period, and it canalized into a single term the pugnacious desire of the young writers for literary renovation.

The sense of renewal or of new directions is probably the central force in all groups, and it is in this somewhat abstract sense that the term *vanguardism* has fundamental meaning. For example, Enrique López Albújar uses the term in this way in a 1930 interview, in which he responds to a question about new poetry:

> En realidad no hay poesía vanguardista. En el tiempo nada está a la zaga. Y en el arte, menos. No hay sino bueno y malo, grande y pequeño. Cosas que acaban y cosas que principian. Una cadena interminable y espiráfica, en la cual el último eslabón que se ad-

hiere no puede jactarse de ser el definitivo porque detrás viene el que lo desmentirá. Ahora, si por vanguardismo se entiende la manera de decir extravagancias ideológicas y ortográficas, como la de firmar en minúsculas, esto no pasa de pueril y hasta de inoriginal. En los archivos de las notarías de Lambayeque hay infinidad de escrituras con ortografía de esta clase. Gran parte de los indios jayancas, morropanos y motupes firmaron así. Posiblemente había ya en estos ascendientes un soplo de vanguardismo. Si es así, habría que reivindicar para estos indígenas el honor de ser los precursores de cierta rama vanguardista.

Pero si el vanguardismo se toma el sentido de renovación de la técnica literaria o de señalamiento de nuevos rumbos artísticos, hay que convenir en que el vanguardismo es una verdad. Mas no una verdad definitiva, sino una verdad transitoria, necesaria para anudar los hilos del pensamiento, rotos por la tensión de ideas largo tiempo usadas.[62]

In Spanish America the terms *vanguardismo, vanguardista, de vanguardia,* and even *vanguardizar* are used with great frequency in discussing the new modes of literature. In almost every case the intent is to generalize,[63] and single figures or national areas are not specifically referred to.

In Argentina, for example, Manuel Gálvez made the following statement:

La literatura de vanguardia comprende todas las escuelas surgidas en los últimos veinte años, desde el futurismo hasta el superrealismo. Aquí hemos llamado a este movimiento: nueva sensibilidad. Pero hay un vanguardismo no escolástico, que consiste en recibir las influencias de las orientaciones esenciales, pero sin adherirse totalmente a una escuela.

Entre los escritores que hemos precedido al vanguardismo, es frecuente repudiar las nuevas ideologías literarias, aunque reconociendo el valor promisorio de algunos de los líderes juveniles. Es un error. Las modernas tendencias estéticas contienen verdades fundamentales. Después de algunos años, y ahora que el vanguardismo comienza a ser cosa juzgada, podremos advertir su trascen-

62 *La Sierra,* 1930, 47.

63 An important exception is the Boedo-Florida dispute in Buenos Aires, discussed above, in which *vanguardista* is used interchangeably with *ultraísta* and *martinfierrista.* See, for example, the article by José C. Picone, "La usurpación vanguardista y la literatura de Izquierda," *Claridad,* 8 (no. 181, 27 April 1929).

dencia. La literatura necesitaba una renovación geológica. Sin el vanguardismo, hubiéramos seguido haciendo lo mismo que en el siglo XIX. [64]

In Chile the term was in current use by 1920, as indicated by the translated comments of the French poet Nicolas Beauduin which appeared in *El Mercurio*.[65] In 1930 the Chilean critic Angel Cruchaga discussed the term in some length. He made reference to the continued disputes in regard to the center of activities in the Hispanic world and gave some indication that the concept and the term were still much under discussion in Chile:

> No hace mucho, las revistas de España y las del Nuevo Mundo comentaron exaltadamente el tema de moda: "la ubicación del Meridiano de la Lengua Española" y las opiniones nunca llegaron a unificarse.
>
> Ahora las publicaciones de Madrid discuten acaloradamente el concepto de "vanguardia," y mientras muchos escritores niegan que haya existido esa vanguardia, o sea, la actitud extrema de lucha en el movimiento de las ideas estéticas, algunos le asignan una situación precisa que difícilmente podría negarse, ya que ese concepto es como el afán constante de la juventud que en todos los climas y épocas ha tratado de superarse y de vislumbrar un camino en la originalidad. . . .
>
> Entre nosotros también se ha analizado el concepto de vanguardia, pero ante esta palabra que implica el gesto del explorador o del heraldo que busca nuevos mundos, los comentaristas han sonreído o se han horrorizado como si ella significara una completa obscuridad o fuera el anticipo de caos.[66]

In Peru, Aurelio Miró Quesada S. uses the term to refer to the belligerent first phase of the period and to suggest the necessity for a more mature utilization of the gains made: "El movimiento 'vanguardista' se presentó como un estruendo, una beligerancia, una actitud. Protesta del momento, tenía que acentuar el tablado y el gesto. No le bastaban los trabajos menudos. Necesitaba el decordo,

[64] Manuel Gálvez, "De vanguardia," *Número*, no. 2 (February 1930), 1.

[65] Translated from *La bataille littéraire* in *El Mercurio*, 26 September 1920, as "La nueva poesía y Vicente Huidobro." Also for early documentation of the term, see Saúl Yurkievich, "*Rosa Náutica*, un manifiesto del movimiento de vanguardia chileno," *Bulletin de la Faculté des Lettres de Strasbourg*, 46 (1968), 649–55.

[66] Angel Cruchaga, "En torno a la vanguardia," *Letras* (Santiago), 3 (no. 25, October 1930), 13.

el acompañamiento de la orquesta, para elevar su aria insistente hasta los más inéditos confines. Pasada la etapa del preludio sería ya más fácil empezar la función." [67]

In an article written from Paris in 1927, César Vallejo expresses the idea that, though at one time necessary, vanguardism has fulfilled its historic purpose. He decries the insistence of those who would continue an appeal to contemporary idols:

> Todos y no por snobismo sino sinceramente, vanguardizan en política con los comunistas integrales, en economía con el marxismo, en literatura con el superrealismo, en música con el yaz-band, en artes plásticas con los negros, en ciencia pura con Einstein, en ciencia aplicarda con el cinema, en gimnástica con el tennis. El pueblo goza ante todo esto hasta el espasmo. Como se vé, ya no existe lucha alguna entre los hierofantes de estas nuevas modalidades de vida y la vasta y cabezuda clientela. Tales revoluciones han logrado una victoria absoluta. Su jornada histórica, en cuanto espíritu revolucionario, está, pues, cumplida.
>
> ¿Qué se quiera más? No vemos la causa del espectáculo que ofrecen esos revolucionarios, cuando saltan a mitad de los grandes bulevares a gritar, con voz de Daniel en el pozo de los leones:
>
> —En verdad os digo que las vanguardias salvarán a los hombres. En verdad os digo que los vanguardistas son los enviados de Dios. Abominad a los que no creen en Charlot, en Josephine Backer, en Lenin, en Einstein, en Suzanne Lenglen, en el radio, en los versos con punta, en la Tour Eiffel, en Tunney, etc. . . .[68]

Ecuadorian writers and critics used the term frequently as a generalizing mechanism. For example, Alfonso Rumazo González made these comments in 1930: "Entonces a las antiguas escuelas se sucedió el afán modernista en sus múltiples formas: intimismo, simbolismo, versolibrismo, musicalismo, creacionismo y en general las múltiples facetas del vanguardismo que al fin y al cabo no es sino la expresión literaria de la emoción modernizada."[69]

In Mexico the term was used as early as 1921. The best example

---

[67] Aurelio Miró Quesada S., "Cuaderno de arte nuevo," *Nueva revista peruana*, 1 (no. 1, August 1929), 61.

[68] César Vallejo, "Los idolos de la vida contemporánea," *Mundial*, no. 358 (22 April 1927), 5.

[69] Alfonso Rumazo González, "La evolución de la poesía en el Ecuador," *Revista de sociedad juridico-literaria*, 39 (no. 128, January–June 1930), 104.

of this use is probably the stridentist publication *Actual No. 1,* which has the subtitle *Hoja de vanguardia.* In a prologue Maples Arce makes the following generalizing comment: "En nombre de la vanguardia actualista de México, sinceramente horrorizada de todas las placas notariales y de rótulos consagrados del sistema cartulario, con veinte siglos de éxito efusivo en farmacias y droguerías subvencionadas por la ley, me centralizo en el vértice eclatante de mi insustituible categoría presentista, equiláteramente convencida y eminentemente revolucionaria, mientras que todo el mundo que está fuera del eje, se contempla esféricamente atónito con las manos torcidas. . . ."[70]

In Brazil the question is more complicated. The term *vanguardism* was apparently not used there nearly as much as it was in the Spanish American countries, perhaps because *modernist* often had both specific and general meanings. However, there was some awareness of *vanguardism* and of its generalizing function. One example is the article by Peregrino Júnior, which was prepared in Spanish for publication in *Martín Fierro* and which also appeared in 1928 in the Brazilian journal *Verde.* He describes the modernist movement in Brazil, together with its main figures, journals, and critics. At several points in the article he uses the term *vanguardismo* or *vanguardista* to describe the modernist movement and at the same time to suggest a basis of comparison with similar groups outside Brazil: "Después hablaremos más detenidamente sobre esas diversas corrientes en que la actualidad literaria de nuestra gente de vanguardia, mostrando la significación de sus ideas, de sus programas y de sus obras. Desde ya, por otra parte, debo decir, para ser exacto y honesto, que ninguna generación, en ningún tiempo, realizó en el Brazil una obra tan bella y tan fascinante, como la que están realizando en esta hora los modernistas."[71]

Later commentators on the modernist movement in Brazil have helped somewhat to clarify this point. I have already mentioned the article of Stefan Baciu, who considers in some detail the possible relationships of Brazilian and Spanish American groups. Even more interesting, however, for its use of the term *vanguard* is the talk

---

[70] Quoted by Schneider, *El estridentismo,* p. 36.
[71] Peregrino Júnior, "El vanguardismo en el Brasil," *Verde,* 1 (no. 5, January 1928), 16.

delivered by Clarice Lispector in which she attempts to make some connections between modernism and other movements in Brazil and the concept of the literary vanguard. She insists on the idea of liberation as a part of the vanguardist spirit and uses the Brazilian modernist period as an illustration of the term:

Tive que pôr de lado a palavra vanguarda no seu sentido europeu. Pensei, por exemple, se o nosso movimento de 1922—o chamado movimento modernista—seria considerado vanguarda por outros paises em 1922 mesmo. Nesse movimento a experimentação característica de uma vanguarda seria reconhecida como tal por outras literaturas? O movimento de 1922 foi um movimento de profunda libertação. Libertação significa sobretudo, um nôvo modo de ver. Libertação é sempre vanguarda. E também nessa de 1922 quem estava na linha de frente se sacrificou. Mas libertação é, às vêzes, avanço apenas para quem se está libertando e pode não ter valor de moeda corrente para os outros. Para nós, 1922 significou vanguarda por exemplo, independente de qualquer valor universal. Foi movimento de posse. Um movimento de tomada de ser, de um dos nossos modos de ser, o mais urgente daquela época, talvez.[72]

Conclusion

The chronologies and terms which I have attempted to examine here are varied on the one hand and susceptible to unification on the other. National realities are strong, but the same cultural and literary influences have an effect in all of Latin America. The search for new expression in the 1920's and 1930's can be characterized, I feel, under the general rubric of *vanguardism*, and it is possible to see Brazilian *modernismo, creacionismo, estridentismo, ultraismo*, and *superrealismo* as various facets of the same literary and cultural whole. As well, Vicente Huidobro, Pablo Neruda, Jorge Luis Borges, César Vallejo, José Carlos Martiátegui, Manuel Maples Arce, Xavier Villaurrutia, and Nicolás Guillén can be seen in context with Mário de Andrade, Oswald de Andrade, Carlos Drummond de Andrade, Jorge de Lima, and Augusto Frederico Schmidt.

An international approach to the study of the vanguardist period reveals diversity and unity, originality and importation, nationality

[72] Clarice Lispector, "Literatura de Vanguarda no Brasil," in *Movimientos literarios de vanguardia en Iberoamérica*, p. 111.

and universality, success and failure. More than any one thing, however, it makes clear the importance of the writers of this generation, who in their experimentation and in their maturity have contributed in a fundamental way to the development of Latin American literature in the twentieth century.

Graça Aranha
and Brazilian Modernism

Anoar Aiex

In his famous lecture on the modernist movement in Brazil, Mário de Andrade observed: "A transformação do mundo, com o enfraquecimento gradativo dos grandes impérios, com a prática européia dos novos ideais políticos, a rapidez dos transportes e mil e uma outras causas internacionais, bem como o desenvolvimento da consciência americana e brasileira, os progressos da técnica e da educação, impunham a criação e mesmo a remodelação da inteligência nacional."[1] Andrade uses this inventory of historical and social developments in describing the internal and external causes of the Brazilian modernist movement. The external causes cited are the development of the First World War; the appearance of such political ideologies as communism, fascism, and nazism, all of which ran contrary to economic liberalism; and the awakening of an American conscience with the first Pan-American Congress in 1888 and the Mexican Revolution in 1910. The internal causes he mentions are the industrialization and economic progress of Brazil; the development of transportation, communications, and sanitation; and the occurrence of the first general strike in São Paulo in 1917.[2]

The convergence of these events, according to de Andrade, ex-

[1] The lecture, "O movimento modernista," is from 1942 and was later included in *Aspectos da Literatura Brasileira* (São Paulo: Martins Editôra, 1959).

[2] See Mário da Silva Brito, *História do Modernismo Brasileiro*, vol. 1, *Antecedentes da Semana de Arte Moderna* (Rio de Janeiro: Editôra Civilização Brasileira, 1964), pp. 24–28.

plains the collective protest of the Semana de Arte Moderna, which took place in São Paulo in February, 1922. With that event, then, the modernist movement was officially established; in close connection with the development of Brazilian politics and society,[3] it continued until 1954, when, in the opinion of Tristão de Ataíde, it was brought to a close by the death of Mário de Andrade, the end of the Second World War, and the redemocratization of the country with the collapse of the Getúlio Vargas regime.[4]

It is well known that modernism was predominantly a literary and artistic movement and that it fought against Parnassian-symbolist poetry, against prose fiction which held itself aloof from the national reality, and against plastic arts which were overly academic. The movement later took on an accentuated national coloring and attempted to interpret artistically both the present and the past of Brazil. This search for origins transformed the modernist leaders into interpretative essayists on the national past and its meaning. It is this thought to which Cruz Costa refers when he says: "Uma perspectiva mais clara do destino nacional toma corpo em função mesmo da cultura européia. Será mais um passo no nosso progresso de consciência."[5]

The essay as a literary form was amplified considerably in the modernist period and was extended to history, sociology, economics, and philosophy. I do not intend to touch here on all these areas, but rather to limit the scope of this study to the interpretation of Brazilian reality in the philosophical essay.

The presentation of the problem in these terms needs some clarification. The history of philosophical ideas in Brazil, as in other Latin American countries, depends on the currents and schools of European philosophy. It is entirely to be expected that this should

---

[3] The "Copacabana" fort uprising in 1922, the antioligarchical revolution of 1930 and the counterrevolution of 1932, the communist revolution of 1935 and the fascist "Intentona" of 1937, the "Estado Novo" of 1938 and the redemocratization of 1945 shook Brazil in her political and social structure. These events reflected the political positions of various modernists, characterized as rightist, Catholic, and leftist, according to Emílio Salles Gomes in Wilson Martins, *A Literatura Brasileira*, vol. 6, *O Modernismo* (São Paulo: Cultrix Editôra, 1965), pp. 134–35.

[4] Alceu Amoroso Lima [Tristão de Ataíde], *Quadro Sintético da Literatura Brasileira* (Rio de Janeiro: Agir, 1959).

[5] João Cruz Costa, *Panorama da História da Filosofia no Brasil* (São Paulo: Cultrix Editôra, 1960), p. 73.

be true, for philosophical systems can be characterized by their sense of universality. There are, nevertheless, attempts to fragment this commonality by creating a national philosophy capable of reflecting the soul of a particular people and by modifying ideas in contact with a different historical and social environment. It is with this intention that Brazilian thinkers search their history for the roots of a national philosophy. They believe that delving into the past offers answers sufficient to explain the contradictions of the present and to prepare the way for the future.

However, since such an undertaking in the modernist period was a part of the search for origins as well, Brazilian essayists took from European culture the tools necessary to form their own philosophy from a nonphilosophical past. Such a phenomenon occurred with orthodox positivism, for example. Cruz Costa calls this attitude in the development of a history of ideas in Brazil, as well as in modernism, an "experiência americana."[6]

The history of ideas in Brazil also presents another aspect, namely, the past being seen through a superimposed philosophical model rather than revealing itself as its own model. With respect to this idea, Bento Prado, Jr., affirms that the "Brazilian experiment" can be characterized as a "temporalidade invertida: nessa a reflexão precede a percepção, a filosofia da filosofia precede a própria filosofia."[7]

In addition, the attempt to understand the roots of the past in order to establish a national philosophy causes the essayist to adopt generally a psychological and historical position. A national philosophy is seen as the expression of the national soul, which maintains its reality unchanged throughout its entire history. The historical point of view presupposes, therefore, the continual development of national awareness based on the concept of historical continuity. It is Cruz Costa's opinion that a certain pragmatism from Portuguese origins continues to be the fundamental matrix of Brazilian thought in the course of its historical development.[8]

It appears, however, that historical perspective is not sufficient to

6 João Cruz Costa, *Contribuição a História das Idéias no Brasil* (Rio de Janeiro: José Olympio Editôra, 1956), pp. 14–15.

7 Bento Prado, Jr., "Il Problema Della Filosofia in Brasile," *Rivista di Filosofia e di Cultura*, nos. 109–10 (January–March 1969), 87–104.

8 Cruz Costa, *Panorama da História* and *Contribuição a História*.

explain Brazilian thought during the modernist period. The essayists of that time did not adopt the same attitude about their relationship to the past or about the meaning of nationalism. For some, the
present was significant solely as a function of the past,[9] or it was to be
seen as a process of breaking with the past.[10] Others proclaimed the
need to bring about a severing of connections with the past, especially in those areas having to do with Portuguese influence. It was
necessary to Brazilianize the culture of Brazil.

The Essays of Graça Aranha

As a writer of undisputed reputation since the publication of his
novel *Canaã* in 1902, Graça Aranha was willing to wager his name
and prestige on the renovating ventures of the young rebels of the
Semana de Arte Moderna, and he placed his first bet with the opening speech of those proceedings, which he entitled "A Emoção
Estética na Arte Moderna." As an active member of the Brazilian
Academy of Letters, he pursued the same line some two years later
by delivering a lecture entitled "O Espírito Moderno" on June 19,
1924. On July 3 he presented a project to the academy which set out
a proposal for reforming its activities. The principal items of that
proposal were the following: (1) that the dictionary which the academy intended to prepare should be called *Dicionário Brasileiro da
Lingua Portuguêsa* and should include words and phrases of the
current Brazilian language, improperly called Brazilianisms, and
exclude *"portuguesismos,"* that is, words and expressions used in
Portugal alone; and (2) that the academy should not accept in its
literary contexts (a) Parnassian, arcadian, or classical poetry; (b)
poetry, novels, short stories, or other fictional work with mythological themes, except those which had to do with Brazilian folklore and
were handled from a modern point of view; or (c) works of foreign
history, whether ancient or modern. Works of Brazilian history had
to be treated with a modern critical spirit capable of understanding

[9] One finds implicit in *Casa Grande e Senzala* (4th ed., 2 vols. [Rio de Janeiro: José
Olympio Editôra, 1943]) the position assumed by Gilberto Freyre later in *O Mundo
que o Português Criou* (Rio de Janeiro: José Olympio Editôra, 1941) and *New World
in the Tropics* (New York: Knopf and Random House, 1959).

[10] Sérgio Buarque de Holanda, *Raízes do Brasil*, 5th ed. (Rio de Janeiro: José
Olympio Editôra, 1969).

how to situate the past and how to break from its influence. When this project was rejected Graça Aranha separated himself from the Brazilian Academy of Letters. In a speech entitled "O Espírito Acadêmico" and in a letter dated October 18, 1924, he declared the academy obsolete and completely divorced from any desires for philosophical, social, and artistic change in Brazil.[11]

The episodes of 1922 and 1924 are only a few of many events which marked the life of Graça Aranha and characterized him as an independent spirit and a nonconformist in his relationships with the established order. It is precisely because of this strain of rebellion that he took upon himself at the same time certain responsibilities in the direction of the modernist movement. He had an open mind about the sociointellectual realities of Brazil, and he was seriously concerned about the historical destiny of nationalism. He attempted to absorb these new realities and to situate them within a larger context of ideas which he had already formulated. These attempts can be detected in his literary development, beginning with the publication of his first work, the preface to a book by Fausto Cardoso, *Concepção Monística do Universo* (1894), and continuing with his novel *Canaã*, the collections of essays *Estética da Vida* (1920) and *Espírito Moderno* (1925), and the novel *A Viagem Maravilhosa* (1931). Graça Aranha intuited in his essays and illustrated in his fictional work the bases of his aesthetic view of the world, which he not only accepted as the foundation of his thought but considered as the ideological model for his interpretations of Brazilian reality and modernist philosophy.

Intelligence and Imagination

In looking at the problem of meaning in human life, Graça Aranha assumes that man, while he lived in a state of complete innocence, was perfectly integrated with his universe and thus had a sense of homogeneity of his own being and nature. This integrity was broken at the very moment in which man became conscious of being

---

[11] Jose Pereira da Graça Aranha, "O Espírito Moderno," in *Obra Completa* (Rio de Janeiro: Instituto Nacional do Livro, 1969), pp. 740, 744, 756, 760, 761. Hereafter, all references to Graça Aranha's works are cited by author, essay title, and pages from this edition.

something apart from the other things in the universe, and at that moment he felt a sense of anguish. There remains still in his spirit the desire to return to that primitive unity, and this desire gives rise to religion, philosophy, and art.

Before attempting to show how these disciplines propose to solve the problem, it is appropriate to examine the philosophical currents which influenced Graça Aranha and the ways in which they made it possible for him to reintegrate the specific within the general.

From 1882 until 1886 Graça Aranha studied law in Recife under the formal and informal direction of Tobias Barreto. More than forty years later, Graça Aranha referred to that period with great enthusiasm: "nunca mais me separei intelectualmente de Tobias Barreto." He added that the principal lesson taken from Barreto was that of being able "pensar com audácia," which allowed him to break away from the "velha mentalidade brasileira" through use of the principles derived from "transformismo, monismo e determinismo."[12]

This system of ideas is reduced by Clóvis Bevilaqua to the single expression "reação científica," which is born from the "espírito positivo" and its heterodox offspring—that is, separated from Comte's orthodox positivism. These ideas take on an important role as the common denominator of the "idéias novas," that is, "positivismo, evolucionismo, determinismo e monismo, o *cientificismo*: a supervalorização da ciência passa a ser o ponto de encontro do pensamento nôvo."[13]

It was precisely by means of this *cientificismo* that Tobias Barreto, the principal figure in the Recife school, attacked the old Brazilian mentality represented by the spiritualist terms *eclecticism* and *Thomism*. He assailed the Brazilian followers of Victor Cousin, whose influence on Brazilian thought lasted from 1830 to 1970,[14] and he also considered correctly that the eclectic current attempted to bring about a kind of peace treaty among all belligerent systems. He indicated that the rhetorical style of the eclectics had the gift of

12 Graça Aranha, "O Meu Próprio Romance," p. 573.

13 Luis W. Vita, *Antologia do Pensamento Social e Político no Brasil* (São Paulo: Editorial Grijalbo, 1968), p. 197.

14 *Ibid.*, p. 87. See also chapter 3 of Antônio Paim, *História das Idéias Filosóficas no Brasil* (São Paulo: Editorial Grijalbo, 1967).

attracting unprepared minds, furnishing them with a large dose of knowledge with the obvious advantage of saving them the trouble of thinking.[15]

Thomist thought was introduced into Brazil in the colonial period and continues its influence to the present. Although its historical development has not been rectilinear, it received new encouragement from the encyclical *Aeterni patris* of Leo XIII, published on August 4, 1879, on the form of Neothomism.[16] Barreto made it very clear that the adherents of Thomist thought were men with their backs turned to the future,[17] and he argued against their thesis that attempted to reconcile faith and reason. He indicated that there was a fundamental difference between religious sentiment and scientific learning, and he defended the dichotomy between belief and science or between faith and reason.

In sum, Barreto's criticism of Cousin's Thomist spiritualism brings to the debate on philosophical thought a grouping of ideas of scientific origin, around which the philosophy of his time turned. This influence was absorbed by Graça Aranha and gave him the fundamental bases of his thought. I have chosen to reduce those bases in this essay to the term *intelligence*.

During the period between Baretto's intellectual activity and the elaboration of Graça Aranha's thought, European culture also underwent new changes set in motion at the end of the nineteenth century and crystallized in the period of the First World War. Those changes had to do with the crisis of science as the solution for human problems and as the generating force of values and ideals in Western society. Other currents emerge from this crisis, such as vitalism, intuitionism, and spiritualism, which together made more evident the irrational elements which operated in the comprehension and solution of human problems.

To the degree that he was influenced by these tendencies, then, perhaps by the books of Émile Faguet, *En Lisant Nietzsche*, and Le Roy, *Une philosophie nouvele*, which spreads the ideas of Bergson, and perhaps by his travels through Europe, where he met Maurice

---

[15] Tobias Barreto, *Obras Completas*, vol. 1, *Estudos de Filosofia* (Rio de Janeiro: Instituto Nacional do Livro, 1966).

[16] Vita, *Pensamento Social e Político*, p. 118.

[17] See, for example, Barreto's essays "A Religião perante a psicologia" and "A ciência da alma ainda e sempre contestada" in *Estudos de Filosofia*.

Barrés and absorbed the artistic orientations of Marinetti,[18] Graça
Aranha developed another dimension in his philosophical thought,
which I here call "imagination."

Having described these developmental influences on Graça Aranha, I can now return to his own philosophical ideas. In his view,
religious sentiment exists in man as a function of the terror which
the mystery of worldly things causes in him. Because of their lack
of scientific explanation for such phenomena, primitive people had
recourse to animism, which is the attribution of one or several souls
to all beings in nature. This animism becomes the basis for all religious forms, but has in each a different significance. If primitive
man attributed a spirit to each being, the pantheist assumes the
existence of spirituality in all nature, and the Christian considers
spiritual power as a force which transcends and acts upon natural
phenomena. From this process of approximation between the natural and the spiritual there is born a unifying passion or relation
which again precipitates man into a state of "inconsciência inicial."[19] Therefore, when religion reaches a maximum point of spirituality it brings about in man a return to the point of origin—a
process for which an explanation was sought in conscious integration of the specific within the general, or of man within his totality.

To the degree, therefore, that science increases its explanation of
natural phenomena, religious sentiment begins to show its insuffi-
ciency and gives rise to philosophy. Working from the direct correlation between scientific interpretation and philosophy, Graça
Aranha assumes that the human spirit is emancipated from "monismo religioso" in order to accept "monismo filosófico."[20] Therefore, the results of each particular science do not interest him as
much as a single scientific system which makes possible a unified
explanation of specific phenomena, because science, in the view of

[18] In the same way that Faguet interpreted Nietzsche in 1905, based upon a "critique des obstacles: les religions, le rationalisme et la science, la morale," Graça Aranha
proceeds in "Estética da Vida." The nationalism of Maurice Barrés is discussed by
Graça Aranha in two articles: "Maurice Barrés" (1925), pp. 784–89, and "Meu amigo
Barrés" (1928), pp. 866–74. In May, 1926, Graça Aranha presented Marinetti when
the latter gave a lecture in the Teatro Lírico do Rio de Janeiro. This presentation,
which supported the vitalist foundations of Marinetti's thought but not his political
position, was published as a preface to Marinetti's *Futurismo: Manifesto de Marinetti
e seus companheiros* (Rio de Janeiro: Pimenta de Mello, 1926).

[19] Graça Aranha, "A Estética da Vida," p. 592.

[20] *Ibid.*

Graça Aranha, has the function of dividing the idea of totality in fragments[21] in order to be able to analyze them with experimental methodology,[22] which in turn will produce an explanation based on the scheme being used. Physics proceeds in this fashion, for example, when it isolates "matter" from "energy"[23] in order to explain them as independent phenomena. Such a method is seen by Graça Aranha as an obstacle to what he calls "explicação sintética do Todo."[24]

Finally, in Graça Aranha's opinion, art can bring about an integration of man and his totality. However, difficulties appear when one seeks to define art, since the innumerable definitions which have been used destroy the sense of universality caused by aesthetic experience. Graça Aranha takes exception, in the first place, to the tenet that "o sentimento estético" should be subordinated to the idea of "utilidade social," and he is of the opinion that such an idea does not explain the origin or the purpose of art. He prefers, then, a concept of disinterested art in which utility is one characteristic of scientific knowledge which has to do with the technical development of society. Second, he finds that art cannot be restricted to the idea of "play" since this aspect is only one of its effects and not the cause of artistic creation. Third, the problem becomes even more mysterious when one attempts to identify aesthetic emotion with the idea of beauty, either because of the inherent difficulties and definition of beauty or in order to limit the scope of artistic creation.[25]

From this analysis of Graça Aranha's ideas, we can conclude that religion, philosophy (as residues of these specific sciences), and art reveal themselves as obstacles which impede the return of the human spirit to its primitive unity. In order to overcome those obstacles, nonetheless, it is essential to base those disciplinary views on an intuition which is wider and more general. As Graça Aranha writes, "a função essencial do espírito humano—é a função estética, e que só esta explica o Universo e a nós mesmos."[26]

For Graça Aranha the term *aesthetic* has a specific meaning:

21 *Ibid.*, p. 591.
22 *Ibid.*, p. 613.
23 *Ibid.*, p. 585.
24 *Ibid.*, p. 599.
25 *Ibid.*, pp. 599–609.
26 *Ibid.*, p. 616.

"spectacular." Therefore, having been unable to find an irrational explanation for the universe (since this would produce a dualist philosophy with separation of subject from object or conscience from totality) he bases his intuition of the universe on the monist philosophy, which causes him to visualize the universe as a "representation" or "a spectacle."[27] According to Francovich, Graça Aranha agrees with Bergson that man exists in an "oceano imenso de imagens, que constituem por definição o que chamamos realidade."[28] Reality is thus an appearance, a succession of images, a representation, a spectacle.

The aesthetic conception of the universe, which in turn serves as an aesthetic foundation for man, does not bring any absolute notion, whether it be moral or religious. On the contrary, it consists of a perfect interplay of forces. As an integral part of that play, man is also a transitory representation of fantasy, but with the ability to be aware of his part in this universal representation. In other words, as Graça Aranha writes: "O universo se projeta no nosso espírito, como uma imagem, um espetáculo."[29]

An aesthetic of life presupposes, at the same time, man's acceptance of certain moral principles. First, he must resign himself to cosmic fatality; that is, he must situate himself in the same transformational process as other things in the same universe. Second, he must become a part of the earth in order to see himself as an expression of the physical milieu. Third, he must unite himself with other men as an indication of human solidarity and as the mechanism for the formation of society.[30]

Graça Aranha's acceptance of this elemental ethic should not imply an admission that the spirit is passive. On the contrary, one takes from the aesthetic contemplation of the universe new incentives for action, since it is only through spiritual activity that man can attain the desired unity. Graça Aranha comes close in this idea

---

27 *Ibid.* The intuition is one of a Bergsonian sense: "On appelle *intuition* cette espéce de *sympathie intellectuelle* par laquelle on se transporte à l'intérieur d'un objet pour coincidir avec ce qu'il a d'unique et par conséquent d'inexprimable" (Henri Bergson, "Introduction à la métaphysique," *Revue de métaphysique,* January 1903).

28 G. Francovich, *Filósofos Brasileños* (Buenos Aires: Editorial Losada, 1943), p. 107; Aníbal Sánchez Reulet, *La filosofía latinoamericana contemporánea* (Washington: Pan American Union, 1949), pp. 141–43.

29 Graça Aranha, "A Estética da Vida," p. 614.

30 *Ibid.,* pp. 595–98.

to the Dionysic attitude expressed by Nietzsche,[31] since he understands that the aesthetic experience is a vital part of man and becomes a sum of experiences which is cast as Phaeton's carriage moving toward light and outer space.[32]

It is, then, with this model that Graça Aranha faces Brazilian reality, first bringing about a diagnosis of Brazilian mental experience and then indicating the path to be followed in order to approach a vital aesthetic of life.

Nature and Man

A study of Brazilian mentality is begun by Graça Aranha through a speculation on collective psychology, which leads him to describe different people by their stereotypes: Roman pride, English energy, French clarity and precision, and so on. From this analysis he arrives at the conclusion that for his own country "o traço característico coletivo é a imaginação. Não é a faculdade de idealisar, nem a criação da vida pela expressão estética, nem o predominio do pensamento; é antes a ilusão que vem da representação do Universo, o estado de magia, em que a realidade se esvai e se transforma em imagem."[33]

For Graça Aranha, therefore, imagination becomes the most important characteristic of Brazilian man and has two specific aspects: magic which destroys reality and passivity which impedes action. In an attempt to clarify these factors he returns to the problem of the origin of Brazilian imagination and bases himself on the following elements: (1) racial formation, (2) influence of tropical nature, and (3) social history of Brazil. He considers that each of these three elements transmits, each in its own way, the biological components of Brazilian imagination. Oscillating between a pedestrian attitude, born of agrarian culture, and the expansionist dreams of maritime discovery, the "alma portuguêsa" gave to the Brazilian "sentimento realista e a miragem." The African heritage, joined with the Portuguese, invented a world peopled by myths and gods which helped overcome the fear caused by tropical surroundings.

---

[31] In the *Origem da Tragedia*, Nietzsche makes a distinction between *apolline* and *dionysian*, the first being the symbol of serenity, lucidity, and equilibrium of reason, while the second is impulsiveness, overflowing, and affirmation of life.

[32] Vita, *Pensamento Social e Político*, pp. 349–50.

[33] Graça Aranha, "A Estética da Vida," p. 619.

The indigenous Indian race, one of the barbaric elements of Brazilian civilization, filled the space between the human spirit and nature with fantasy and images.[34]

These contributions at the same time underwent other modifications as they came in contact with the exuberant natural setting of the tropics. With a sense of fear in those surroundings, the "espírito do homem rude" constructed a "mitologia selvagem" and was able to combine European and African legends with the mythology of the American jungle. With those beginnings as a defense mechanism, the Brazilian then confused objective reality and dreams and began to interpret nature through "objetivismo mitológico,"[35] which Graça Aranha represents as an obstacle between man and nature.

Graça Aranha considers the social history of Brazil as one chapter in "a história dessa imaginação," and he believes that the Portuguese colonizer was attracted primarily by a fascination for gold which was his beginning point among other "miragens."[36] By characterizing the colonizer primarily as an adventurer, Graça Aranha nonetheless shows one of the former's positive contributions: the discovery and the settlement of Brazilian territory.

However, the negative influence is predominant. The myths invented by man's imagination do not integrate him with nature; on the contrary, they establish "uma descorrelação insuperável entre o meio físico e o homem."[37] Therefore, the Brazilian must engage in three spiritual tasks. First, "vencer a nossa natureza," since at times he is dazzled by nature, and feeling himself in many ways an exile he develops a paradoxical view: the exuberance of tropical nature generates in him a feeling of sadness. Second, the Brazilian must eliminate from "nossa metafísica" the inherited elements from Indian and African cultures, which produce a mystical excitement that submerges man in ingenuous fetishism, and the immobilization of the human soul, which brings about inertia and the inability for any kind of spiritual conquest. Third, the Brazilian must exclude from "nossa inteligência" those barbarous elements which condition him for "uma fuga idealista," which is in opposi-

34 *Ibid.*, pp. 620–21.
35 *Ibid.*, p. 621.
36 *Ibid.*, pp. 621–22.
37 *Ibid.*, p. 623.

tion to the Portuguese sense of reality. With those beginnings, the lack of communication between artist and nature can be characterized by the melancholy lyricism of Brazilian poetry, a prose fiction which distinguishes between written and spoken language, and an absence of the plastic arts in Brazil.[38]

The struggle against nature, metaphysics, and intelligence can be reduced, in the ultimate instance, to a broader conflict: man and nature. Communion between the two can be brought about, according to Graça Aranha, only by a cultural process: "a cultura libertará o nosso espírito."[39]

Civilization and Culture

Graça Aranha defines culture as intellectual development, and he makes a fundamental distinction between "civilização de quantidade," which is valuable only for its material progress, and "civilização da qualidade," which embraces at the same time both material and spiritual development. As might be expected, he prefers the latter: "Uma civilização em que se forme uma elite de filósofos, de artistas e religiosos, será superior a outra em que as preocupações dos indivíduos forem de ordem material, composta de negociantes, de industriais, de agricultores e mesmo de guerreiros."[40] This view of culture implies an aristocratic view of society and at the same time approaches the platonic conception.[41] Nevertheless, Graça Aranha adopts a more realistic hypothesis: "Este momento do Brasil reclama o máximo de instrução, e de ciência, que liberte os homens da barbarie americana e da servidão européia."[42]

Reflecting in this way the ideals of a Brazilian intellectual elite at the end of the nineteenth century and the beginning of the twentieth, Graça Aranha assumes that with scientific culture Brazilian man can begin the process of conquering and liberating nature. He also makes the point that such a scientific culture could

[38] *Ibid.*, pp. 629, 632.
[39] *Ibid.*, p. 634.
[40] *Ibid.*, pp. 635–37.
[41] Graça Aranha's connection with Plato can be examined in two aspects: the aesthetic of life as an ideal to be reached, and the conception of a society governed by an intellectual elite. See, for example, chapters 4 and 7 of *La Republique* (Paris: Société d'Édition les Belles Lettres, 1949).
[42] Graça Aranha, "A Estética da Vida," p. 656.

result in the Americanization of Brazil, if it should be oriented exclusively toward the accumulation of material goods. He reaffirms, therefore, his educational ideal: to conserve within an American Brazil a certain Latin spirituality.[43] At the same time he mentions the Brazilian's necessity to free himself from "European servitude." He considers this problem in three aspects, and I will touch on the first two immediately. First, he makes reference to the idea that the discovery of Brazil awakened the avarice of foreign businessmen, and he shows that this same thing happened in all of America: "era simples destino econômico, terras de produção material, de trabalho e de riqueza."[44] He also feels that the Brazil of his time was continuing in the same routine pattern: to be the supplier of raw materials which were necessary to the industries of other countries. He interprets this situation as a failure on the part of Brazilian statesmen and businessmen, because rather than having an "espírito industrial" they possessed only an "educação literária,"[45] which was completely separated from the vital problems of the country.

He takes up as a second aspect the development of labor in Brazil through immigration from Europe and considers the effects of that immigration on the Brazilian people. If the white man were not absorbed by the mestizo, Graça Aranha believes that there would be a conflict between a Brazilian "sub-race" and new European immigrants. However, this danger can be eliminated if the "quadro da nação," which he identifies with the mestizo, can be preserved: "Não permitamos que dento dêle reine a alma dos outros povos, e a nossa própria alma seja expulsa e exilada da terra que lhe criou a expressão ainda incerta, mas ardente e luminosa."[46] In his acceptance in these terms of the maintenance of the spirit of a people throughout history, Graça Aranha manifests again his historicist point of view: "O futuro não entenderá mais o passado. . . ."[47] It is within this framework that he analyzes the problem of nationalism

---

[43] *Ibid.* I refer particularly to the movement to enlighten and transform the country through science and culture. This is what Silvio Romero meant: "nossos erros não nascem tanto de nossa maldade como de nossa ignorância" (Vita, *Pensamento Social e Político*, p. 197).

[44] Graça Aranha, "A Estética da Vida," p. 651.

[45] *Ibid.*, pp. 658–59.

[46] *Ibid.*, p. 656. One of the themes of the novel *Canãa* is the problem of the relation of the white and the mestizo.

[47] *Ibid.*

in contrast to international communism. His central thesis consists of showing the necessity of maintaining intact the concept of nation: "será dentro do quadro nacional que se fará a transformação econômica do mundo."[48] Later, however, he takes somewhat the same position in two interviews, but with a fundamental difference: "Será dentro do quadro das nações que se dará a luta de classes para o ideal socialista."[49] This commentary reveals that he followed the great issues of his time closely and that he saw them from a broad perspective, as was also apparent in his attempt to reconcile the economic doctrine of communism with the idea of nationalism.

Within the same scheme of the development of ideas, Graça Aranha returns to the theme of Portuguese influence in Brazilian historical development, and he discusses it from two points of view. First, he argues for political and economic union between Portugal and Brazil and judges that both homelands reveal the identity of the Portuguese race, which was able to combat German influence. He understands that in the formation of the Brazilian people the impetus transmitted by the Portuguese, with their labors of conquest and territorial settlement, subsists as the fundamental racial strain which is revived in modern Brazil. In this way "a lei da constância vital" of the Portuguese, which for Graça Aranha signifies racial continuity, resulted in the unification of the two homelands in one single race. He extends his historicist attitude in this way by not distinguishing one people from another and by accepting continuity in spite of different environmental influences. It is appropriate to remember that when Graça Aranha talked about the negative aspects of Brazilian metaphysics and intelligence, he made it clear that these defects originated in the "barbaric races" (African and Indian) and not in the Portuguese. Basing himself on this ethnological illusion, shared by several Brazilian intellectuals of his time, he affirms that the "união política de Portugal e do Brasil, consequência da unidade moral das duas nações, seria a grande expressão internacional da raça portuguêsa."[50] In his view, this unification could produce the breakdown of tariff restrictions in

48 *Ibid.* p. 649.
49 In Mário da Silva Brito, *Angulo e Horizonte* (São Paulo: Martins Editôra, 1969), pp. 101–5.
50 Graça Aranha, "A Estética da Vida," pp. 640–43.

Portuguese ports against the importation of Brazilian industrial products, the diffusion of the Brazilian spirit in the European world, and the preservation of a Latin spirit in the American world.

From the point of view of art and literature his attitude is different. It is here that he takes up the third aspect of "servidão européia," and with the inclusion of Portuguese cultural influence he assumes the necessity of bringing about a break with the past. In his essay "O Espírito Moderno" he writes: "Em vez de tendermos para a unidade literária com Portugal, alarguemos a separação. . . . Não somos a câmara mortuária de Portugal." In a similar fashion he expresses himself against European influence in general: "A cópia servil dos motivos artísticos ou literários europeos, exóticos, nos desnacionaliza." Taking that point of view, he is moved to affirm that "o modernismo é a função do nacionalismo." He does not understand nationalism to mean an intellectual's identification with a barbaric world or his affiliation with primitivism, since this would be derived from "um ato da vontade, um artifício como o arcadismo dos acadêmicos." However, he does feel that to be Brazilian is "sentir todo como brasileiro, seja a nossa vida, seja a civilização estrangeira, seja o presente, seja o passado." From these affirmations comes his comprehension of the "Brazilian experiment" mentioned earlier or, in other words, that the European culture which is a part of his formation should not serve to prolong Europe but rather to meld it with the elements derived from the new sociocultural environment. On the other hand, he assumes that modernism should not be limited to art and literature but should be a total transformation: "filosófica, social e artística."[51]

Basing this philosophy on his aesthetic intuition of the universe, Graça Aranha finds that modern art, for example, can bring about the universal unity which he seeks as long as it is derived from "objetivismo dinâmico." In order to explain that term, he again takes up the problem of art and nature and proposes that in its artistic meaning "a natureza é tudo o que se apresenta aos nossos sentidos como exteriores a nós." The relationship between the artist and nature, in his view, can begin in an imitation of nature, but the final purpose of art consists in being liberated from that imita-

[51] Graça Aranha, "O Espírito Moderno," pp. 753–57.

tion. The Brazilian, at the same time, is not only inclined to imitate nature as someone subordinated to it, but is in effect a prisoner of aesthetic subjectivism and in some sense continues the impact of romanticism. In order to overcome such an attitude, therefore, the Brazilian artist must bring his subjectivism together with a necessary objectivism in order to construct a work of art in which "a cultura o libertará da Natureza, para dar-lhe forma artística, forma espiritual, peculiar, como um organismo nôvo, vindo da fôrça criadora do homem."[52]

Conclusion

Oscillating between reason and imagination, but with definite tendencies toward the latter because of the vital bases for his thought, Graça Aranha worked out his aesthetic intuition of life with which he attempted to interpret Brazilian reality. Facing that reality as an aesthete not imprisoned in universal categories,[53] he viewed it as a process of forms in search of a definition. The definition of that reality, in his presentation, had to be understood and formulated through an understanding of culture and industrialization and a defense of nationality. Graça Aranha was, in sum, a thinker well fitted for the discussion of general ideas and for the formulation and free discussion of the great number of cultural problems which were of interest in the Brazil of his epoch.

[52] *Ibid.*, pp. 746–50.
[53] Vita, *Pensamento Social e Político*, p. 350. See Alfredo Bosi, *O Pré-Modernismo* (São Paulo: Cultrix Editôra, 1966), and José C. Garbuglio, *O Universo Estético-Sensorial de Graça Aranha* (Assis: Faculdade de Filosofia, Ciências e Letras, 1966).

Notes on Regional and National Trends in Afro-Brazilian Cult Music

Gerard H. Béhague

Taking as a premise that "the music of the Negro cult-groups of Bahia follows the fundamental patterns of West African and New World Negro music everywhere,"[1] most ethnomusicologists, folklorists, and anthropologists have worked mainly on the problem of African retentions in Brazilian Negro music. Melville Herskovits, Nina Rodrigues, Artur Ramos, and others have represented the school of thought that emphasized African retentions in Afro-Brazilian culture. Others, such as René Ribeiro and Franklin Frazier, have tended to deemphasize the retention thesis by successfully showing that as Brazil becomes urbanized and industrialized, ties to African culture tend to break down.

Most writers agree upon the syncretistic nature of Afro-Brazilian cults and stress what has been preserved of African religious practices in the *candomblé*, the *xangô*, and the *pajelança*.[2] But what they

This chapter is the result of field work specifically in the area of Salvador, Bahia, and Recife, Pernambuco, carried on during the summers of 1967 and 1970 with the help of the Center for Latin American Studies, the Center for International Comparative Studies, and the Research Board of the University of Illinois. At the time of this writing a large-scale collection of *candomblé* repertory is being gathered in the Salvador-Bahia area with the support of a Guggenheim Foundation fellowship and a grant from the Foreign Area Fellowship Program (SSRC).

[1] Melville Herskovits and Frances Herskovits, *Afro-Bahian Religious Songs from Brazil*, Archive of American Folk Song Record No. L13 (Washington: The Library of Congress, n.d.).

[2] Brazilian cult terminology varies a great deal among regions and cult groups. In Bahia *candomblé* designates the cult in general, the actual locale of the cult house,

have neglected (the only possible exception being Mário de Andrade in his essays in *Música de feitiçaria no Brasil*) is the study of the native elements of the cults. By "native" we mean, above all, those aspects that could be isolated as belonging to a local tradition (Amerindian or *caboclo* as found in some components of the Caboclo cult and the *pajelança*) and those of possible non-African provenience in the most traditional cult groups, especially in Bahia. Although it would be inaccurate in our context to consider African retentions as foreign elements, this study aims at elucidating recent changes brought about in cult-music repertory from the local scene itself and made up of African-derived folkways which are in themselves an integral part of the native elements.

In the Latin American context, the definition of black music is an extremely complex one. First of all, the general acceptance of what constitutes, culturally and ethnically, an Afro-American is not as unequivocal as it is in North America. There are some examples in Central and South America of black groups, such as the Caribs of Honduras and Nicaragua who are black representatives of an Indian culture, whose African cultural identity is virtually non-existent. Conversely, important nonblack segments of certain communities, such as, for example, some East Indian groups in Trinidad or the Cayapa Indians of western Ecuador, have perfectly definable African-related cultural traits. In Brazil, Negro acculturation has been considerable and has affected other ethnic groups and a wide range of mixed groups. In such a case we are confronted with ethnically diverse groups which have a remarkably homogeneous "black" culture. Race alone cannot, then, be considered a valid criterion in discussing Afro-American music in Latin America.

The various definitions of the term *cult*, as given in standard dictionaries, have serious limitations, and none explain the actual nature of Afro-Brazilian religions. Most of all, in its generalized meaning, the word *cult* is defined as a religion that is considered or held to be false or unorthodox. The implication seems to be that

and certain public ceremonies. Traditional, African-related cult groups include the Ketu, Gêge, Ijesha, and Angola (or Congo-Angola) *candomblés*. *Caboclo* is the general term used to indicate "mestizo," either half-breed of Indian and white or mulatto; hence, *candomblé de caboclo* is the cult of such acculturated groups. In addition, in such a cult *caboclos* are also the deities worshipped. *Xangô* is the generic name for cult in the state of Pernambuco, and *pajelança* specifically in the Amazon area.

non-Christian religions in predominantly Christian countries are relegated to a lower rank in a scale of values. Other such subjective criteria include the degree of "exoticism" or "deviance" that a religious group's beliefs and behaviors supposedly exhibit. Social scientists regard a cult essentially as a small religious group made up primarily of lower-class people, guided by a charismatic leader, and concerned with problems of the individual rather than those of the community. More satisfactory criteria offered in devising a typology of religious groups are the inclusiveness of membership and the amount of support given to social integration. With such criteria most societies seem to have religious groups that can be labeled "cults" without tacit value judgments.

Liturgical Setting

Afro-Brazilian cults involving deities (orixás, vodouns, saints) have been transferred from the West African homeland, but their character has often suffered substantial change in the process. Among the various communities a cult implies the recognition of African deities and a system of belief which is essentially African. Syncretism, however, has taken place almost everywhere in the country in varying degrees. Most cults show features of Christian belief systems, although not necessarily a recognition of a Christian god or saint. Often, as a result of sociohistorical accommodation, a Catholic saint has been assimilated into the personality of an African deity, but the equivalence of saints and deities is by no means homogeneous throughout the country, or, for that matter, throughout the Latin American continent.[3] Frequently cultists consider themselves even better Catholics than the people who only go to church.

West African religions as developed in Brazil are nowadays considered "monotheistic,"[4] animistic in nature, and comprising a

[3] Numerous studies of this equivalence in various areas of Latin America and the Caribbean are available. See especially Herskovits, Edison Carneiro, A. Ramos, René Ribeiro, Roger Bastide, and Pierre Verger.

[4] The concept of polytheism and paganism (idol worship) had to be revised in relation to Afro-Brazilian cults since the cult of saints in popular Catholicism is analogous to that of the orixás who serve one supreme God, Olorun of the Nagos and Zambi of the Angolas and Caboclos. Olorun is not an orixá as previously believed (see A. Ramos, O Negro Brasileiro, vol. 1, Etnografia Religiosa [Rio de Janeiro, Editôra Nacional, 1940]).

pantheon of major and lesser deities, each being worshipped with characteristic ceremonies, food offerings, songs, and drum rhythms. The most obvious African traits pertaining to such ceremonies include the ritual uses of blood (animal sacrifices to feed the *orixás*, the drums, etc.), initiation rites, ritual uses of plants and leaves, ritual dancing with a highly symbolic choreography, personification of the *orixás* through spirit possession, cults of the dead, and others. The most outstanding Christian or reinterpreted Christian elements include, in some cult groups, the use of the Bible, Catholic prayers, the cross and crucifixes, candle burning, and saint lithographs and shrines. Misconceptions about Afro-Brazilian belief systems, epitomized by the term *black magic*, arise because most cult leaders practice some aspect of folk medicine (herbalism). Within this system the *orixás* are considered to be the intermediators for the devotees with the supreme god inaccessible to men. The *orixás* symbolize natural forces.[5] Their attributes are often confused in the minds of the believers.

The regional cults of Bahia, which maintain the closest relationship to Africa, include the Ketu (Nagô) and 'Jesha (Ijesha or Ijexá) cults, both derived from the Yoruba of Nigeria and Dahomey, the Gêge (Ewe) cult from Dahomey, and the Congo-Angola cult, known simply as Angola in Salvador and Rio de Janeiro. In Pernambuco and other northeastern states the Yoruba cult is known as *xangô*.[6] The other cults which have spread throughout the country are the Caboclo cult, called Caboclo-Guarani, a restrictive term, by Herskovits, and the nationally omnipresent Umbanda, which originated presumably in this century. Both Caboclo and Umbanda are genuine expressions of national popular religions. Umbanda shows varying degrees of mixture of Catholicism and the Caboclo cult, spiritualism and occultism, and other features.[7] Umbanda practice

5 Pierre Verger, *Notes sur le Culte des Orisa et Vodun* (Dakar: Institut Français d'Afrique Noire, 1957).

6 William Bascom, *Shango in the New World* (Austin: African and Afro-American Research Institute, 1972).

7 The extensive literature on Umbanda attests to its popularity. Recent estimated figures (1972) point to about 32,000 Umbanda houses in Rio de Janeiro alone. There exist, in addition, numerous societies or associations, such as the Federação Espírita Umbandista do Brasil, the Associação Federativa de Umbanda do Brasil, the Escola Superior Iniciática de Umbanda do Brasil, and the Movimento de Unificação Nacional pró Religião de Umbanda (MUNRU).

includes, above all, the cult of souls (spirits) which are believed to come to earth to reincarnate themselves in order to help men. Recent stylistic changes in the music of the Caboclo cult and the constant elaboration of the repertory of the Umbanda groups illustrate the cultural integration of the northeastern area, that is, the effective penetration of national values into a strong regional and urban cultural setting. Specific examples of these changes will be given in a future study.

One common denominator in all groups is the fundamental belief that the destiny of the world is controlled by the *orixás*, although man is not "a passive agent in relation to his destiny, for through divination he can discover the secrets of that destiny, and learn how to cause it to favor his ventures, his well-being, and his status in the group among which he lives."[8] A specific act of all cults is, of course, the spiritual possession of the initiates by the deities. Men and women are affected by this essentially psychological condition, and a wide variety of expressions of this phenomenon can be observed from the simple occasional faintings to the most violent explosions with classic convulsions. For the devotee, this seizure indicates the "entering" of the deity into her (or his) head.

Initiation into the cults can only be accomplished after a series of tests has been performed to discover the deity to be served by the prospective initiate as well as idiosyncratic traits of the candidate. Initiation requires a period of retreat in the cult house (also called *candomblé* in Bahia) which varies greatly from group to group. Under these rites, intensive training is given in cult language, the *iaô*'s (initiate's) responsibilities toward her *orixá*, cult song repertory, and dancing. Most of the initiates are women, and the preparation for the initiation ceremonies is mandatory. A very specific song repertory operates in such rites.

Musical Functions

In all ceremonies (public and private) of Afro-Brazilian cults, music is of transcendental importance, and no worship would be possible without it. Its basic function is to call the gods, whether in purifica-

---

[8] Herskovits and Herskovits, *Afro-Bahian Religious Songs*, p. 9.

tion, initiation, communion, social, or funeral ceremonies. Every single act of the liturgy is accompanied by ritual songs or drum music, thus constituting a very extensive repertory. An initiate (known as *iaô* from the time of initiation up to seven years afterwards and *ebomin* after the seventh year) learns the drum rhythms and special canticles of the *orixá* who rules the house (*santo da casa*) with which she is associated. She also has to know the specific repertory of her own *orixá*, not only according to the tradition of her cult group ("*nação*") but frequently according to that of other groups as well. In addition, canticles and rhythms for all *orixás* (and sometimes *caboclos*) have to be learned, for no participation in the *candomblé* ceremony would be possible without this knowledge. After the arrival of the *orixá*, greetings take place through appropriate canticles, all set in a very logical sequence. After the possessed initiates have been dressed as *orixás* (each with her or his appropriate colors, emblems, and tools) the cult leader sings a special canticle inviting them to enter into the "*barracão*" (the main dancing room of the house) and dance. Then, in turn, each *orixá* dances to specific rhythms and a series of special songs (three to seven songs for each).

In the Ketu and Gêge cults this large repertory is traditional and seems to have been retained with few changes, although alterations in performance practices in the last thirty years have occurred. Transcription and analysis of recordings made in the 1940's (Herskovits) and 1950's (Ribeiro and others) have allowed, among the various cults, a typological-analytical system to be used in song classification and have pointed toward an assumed "old" style, characterized by usually short melodic phrases, constant repetitions with variants through ornaments, and a singing style involving falsetto and a hard, metallic quality of vocal production, especially in female choruses. More recent field recordings among the same groups (1970) give evidence that little change has taken place; that is, the same songs continue to function according to tradition. But the testimony of several cult-house leaders (*pai de santo, mãe de santo,* or *babalorixá, iyalorixá*) indicates that many songs attributed to a given deity have disappeared from the repertory or that younger *babalorixás* simply do not know the complete repertory. Incidentally, the leaders are the supreme authority, both spiritual and temporal, of a given group. They are themselves the leading singers (and often dancers) and are responsible for transmitting the knowledge of the vast cult repertory and for the supervision of music teaching in the house. They also represent the key to the degree of orthodoxy in their particular *"terreiro"* (temple).

Since the Caboclo and Angola cults are more readily open to innovations, new songs are being incorporated into their repertories. Generally, these are not composed songs as such. What we find is an apparent stylistic transformation by innovation, which takes place when an initiating *iaô*, in a state of possession, sings her own song to the deity to which she is being initiated. Although generally such songs are "invented" more or less according to traditional patterns, many elements foreign to the tradition (but certainly familiar to the songmaker) appear in them—for example, texts in the vernacular, longer melodic phrases, alternation of stanzas and refrain, and general performance characteristics closely related to urban, folk, and popular musical expressions such as carnival street music. The process whereby such "improvised" songs become part of the current repertory has been observed exclusively in Pernambuco among the Caboclo cult groups and remains to be investigated.

The most obvious common stylistic trait of "old," "new," or "heterogeneous" song types of the various cult musics in Brazil is the predominant call-and-response pattern. The leader or solo singer is often the *babalorixá* or *iyalorixá*, but also the master drummer for the first part of the public ceremonies. Anyone, however, can lead the singing (*"tirar a cantiga"*) as an homage to the *orixás*. The chorus is usually composed of women and sings in a monophonic fashion. Among the most acculturated groups (Caboclo and Umbanda) heterophony is not uncommon but consists essentially of parallel thirds at the end of the choral phrases. Often soloist and chorus overlap. Within the framework of the solo-chorus alternation, the form is frequently based on the repetition of a single phrase, with some minor variations through ornamentation. Examples of this particular element abound in the traditional performance of the Ketu cult repertory in Salvador, as collected in the oldest houses as well as smaller or more recent ones. In such cases, the soloist is likely to present a theme with variations as the basis of her tune. Most of the time leader and chorus use the same tune, sometimes related tunes (in an antecedent-consequent type of phrasing), and more rarely completely unrelated materials. The large majority of songs follow the strophic form in most regional cults, while in the Caboclo and Umbanda *candomblé* (as observed in Salvador and Recife) the alternation of stanzas and refrain seems to be the norm. The Ketu and Gêge song repertory reveals frequent tetratonic and pentatonic scales, without semitones, and, less commonly, hexatonic formations. Diatonic scales, especially the European minor scale, are found in many songs of the most acculturated groups, representing the national trend. The tonal ranges of the melodies vary a great deal. The Gêge cult songs show a marked tendency toward wide range (more than an octave), while the 'Jesha and Angola cults have songs that average less than an octave. Umbanda songs have typically short melodic range. The melodic contours reveal a definite tendency toward generally descending patterns, but frequent pendulumlike movements are also characteristic in both Ketu and Gêge songs. Umbanda melodies frequently follow a smooth, conjunct motion and present narrower ranges than the Ketu and Gêge melodic material. In the latter, melodic intervals are frequently quite large, and whenever the responsorial pattern is present the melodic phrases tend to be short—an obvious African retention. But with solo songs the melodic line becomes longer and more complex.

Tempo varies considerably from one cult group to another, and, within the same cult, in accordance with a particular song cycle. The idiosyncrasies attributed to a given *orixá* (whether young or old, temperamental or peaceful, and so on) influence the tempo of such song cycles. Gradual tempo acceleration in many songs and much drum music as well is rather frequent, depending on their particular ritual function. The singing styles of most Afro-Brazilian cultists are essentially similar to the relaxed, open manner of singing common in West Africa. Female voices present a characteristically hard, metallic quality, with a preference for the upper range of the voice. Falsetto, while used by both soloist and chorus, is not as common nowadays as it used to be, according to the testimony of cult leaders in Salvador. The vocal quality found in the nationally oriented cults (Caboclo and Umbanda) is, on the other hand, quite different from that in the regional cults. Placement of the voice tends to follow that of Luso-Brazilian folk traditions, with an occasional use of vibrato. Soloists especially favor a ringing voice.

The song repertories of Afro-Brazilian religions have never been fully codified for the simple reason that it is an enormous task to consider the large body of songs found in each cult group. In the public ceremonies (*candomblé* itself) cycles of songs are performed in a ritual order, known as the *orô*. Including three to seven songs for each *orixá*, the *orô* starts inevitably with Exú (Elegbara of the Ewe) and ends with Oxalá in the Yoruba-derived cults. Among the Caboclo *candomblés* and the Umbandas the ritual order is not as strict. For example, while in the Ketu cults the order Ogum, Oxossi, Ossanha, and so on, is strictly followed, we have witnessed the most unbelievable departure (that is, liturgically illogical) from that order in the more national cults. There seems to be less concern nowadays, in the smaller cult houses, for the proper order of the *orô*.

Song texts appear in various languages, from Yoruba (Nagô) in the Ketu cults, Fon (Gêge), and various Congo dialects (Angola) to Portuguese, or a combination of all of these. A peculiar dialect is used by the Caboclos, who call it Guarani. Typically, song texts are simple praise or imprecation directed to the *orixás*, or they refer to mythical episodes or specific life events of the deities or to their most remarkable feats, following West African mythology and often reinterpreted in Brazil through the influence of popular Catholicism.

By comparing the Ketu-Gêge material with Caboclo and Umbanda music accompanying the rituals, we realize immediately why the latter have transcended the regional focus of the former. The songs of Umbanda, especially, show some of the drastic changes that have occurred in the ritual music of those cults. It is as if there has been a rapprochement between purely old-African ritual materials and folk music characteristics of the mestizo tradition at large. The song texts of Umbanda are almost always in the vernacular, with refrains using occasional Yoruba words. Musical phrases tend to be more regular (four- to eight-bar phrases), melodies are often cast in the major-minor European modal system (with occasional retention of pentatonicism), and the rhythmic accompaniment, while syncopated, is steady and rarely presents any kind of hemiola rhythm.

The single most important ritual and musical element in Afro-Brazilian cults (particularly the regional ones) is the drumming. Drums (*atabaques, tabaques, ilus*) are considered sacred instruments. They still undergo ritual baptism by means of animal sacrifices after their construction and receive food offerings at least once a year. While perhaps not as elaborate and precise as in the 1930's, the baptism of the drums continues to have the symbolism ascribed to it by Herskovits in the following passage:

> A drum is baptized shortly after its completion. It must have a godfather and a godmother (a *padrinho* and a *madrinha*), selected by the head of the house from among its personnel. If the new drum, or new set, is the gift of an individual, he will be designated for one of these roles. With the godparents standing on either side, the priest or priestess takes holy water, obtained from a Catholic church, and, speaking entirely in the African tongue employed by the group in its rituals, blesses the drums while sprinkling them with the sacred liquid. A candle, held by the godmother, is then placed on the floor in front of the drums, where it is allowed to burn out; each drum is decorated with a bouquet of paper flowers, allowed to remain in place for awhile.[9]

My observations of several drum baptisms indicate different practices nowadays, and the repertory of songs involved in such a ceremony will be the subject of a future study. This complex ritual involving the drums is essential since they alone receive the power to communicate with the deities. In most cult groups, drums are played in a battery of three, in conjunction with an iron gong or a rattle. They vary in size and shape among the various cults, but the trio always comes in three different sizes.[10] In the Ketu and Gêge cults they are played with sticks called *aghidavis*, while *caboclos* and *umbandistas* use their hands most of the time, as do *alabés* (drummers) of the 'Jesha and Angola groups. The largest drum (generally 1.10 to 1.40 meters high and about 35 to 40 centimeters in head diameter), called the *rum* by the Ketu of Bahia, is played by the master drummer. The medium-sized drum, known as *rumpi*,

---

[9] Melville Herskovits, "Drums and Drummers in Afro-Brazilian Cult Life," *Musical Quarterly*, 30 (1933).

[10] Exceptions to this statement were seen in several *xangô* cult houses of Recife, where the three *ilus* are identical.

and the smallest one, the *lê*, usually repeat a single steady rhythm. As a contrast, the *rum* (also the lowest in tone) varies its beats, determining the various changes in the choreography and producing some of the complex rhythms typical of Afro-Brazilian musical styles. The gong, variously called *agogô* or *gã*, or the rattle sets the fundamental beat or pattern of each rhythm, joined by the *rumpi* and the *lê* and finally by the *rum* a few seconds later. Herskovits has pointed out that the melody of the song is but the accompaniment to the rhythm of the drums in the Ketu-derived cults. While this is true from a strictly musical viewpoint, the song itself assumes the leading role liturgically. Emphasis on rhythm, however, is an obvious African heritage. Each cult, dance, ceremony, or deity has its characteristic rhythms in the Ketu-Gêge cult groups. The Angola groups have basically three rhythms accompanying the song repertory. These are the Congo, Cabula, and Barravento rhythms, frequently borrowed by the Caboclos in their rituals.

Drum music *per se*, that is, beyond an accompanimental function, does exist in large quantity. Its major function is to "call" the *orixás* and to bring on possession, in addition to providing materials for the many ritual dances. Cross rhythms and polyrhythms form the major substance of that music. The meters are most commonly duple, but often triple, and the hemiola rhythm, African par excellence, finds its way into much of the drum music repertory. While there is no definite evidence of the retention in Brazil today of the African talking drum techniques, it is believed that the various ritual drum patterns (attributed to each deity) were, originally, rhythmic renditions of the melodic shape of certain phrases of Yoruba, which is a tone language. Such renditions would have been learned, memorized, and transmitted by use of onomatopoeias.

Specific rhythms correspond to specific dances by the personalized *orixás* after possession has taken place. Each rhythmic pattern has a name; for example, Opanijé is the rhythm for the *orixá* Omolú; Aguerê (also called Xagum) is the rhythm for Iansã and Oxossi; Alujá, Tonibobé, and Bajubá are for Xangô; Agabi is for Xangô and Ogum; and Igbim is for Oxalá. Within the *orô*, specific rhythms have well-determined ritual functions. For example, the pattern Bravum is played in the *orô* for Gêge "saints" (Omolú, Oxunmaré, Roko, and Nanã), while the Avaninha rhythm (also known as Ramunha) is used for the entry and exit of the *orixás* from the *barracão*. The pattern Adarrum (a name designating the drum itself) has the function of calling all the *orixás* at the same time. Few devotees can resist the call of the Adarrum.

Within the social structure of the Afro-Brazilian cults, women have a particularly important position. In the Ketu and Gêge cults, while many leaders are men, the great majority of the members are women, as are most initiates. Drummers (only men) also enjoy an exalted position. They are first-rank musicians and are essential to the cult ceremonies. The master drummer not only knows the full repertory of his own cult group but generally that of the other groups as well. "It is he who brings on possession through his manipulation of these rhythmic intricacies, yet he himself never becomes possessed."[11] Drummers go through a series of tests before they are allowed to perform in ritual ceremonies. Their acceptance into the cult is publicly signified by means of a "confirmation" ceremony. A drummer may become a master drummer after many years of experience and only under certain circumstances, for it is considered a very special privilege. In smaller Nagô-Gêge houses, and among the Angola and Caboclo groups, however, we have observed rather loose rules concerning the master drummer (*alabé*). Almost anyone who happens to be available can play the *rum*.

Conclusions

In partial conclusion, in order to gain insights into the social bases of *candomblé* musical styles, it seems crucial to consider that such styles are the result of an ethnically and culturally heterogeneous milieu. The causes for the present orientation and the stylistic changes in ritual music may well relate to the complete identification and integration of cultists with the urban environment in which they live. Ethnomusicologists have stressed in recent years, and showed in the most varied contexts, how much song style portrays levels of human adaptation. Alan Lomax states: "Each performance is a symbolic reenactment of crucial behavior patterns upon which the continuity of a culture hangs. . . . Many levels of this symbolic behavior are brought into congruency with some main

11 Herskovits, "Drums and Drummers," 477.

theme, so that a style comes to epitomize some singular and notable aspect of a culture, by which its members identify themselves and with which they endow many of their activities and their feelings."[12]

Postulating, therefore, that features of song style symbolize significant traits in culture, we hypothesize that the Caboclo and Umbanda cults are becoming a group-identity symbol acceptable to the majority of Afro-Brazilians in the area of Salvador and Recife because their very nature tends to fill the gap between the traditional regional (that is, the most clearly African-derived) *candomblé* and the national cult current. At least the musical traits of such cults, which show an obvious stylistic integration with nationally predominant popular music, tend to confirm that assumption. The causes of this integration are being studied as of this writing.

Charles Seeger has always advocated that musicology concerns itself with processes of variation in the components of a music text on the one hand and a social context for music making on the other. In this study I have examined the general traits and tendencies of the music text. Since *candomblé* is indeed a world in itself, a thorough study of the contextual factors will require considerably more time.

[12] *Folk Song Style and Culture* (Washington: American Association for the Advancement of Science, 1968), p. 8.

The Black Presence
and Two Brazilian Modernists:
Jorge de Lima and José Lins do Rêgo

Richard A. Preto-Rodas

The subject of this essay is the literary use of Afro-Brazilian motifs in the works of two outstanding Brazilian writers of the second quarter of this century. Both Jorge de Lima, as a poet, and José Lins do Rêgo, as a novelist, have won a prominent place in anthologies and literary histories concerning Brazil for their contribution to the cultural movement known as modernism.[1] Both writers derived considerable inspiration from the Negro experience in their country, and the poet has especially been identified as a pioneer in his portrayal of Afro-Brazilian aspects of the national culture.[2] The following pages will analyze the perspective of both writers in their literary view of the Negro. The works which will concern us include those of Jorge de Lima's poems expressly based on Afro-Brazilian motifs and Lins do Rêgo's novel *O Moleque Ricardo*. Since the poet's milieu is the plantation, while the novel is situated primarily in a large city, the two perspectives, as examined here, will accordingly encompass the very different worlds of rural and urban life as backgrounds for the black situation in Brazil.

[1] For an introduction to their contribution to modernism, see Wilson Martins, *A Literatura Brasileira*, vol. 6, *O Modernismo* (São Paulo, 1965), especially pp. 204–9, 272–76; John Nist, *The Modernist Movement in Brazil* (Austin, 1967), pp. 146–60 (for Jorge de Lima); and José Aderaldo Castello, *José Lins do Rêgo: Modernismo e Regionalismo* (São Paulo, 1961).

[2] See José Fernando Carneiro, *Apresentação de Jorge de Lima* (Rio de Janeiro, 1967), pp. 17–20.

It would, of course, be misleading to imply that before de Lima and Lins do Rêgo the Negro and the nonwhite in general were absent from the literary panorama of Brazil. Even the casual student of Brazilian literature is familiar with the Indians and Negroes of nineteenth-century writers like Gonçalves Dias and José de Alencar. The black especially is a familiar figure in the late nineteenth century, thanks to the ringing verses of abolitionists like Luis Gama and Castro Alves. What *is* different is the authentic flavor of de Lima's black-inspired poetry, which is worlds away from the Hugo-esque rhetoric of Castro Alves and its social romanticism. In fact, until the generation of Jorge de Lima and José Lins do Rêgo, Brazilian letters in general betrayed a certain artificiality and tended to reflect European attitudes and literary movements with a consequent loss of cultural autonomy. As the critic Monteiro Lobato once remarked, the Indians of de Alencar and Gonçalves Dias are really Roman senators covered with toucan feathers. And the reader of abolitionist poetry is generally left with the impression that all slaves were sensitive members of royal families before falling prey to sadistic owners.[3]

The reassessment of perspectives prompted by modernism's search for cultural autonomy could hardly avoid the contribution of the Afro-Brazilian, especially in the northeast, where both de Lima and Lins do Rêgo were born and raised.[4] The area's sugar-based economy had resulted in a plantation society from the dawn of national history, with millions of laborers imported primarily from what are now Senegal and Angola. Both writers were products of the waning days of the plantation society; they were cared for by black nurses and surrounded by black servants, many of whom had been slaves until the emancipation of 1888. Thus, both writers were members of the white aristocracy: the grandfather of José Lins do Rêgo had been governor of the then-province of Paraíba, and Jorge de Lima was fond of boasting that his grandmother had once waltzed with the emperor Dom Pedro II. However, unlike the North American plantation aristocracy, both men were themselves

---

[3] See Lobato's perceptive comments on would-be expressions of literary autonomy in *Urupês* (São Paulo, 1962), pp. 277–79.

[4] See Martins, *O Modernismo*, especially the section "Nacionalismo e Regionalismo," pp. 137–56.

of mixed racial ancestry. In Brazil, being white does not exclude signs of African antecedents. In fact, the aristocratic Jorge de Lima has been described by more than one foreigner as a mulatto, and he was probably no less "Afro" than Senator Edward Brooke or the late Adam Clayton Powell.[5] Few writers in any language blend artistic inspiration and personal revery as effectively as do Lins do Rêgo and de Lima. Theirs was a world where small plantations were being fast absorbed by large corporate farms, many of them administered by men they described as blue-eyed interlopers from northern climes. Accordingly, there is a plaintive tone as they reflect upon their own situation, living in an intersection between past and present where ghostly reminders of a pastoral, patriarchal culture clash with the technical efficiency of machines and smokestacks. The traditional rural aristocracy was in eclipse, and its colonels and their crude if uncompromising code of honor were no match for the bureaucracy and industrialization of the modern era.[6] While suspicious of modernism's cosmopolitan aesthetics and irreverence for the past, both poet and novelist joined forces with other prominent northeasterners, like the socioanthropologist Gilberto Freyre, to seize upon the movement's spirit of freedom and explore local reality. In this way they hoped to resist the non-Brazilian aspects of contemporary life which threatened their region's contribution to a national culture. The result was a congress which met in 1926 in Recife under the banner of Freyre's regionalist *Manifesto*. Its goal was to enhance local customs and social flavor by distilling humanistic values from immediate reality.[7]

For Jorge de Lima the northeastern adaptation of modernism's

---

[5] For the reference to his aristocratic grandmother, see Gilberto Freyre's "Nota Preliminar" to *Poemas Negros* in Jorge de Lima, *Obra Completa*, vol. 1 (Rio de Janeiro, 1959), p. 342 (hereafter, references to this edition are incorporated into the text); also see Nist, *Modernist Movement in Brazil*, p. 158. However, the poet at times regarded himself as "Ameríndio" (see Povina Calvalcânti, *Vida e Obra de Jorge de Lima* [Rio de Janeiro, 1969], p. 204), while in "Minhas Memórias" he described his siblings and childhood playmates as "morenos . . . [some] quáse saravá . . . [others] côr de jambo" (*Obra Completa*, p. 120).

[6] The poet synthesizes the passing of an era and the increasing hegemony of the United States in several poems. See especially "A Minha América" and "Bangüê," in *Obra Completa*, pp. 227–29 and 352–53.

[7] See Castello, *José Lins do Rêgo*, pp. 27–70, and Martins, *O Modernismo*, pp. 108–16; cf. Renato Carneiro Campos, *Arte, Sociedade, e Região* (Rio de Janeiro, 1960).

freedom meant "o regresso às nossas origens e ao nosso caráter" (p. 79). He pointedly rejected the attempts of an earlier generation to define Brazil as an American nation with a Latin culture and turned to the interior of his state of Alagoas to discover "a realidade física, biológica, racial e religiosa do brasileiro. Caimos em nós mesmos para libertarmos de nós mesmos" (p. 82).[8] And even while avoiding the rhetorical extremes of a committed literature, he acknowledged the social character of his poems, saying, "eu falo do homem, de sua presença no mundo, de suas lutas e sofrimentos, de suas inquietações" (pp. 64–65).

As a result of a strong social and ideological impetus, both writers often betray a stance more appropriate to the anthropologist and the social historian than to the creative writer as such. It is no coincidence that Gilberto Freyre wrote the preface to de Lima's *Poemas Negros*, praising them for exemplifying as complete an expression of African sensibility as can be found in Brazilian literature.[9] At the same time, Freyre emphasizes that a truly Negro literature is impossible in racially mixed Brazil. According to this view, a marginal black literature existing outside the mainstream of national life can develop only in racially divided societies like the United States.[10] Some recent voices, however, submit that notwithstanding racial mixture and goals of modernism, the blacks in de Lima's poems and in Lins do Rêgo's novels do not evidence a completely harmonized view but rather suggest that there is a curious emotional distance separating each writer from the world of his subjects.[11] The validity of this observation, however, can be determined only after a closer look at the Afro-Brazilian that appears in Jorge de Lima's poems and in *O Moleque Ricardo*.

The poet's use of the Afro-Brazilian theme was an immediate success thanks to the universal acclaim which greeted his first "Negro"-inspired poem, "Essa Negra Fulô" (Fulô, the subject's

---

[8] Cf. *Obra Completa*, p. 88, where the poet identifies "a nossa psique, verdade nacional" with "o subsolo da nossa raça."

[9] Freyre's comments are included in his "Nota Preliminar," in *Obra Completa*, pp. 342–47.

[10] For a similar opinion, see Álvaro Lins, *Os Mortos de Sobrecasaca* (Rio de Janeiro, 1963), pp. 65–66.

[11] See below, footnotes 20–23.

name, is a corruption of *flor*, "flower").[12] A kind of long folk ballad with an infectious musical cadence characteristic of the popular group dances of Alagoas, the structure is an incident which typifies the way traditional Brazilian society became racially mixed. The narrator tells of a comely slave girl who many years before was brought to his grandfather's plantation, where she was received by an exacting mistress. Not only obliged to tend to her lady's every need, the girl is also accused of stealing whatever disappears—perfume, handkerchiefs, jewelry, rosary beads—and with each disappearance Fulô is stripped and beaten by the overseer. However, when one day the master sees her lovely naked form, he decides to administer future punishments personally, and the mistress is left to lament another kind of stealing:

> Ó Fulô? Ó Fulô?
> Cadê, cadê teu Sinhô
> Que nosso Senhor me mandou?
> Ah! foi você que roubou,
> Foi você negra Fulô?
> Essa negra Fulô!

The poem's lilting rhythm and air of uncontrived spontaneity is enhanced by the refrain ("Essa negra Fulô! Essa negra Fulô!"), which adds a percussive quality reminiscent of the drumbeats essential for Afro-Brazilian musical expression. More significant for our purpose, however, is the author's perspective, which varies little in subsequent works with a Negro motif. The most obvious topic, of course, is Fulô's subservient state, whether as her lady's maid or her master's concubine. But, although her lot is a sad one, there is a humorous note, especially with regard to her stealing her master's affections from the cruel mistress. Even more basic to our poet's view of the black presence is the fact that Fulô is sensually attractive; indeed, the figure of the seductive black woman is a leitmotif prominent throughout Jorge de Lima's Afro-Brazilian poems. In fact, as any reader of Gilberto Freyre doubtless knows, the sensuous charms of the slave woman is a *topos* of the regionalist *Manifesto*. White

---

[12] For a discussion of the poem's success, see Cavalcânti, *Vida e Obra de Jorge de Lima*, pp. 105–10. "Essa Negra Fulô" appears in *Obra Completa*, pp. 291–93.

children, especially the boys, were awakened to sexual desire at an early age by black nursemaids and house servants who fairly smothered their white charges with caresses.[13]

In his *Poemas Negros* de Lima provides an example of such desire in a curious elegy to Celidônia, an adolescent slave girl from Nigeria who was the first nurse of the poem's speaker until she drowned herself.[14] Each stanza of the poem, entitled "Ancila Negra" (pp. 362–63), begins with the verse "Há ainda muita coisa a recalcar." Nowhere is the poet explicit about what precisely is to be repressed, but he recalls vaguely remembered moments of physical contact between the girl and the little boy who, as an adult, re-creates the ambiguous feeling evoked by "carne perdida / noite estancada / rosa trigueira / maga princesa." He goes on to state her obvious duties, such as rocking him to sleep, taking him to school, and telling him tales of Africa, while other strange, half-forgotten memories of caresses and kisses are also recalled. But, he muses,

> . . . tudo ficou como um sino ressoando.
> E eu parado em pequeno
> mandingando e dormindo

For the poet even the mythical mermaid, no less sensuous than exotic, is a Negro woman, as he points out in "Quichimbi, Sereia Negra." The poem is a verbal portrait of the siren, who here appears in a rhapsody of satin-smooth black skin and carefree sensuality: "Quichimbi, sereia negra / bonita como os amores" (p. 356). So pervasive is the comely slave that even places are sometimes anthropomorphized in the form of sinuous African women. Thus, the city of Salvador, where he attended university, is the goal of a student eager for "o contato de teus membros morenos / e procuro com as mãos, / com os lábios tudo o que é bom de cingir e beijar!" And "Serra da Barriga" (p. 294), a wild, craggy area near his home where runaway slaves had once sought refuge, is re-created lyrically as a gigantic Angolan woman reclining in sensuous curves and awaiting her lover, the slave king Zumbi.

Just as frequent as his allusions to black women's sensuality are

---

[13] See Gilberto Freyre, *Casa-Granda e Senzala*, vol. 2 (Rio de Janeiro, 1961), pp. 393–649.

[14] Apparently the incident actually occurred. See Carneiro Campos, *Arte, Sociedade, e Região*, p. 49.

de Lima's references to Afro-Brazilian cults and their throbbing rhythms. In fact, he often blends sex and pagan religion, as in his poem "Xangô." In honor of the powerful voodoo deity whose name provides the title, Yoruba priests from sundry African tribes chant and beat tom-toms while their followers, mulattoes and lithe black silhouettes, dance wildly. The poet's gaze fixes upon a single girl who is especially taken by the spirit as she shakes and sways while all around her the frenzied whirl rises to a crescendo in a haze of smoke from marihuana and incense. Sexual desire and animal passion merge with religious possession:

> A negra mais nova se espoja no chão.
> . . . .
> Xangô tinha entrado no ventre bojudo
> subira pro crânio da negra mais nova.
> Num canto da sala
> Oxalá sorri.   [p. 251]

The poet achieves the sense and feel of *macumba* in short, percussive verses which combine asyndeton, series of nasal gerund forms, and bilabial consonants with the refrain of Yoruba chants:

> Caboclos, mulatos, negrinhas membrudas
> aos tombos gemendo, cantando rolando,
> mexendo os quadris e as mamas bojudas,
> retumbam o tantã . . .
> Oxum!   Oxalá!   Ó!   Ê!

The same blend of voodoo, rhythm, and sex is found in "Diabo Brasileiro," a poem structured around a ritual for casting spells. All the necessary accoutrements are enumerated: a black hen, a crucifix, gold teeth, and so on. The victim is an evasive woman who has resisted the worshiper's advances: "Capeta," cries the suppliant, "tome galinha preta, / quero dormir com Zefa!" To be sure, sex and voodoo are not inseparable for Jorge de Lima, who composed several other poems inspired by Afro-Brazilian cults where sensuality is absent. Such poems are skillful literary adaptations of initiation rites, incantations, and praise for the deities.[15] All, however, reveal a similar dependence on exotic sights and sounds and are expressed

15 For example, "Benedito Calunga," p. 358; "Obamba é Batizado," p. 365; and "Xangô" (not the same poem mentioned in the text), pp. 369–71.

in a markedly Afro-Brazilian vocabulary arranged in free verse shot through with percussive rhythms. Here, too, the reader finds a reliance on repetition and asyndetic series, devices common throughout his "Afro" poetry, but especially so when he focuses on the Negroes' religion.

Closely aligned to voodoo are the folk superstitions of the blacks. In a world where the dead and the living constitute a single community and the gods inhabit all levels of reality, the repertory of ghost tales is immense. From a very early age the poet thrilled and shivered to the supernatural in its manifold forms of headless mules and assorted monsters. In his poem "O Mêdo" he expresses how fused with his traditional Catholicism were these superstitious beliefs. While his grandmother led evening prayers in the family chapel, the servants and the master's children shuddered and trembled at the very thought of zombies roaming through the deserted slave quarters and were fearful of meeting Zuza, the local fireworks maker, who, as all knew, was really a werewolf. "A gente sabia quem era a mula sem cabeça. / O lobisomem era o Zuza-fogueteiro" (pp. 271–72). In "Democracia," a poem addressed to Walt Whitman, de Lima sings of his eclectic spiritual formation, where imps and spells, water sprites and the evil eye were inseparable from catechism classes and vespers (p. 355). From this union there resulted a Catholicism as African as another heirloom of the past, the foods of the northeast.

Few aspects of his region's distinctively Negro culture were more highly prized by Gilberto Freyre and his followers than the foods and dishes prepared by black cooks.[16] In fact, Jorge de Lima often enhances his poems by combining the motifs of the attractive non-white woman and the exciting ceremonies of voodoo cults with ingredients from the varied Afro-Brazilian cuisine. For instance, in a poem in Novos Poemas simply entitled "Comidas"—a tribute to the famous cooking of Bahia—the poet humorously compares the glories of shrimp casseroles and peppery okra with the equally spicy charms of a mulatto girl and the magic spells of witchcraft: "Iaiá," he asks, "me diga / nessa comida / você botou / mulata em pó?" (p.

[16] See Freyre, Casa-Granda e Senzala, vol. 1, pp. 59–60; vol. 2, pp. 634–44. Cf. Luis da Câmara Cascudo, História da Alimentação no Brasil (Rio de Janeiro, 1967), pp. 177–378.

295). And he goes on to exult: "Bahia, estas comidas têm man-
dinga! / Bahia, esse tempeiro [sic] tem mocó!" The non-Latin
sounds of the names of African foods are used to great effect in a
voodoo incantation ("Poema de Encantação," p. 366), where various
dishes and vegetables, all African in origin, are offered to the gods.
The poet catalogues the exotic sounds in alliterative torrents, where
the lack of connectives underlines the frenzied beat of the great
drums. As the Portuguese will show, the very names are onomato-
poeic and represent the chants and the wild scene which he presents
to his bourgeois reader: "Vos ofereço quisama, quinanga, quilen-
gue, quingombô. / Tomai acaçá, abará, aberém, abaú! / . . . Vos
ofereço quitunde, quitumba, quelembe, quingombô."

In our reference to the ballad "Essa Negra Fulô," certain unpleasant aspects of black subservience to white whimsy were mentioned. And in "Serra da Barriga" the hideaway for runaway slaves
would indicate something less than a peaceful assimilation of masters and slaves. Another narrative ballad, entitled "História," tells
of a black princess abducted by an Arab slaver and sold: "Peça
muito boa: não faltava um dente / e era mais bonita que qualquer
inglêsa" (pp. 354–55). Her very beauty, as can be foreseen, is the
cause of her misery as she is abused by captain and crew of the slave
ship and later by her new master in Brazil, only to be tortured by
her jealous mistress. The girl finally escapes to the bush, where she
becomes a devotee of the god Oxalá. Here, the poet combines motifs
already mentioned as the girl implores the god in Nagô, her tribal
language, to defend her and wreak revenge on her mistress: "Exu
escangalha ela . . . / . . . que eu não tenho defesa de homem" (p. 355).
As in other examples in *Poemas Negros*, thanks to his religious faith
the black bears the oppression of slavery in resignation, with revenge left to the gods. One finds only one reference to a Negro, the
famous Zumbi, who strongly protests his enslaved state, and he is
mentioned in passing in "Serra da Barriga." It is curious, though,
that he should serve as a figure to terrify children. "Serra da Barriga! / Te vejo da casa em que nasci. / Que medo danado de negro
fujão!" (p. 294).[17]

17 For the slave as a fearsome figure in Brazil, see David T. Haberly, "Aboli-
tionism in Brazil: Anti-Slavery and Anti-Slave," *Luso-Brazilian Review*, 9 (1972),
30–46. De Lima exemplifies his country's ambiguity regarding the slave as inspiring
both compassion and fear.

The clearest note of social outrage is found in "Pai João," which appears in *Poemas Negros* (pp. 268–69). It is another of the relatively few allusions to the black male, whom de Lima generally consigns to his role as voodoo priest and worshiper of pagan deities. The central figure, an aged black, is about to die after a life spent in toiling for the wealth of others and in losing his women to the masters in the big house. As the slave progresses from the field and the lash to an old age as house retainer and storyteller for the white children, his wife is appropriated while still young enough to bear mulatto offspring for house servants, and their own nubile daughter loses her strength as wet nurse until she, too, becomes as withered as her father and is assigned to the laundry room. After all this, Pai João's revenge in his dying moments is indeed a mild one, for he merely casts a spell on the night sky, leaving it as starless and dark as his own skin:

> Há uma noite lá fora como a pele de Pai João.
> Nem uma estrela no céu.
> Parece até mandinga de Pai João.

As a summary of the quotes thus far should make clear, the Negro in the rural world of Jorge de Lima most frequently appears as a sensuous woman. The black male appears far less frequently and then is usually a figure in a voodoo ceremony. The suffering slave does appear in several poems, but, save for one exception, he is a resigned believer in an animistic universe. Of special social relevance is his helplessness and the attractiveness of his women, which has led to racial mingling on a large scale. The result is a society pervaded by superstitions, folktales, music, and cuisine of African origin.[18]

The critic Antônio Rangel Bandeira some years ago faulted de Lima for showing no outrage even when creating an outrageous situation like that in "Pai João."[19] While the charge is irrelevant

[18] Cf. Carlos Dante de Morães, *Três Fases de Poesia* (Rio de Janeiro, 1960), pp. 119–20.

[19] Antônio Rangel Bandeira, *Jorge de Lima: O Roteiro de uma Contradição* (Rio de Janeiro, 1969), p. 36. Cf. p. 113, where Rangel Bandeira claims that de Lima looked upon Zumbi "com olhos de casa-grande." Others, sharing the poet's own unconscious ethnocentrism, would disagree. Thus, the Portuguese critic Manuel Anselmo finds a spirit of "firme camaradagem" in "Pai João"; see his *A Poesia de Jorge de Lima* (São Paulo, 1939), p. 54. Similarly, Cavalcânti finds a genuine feeling of brotherhood; see Cavalcânti, *Vida e Obra de Jorge de Lima*, pp. 200–5.

in that it confuses the poet with the man and does not allow for an aesthetic viewpoint, it does underline what has already been mentioned as an emotional distance separating the poet from his subject. Moreover, it would seem that such a detached attitude is quite intentional, since de Lima harshly criticized the abolitionist Castro Alves for the latter's "romantismo social, simplista e verboso" (p. 71). And in his poem "Olá Negro" (pp. 373–74) he inveighs against those writers who converted the Negro into a literary theme with "babosas torrentes de falsa piedade."

One wonders why such pity as that of the abolitionists was necessarily false and what our poet's attitude would have been had he been a contemporary of the social reformers of the late nineteenth century.[20] It does seem clear that the Afro-Brazilian of his poetic world represents an artistic transcription of sociological data with little interior human resonance aside from the writer's own nostalgia for the past. In short, Jorge de Lima has produced a colorful, musical, exotic world seen from the outside. Rangel Bandeira remarks how often the lyrical voice of the poems is attributed to one who sees or watches or espies a scene.[21] What transpires is an ahistorical Negro and his culture, objectivized through the lens of childhood reveries and bathed in the aura of bittersweet nostalgia with which the writer recalls his youth. There is rarely any doubt that a voodoo scene is described from the impartial distance of the spectators' gallery, and even the sentimental eclecticism of a superstitious boyhood is recollected by the committed Catholic who turned to dogma when faced with the terrors of unbelief. The only sense of involvement with the poetic world he creates remains the sensuous appeal of Afro-Brazilian women, and they are certainly sex objects in the fullest sense of the word. Never does he show for them the high regard that he directs to Inês de Castro and other European women who appear in his later poetry.[22]

[20] See Rangel Bandeira, *Jorge de Lima*, p. 69. For more on de Lima's aversion to "social romanticism," see his "Auto-retrato" in *Obra Completa*, p. 71. Yet his own novel, *Calunga*, has been described as a "social novel"; see Anselmo, *A Poesia de Jorge de Lima*, p. 70. And the poet composed a laudatory "Vidinha de Castro Alves" in honor of the same abolitionist poet that he criticized; see Cavalcânti, *Vida e Obra de Jorge de Lima*, pp. 247–51.

[21] Rangel Bandeira, *Jorge de Lima*, p. 68.

[22] Thus, Morães' emphasis on de Lima's "forte coloração exótica" and "fascínio exótico" would seem to conflict with the critic's praise for the emotional authenticity

The detached "tourist's" view which characterizes his poems would explain what a sympathetic critic has described as a puzzling persistence of Parnassian techniques even after the poet abandoned the academic school for social realities on the local scene. Thus, Waltensir Dutra rightfully considers *Poemas Negros* and other works of this period examples of stylized regionalism; that is, exact, correct reproductions of local folklore, quite authentic in their descriptive force but by no means imbued with a distinctive Afro-Brazilian awareness or sensibility.[23] Clearly, the poet feels little common ground between himself and, for example, Pai João. In fact, the same tragic figure, his sad plight safely removed in time, is invoked in a humorous poem celebrating the many holidays in May. With Abolition Day commemorated on May 13, the poet calls for merrymaking with:

> O brasileiro só deve
> pensar mesmo em descansar!
> Quem trabalhou mais que Pai João
> cavando a terra com a enxada?
> Dia 13 de Pai João,
> Meu bem, . . .
> Vamos nos deitar?
> Mês de maio, mês santinho!

But it would be unfair to fault de Lima with unusual insensitivity. At least one modern critic shares his distaste for social romanticism and lauds "Pai João": "Jorge de Lima não esbravejou contra êsses chicotes, não fêz 'meeting' contra êsse chicote à Castro Alves e a

---

which he claims to find in our poet's portrayal of the black. See Morães, *Três Fases de Poesia*, pp. 119–20. For de Lima's religious orthodoxy, see Carneiro Campos, *Arte, Sociedade, e Região*, p. 64.

[23] See Dutra's essay, "Descoberta, Integração e Plenitude de Orfeu," in *Obra Completa*, pp. 13–43. See especially pp. 19–20 for his references to de Lima as one who "estiliza a exatidão do regionalismo ou do folclore." For the same reason, Alvaro Lins regards de Lima's poem "Xangô" as "uma representacão não só visual, mas também plástica dos corpos em delírio numa dança primitiva" (see Lins, *Os Mortos de Sobrecasaca*, p. 64). This coincides with Rangel Bandeira's observation that Jorge de Lima saw things with "olhos turísticos" (*Jorge de Lima*, pp. 36 and 56; cf. Martins, *O Modernismo*, pp. 206–7). For a provocative evaluation of Gilberto Freyre's regionalist *Manifesto*, which stresses the movement's detachment from social realities in favor of the exotic note which I have been tracing in de Lima's poems, see Rui Mourão, *Estruturas: Ensaio sôbre o Romance de Graciliano* (Belo Horizonte, 1969), pp. 184–87.

gente fica querendo bem a Pai João e a todos os pretos velhos que nos contarem histórias, daqui por diante."[24]

Most illuminating are the poet's few references to the black in the future, beyond his lyrical world of childhood revery. Apart from the traditional role as a rural servant, it would seem that the Negro in his vision *has* no future. Like many others of his generation, the poet foresaw an even whiter Brazil, where the Negro presence would eventually disappear.[25] In an essay which he wrote in German and published in Leipzig in 1934, entitled *Rassenbildung und Rassenpolitick in Brasilien*, the writer elaborates his conviction that modern Brazil would continue to suffer a crisis of racial identity as long as the total fusion of white and black remained unaccomplished.[26] However startling it may seem, his conviction is nonetheless expressed in the same poems which have won for him the accolade of exponent of Afro-Brazilian culture. Thus, a curious simile in "Pai João" expresses the absorption of the slave and his issue into the nonblack world:

> O sangue de Pai João se sumiu no sangue bom
> como um torrão de açúcar bruto
> numa panela de leite.

More eloquent, the final poem of *Poemas Negros*, "Olá Negro," is a salute to the slave of yesteryear which begins:

> Os netos de teus mulatos e de teus cafuzos
> e a quarta e a quinta gerações de teu sangue sofredor
> tentarão apagar a tua côr!
> E as gerações dessas gerações quando apagarem
> a tua tatuagem execranda,
> não apagarão de suas almas, a tua alma, negro!

The poet sees a final vindication for the black insofar as he will influence the character of future generations of lighter descendents, creating whites with black souls alive to the music, sensuality, and spontaneity so long absent in the white world. A black ancestry, albeit invisible, will thus be a spiritual antidote to the ills of the

---

[24] See Carneiro Campos, *Arte, Sociedade, e Região*, p. 21.

[25] See Guerreiro Ramos, *Introdução Crítica à Sociologia Brasileira* (Rio de Janeiro, 1957), pp. 148–58. Ramos includes the poet among those who present a less than adequate view of the Afro-Brazilian (see p. 196).

[26] See Rangel Bandeira, *Jorge de Lima*, pp. 55–56.

modern, dehumanized world of technology.[27] Jorge de Lima assures the black man:

> A raça que te enforca, enforca-se de tédio, negro!
> E és tu que a alegras ainda com os teus *jazzes*,
> com os teus *songs*, com os teus lundus!
>
> . . . .
>
> E o teu riso, e a tua virgindade e os teus medos e a tua bondade
> mudariam a alma branca cansada de todas as ferocidades!

One can hardly accuse the poet of the racism that has typified Anglo-Saxon attitudes; for Jorge de Lima the goal, already in sight in his own country, is complete amalgamation. But it is equally true that he is hardly a champion of the Afro-Brazilian's place in a modern egalitarian nation.

That the poet's rendering of the black experience struck a responsive chord is clear from the acclaim he has enjoyed from his fellow northeasterner, José Lins do Rêgo. The novelist praised his colleague's indifference to social propaganda and hailed his poetic world as an authentic version of Brazil, unlike the pastiche created by the city dwellers of "modernismo oficial."[28] Like the poet, the novelist also contributed to Freyre's *Manifesto* of 1926 and its high regard for local realities as a means for creating a truly national culture. Lins do Rêgo's saga of regional society, the so-called Sugar-Cane Cycle, comprising six novels, set the tone for a generation of northeastern writers.[29]

Although one of the Sugar-Cane Cycle, *O Moleque Ricardo* is a departure from the other five works in that it is set not in the interior but in Recife, with all the movement and confusion peculiar to a large city. Another difference concerns the central figure; unlike earlier novels in which the author himself, thinly disguised as the fictional Carlos de Melo, is the protagonist, *O Moleque Ricardo*

[27] A similar view of Negro spontaneity as an antidote for white *ennui* has become a stock theme of modern Negritude; see Lilyan Kesteloot, *Les Écrivains noirs de langue française: Naissance d'une littérature* (Brussels, 1965), pp. 116–18. Jorge de Lima ascribed to poetry the same task, that is, to combat the dehumanization of scientific expertise and specialization; see "Minhas Memórias" in *Obra Completa*, pp. 151–52.

[28] See José Lins do Rêgo's essay "Jorge de Lima e o Modernismo," in his *Gordos e Magros* (Rio de Janeiro, 1942), pp. 6–32. Cf. Castello, *José Lins do Rêgo*, pp. 100–3.

[29] See Fred P. Ellison, *Brazil's New Novel: Four Northeastern Masters* (Berkeley, 1954), pp. 45–79.

is an attempt to view the world through the eyes of a young black from the interior seeking his fortunes in the big city. To be sure, Ricardo is from Santa Rosa, the family plantation of the de Melo clan. Moreover, the novelist declared that both young men shared a similar story of personal suffering, frustration, and ultimate defeat. And even their characterization reveals the same melancholy passivity except when stirred by strong sexual desires. For these reasons, many critics have regarded Ricardo as a black alter ego of Carlos de Melo, a relationship which the author explained in view of their shared childhood and common nursemaid, Ricardo's mother Avelina.[30] But there are differences between them as well. Even in the simple rural environment of Santa Rosa there was a sharp line between the plantation owner's children and other youngsters who, as the author says, "nem o nome de menino podiam usar, os chamados moleques de bagaceira, os Ricardos."[31] Later, in the city, the gap between them widens, for Carlos de Melo appears now and then in O Moleque Ricardo as a law student caught up in social and intellectual circles far removed from the milieu of his boyhood playmate.

The plot is a simple one: the young Ricardo runs away from the farm to seek his fortune in the capital. Until his departure, his is the life of the typical rural black; he is virtually illiterate, the son of an amoral mother who shows great tenderness for her large brood of illegitimate children, each sired by a different father. Life is not unpleasant, even if the owner often loses his temper and the routine of milking cows and running errands promises little excitement. Recife, on the other hand, is a complete change in time as well as in place. There, the blacks often seem as educated as the rural white aristocracy, but they have lost the protective paternalism of the plantation and must struggle against a spiraling cost of living and low wages. Nonetheless, Ricardo's needs are few, and he even manages to save some money by living in the shop of the Portuguese baker who has employed him as a delivery boy. A kind, gentle fellow, he is quick to help others, whether the family of a sick colleague

[30] Castello, José Lins do Rêgo, p. 158.

[31] Lins do Rêgo's preface to the first edition of Usina. Hereafter, references to O Moleque Ricardo are to the volume containing both O Moleque Ricardo and Usina (Rio de Janeiro, 1961) and are incorporated into the text.

or the abused wife of his avaricious employer. His only problem seems to be one of sexual and emotional frustration. His first girl-friend commits suicide for unknown reasons, and the second, Isaura, is a voracious nymphet with no sense of loyalty. The third woman in his life is Guiomar, an only child with social pretensions whom he meets at carnival rehearsals and eventually marries. Despite an unusually comfortable existence—his father-in-law has been well compensated for losing a leg in his work as a watchman at a large warehouse—Ricardo is unhappy. He remains infatuated with the lascivious Isaura, and, to compound his distress, his bride contracts tuberculosis and soon dies. When the young widower returns to the bakery to live, he becomes reluctantly involved in a general strike and is arrested with a few leaders. The novel ends with his imprisonment on the island penitentiary of Fernando de Noronha.

In his study of the impact of modernism on Lins do Rêgo, the critic Aderaldo Castello singles out as Ricardo's dominant char-acteristic an intriguing moral neutrality, much the same attitude that Rangel Bandeira detected in de Lima's *Poemas Negros*.[32] Away from his rural background, the young black is incapable of any commitment to life in the city. He remains docile and sub-servient from beginning to end while all around him rages the violent social upheaval of a large city in an underdeveloped society during the years following the First World War. Ricardo apparent-ly became psychologically static ever since his first realization that the privileges of a household pet, which he had been as a child, would not continue after adolescence. With maturity came the realization that "não valia nada mesmo. Só para o serviço, para lavar cavalos, rodar moinho de café, tirar leite. Negro era mesmo bicho de serventia" (p. 12). Not surprisingly, he is later impervious to calls for social revolution, saying, "Isto vai assim até o fim do mundo" (p. 157).

As in Aesop's fable of the two mice, city life, despite its glitter, pales beside the placid monotony and simple joys of the interior. When the young husband finds himself saddled with a dying wife and a resentful mother-in-law, he seeks relief in remembering earlier years on the plantation, with its safe, if dull, routine: "Ah! se tivesse ficado por lá!" (p. 171). Nor is Ricardo the only Negro

[32] See Castello, *José Lins do Rêgo*, p. 159.

character who regrets leaving the country. When a fellow worker is wounded in a labor dispute, the man's wife laments: "Bem que vivia satisfeita em Limoeiro . . . Florêncio trabalhava na pressa de algodão do Coronel Furtado . . . mas bateu por aqui" (p. 57). She proceeds to describe "here": the horrors of slum life on the mud flats with their periodic flooding, filth, and privation. In this alien place Ricardo can hardly be himself, and even simple physical love and deep sentiment elude him. The loss of these virtues in the impersonal city is especially tragic for him since "tudo que era negro tinha mulher" (p. 53) and "negro sem coração era negro desgraçado" (p. 161).

Clearly, Lins do Rêgo predicated the same traits of the Afro-Brazilian that we have already seen in Jorge de Lima. Besides the black's sensuality and emotional spontaneity, here often frustrated, *O Moleque Ricardo* abounds in references to musical rhythm, superstitions, and voodoo. The only absence is food, which is always in short supply in this novel of grinding urban poverty. Although Ricardo himself is skeptical of voodoo, he is awed and a bit frightened by the magical powers of Father Lucas, the *macumba* priest. The latter is a pivotal character holding up the appeal of the ancestral African cults as a solace to his people's suffering: "Éle dava Deus ao povo, êle dava uma esperança de muito longe no céu, um céu que era para depois de tudo" (p. 183). And there is frequent mention of the mingling of sex and pagan religion, though the more sophisticated milieu of the city results in a presentation of voodoo that is somewhat less telluric than the mysticism of de Lima's poems. Thus, a nonbeliever scoffs at cult meetings with "êles querem papar as negrinhas que vão para lá cair na tremedeira!" (p. 34). Generally, then, the city has a negative effect on the traditional Afro-Brazilian character, which is captured in a more pristine state in de Lima's verses. Now the sensuous Negro woman appears under a veneer of white cosmetics, as when Guiomar prepares for a date with her hair grotesquely stretched flat and her lovely skin ashen under a film of cheap face powder (p. 121).[33] And even the kindly Father Lucas is

---

[33] All the female personages are poles apart in their carefree sensuality from the prudish middle-class woman. Guiomar, in fact, is shown as a nymphomaniac after marriage, and there appears the typical vivacious mulatto mistress of the no less typical lecherous Portuguese immigrant. Like his colleague Jorge de Lima, Lins do

often jailed by authorities who fear his popularity and suspect that the voodoo sessions are really pretexts for sexual orgies (p. 33).

Perhaps the single major difference between country and city is the union movement of the latter, which is a parallel plot in this novel set among a largely Afro-Brazilian labor force. But the author considers it an opiate like *macumba*, and an even less satisfying one.[34] Lins do Rêgo paints a sordid picture of political chicanery as white leaders use the labor movement for their own advancement while university students play at the game of social involvement: "Não podia suportar o contato do povo em comício ou em qualquer parte" (p. 76). There are several comparisons between the cults and the movement: both are collective expressions which seek to redress wrongs but which are equally ineffective. The author shows the futility of both when the strikers are shipped off to Fernando de Noronha, the prison, while on the shore the more traditional blacks chant and sway to the throbbing beat of a new refrain: "Que fizeram êles que vão para Fernando? Ninguém sabe não!" (p. 193).

A considerable portion of the novel is given to carnival time in Recife. The carnival is shown as an outburst of Afro-Brazilian musical celebration, but it is also a rare leveler of the differences separating the classes and colors. When the infectious rhythms fill the streets, "não havia branco e não havia prêto . . . as môças dentro dos automóveis, os que iam a pé, os homens importantes e os iguais a êle, todos como se fôssem de uma mesma casa . . . gente de gravata e de pé no chão" (p. 102).

Like *macumba*, then, the musical holiday is a narcotic for social ills, and even the labor movement and talk of revolution are temporarily shelved until after Ash Wednesday. So inviting is the hilarity that the moody Ricardo heartily joins in, and the normally proper Guiomar astounds him with her provocative behavior. A cooler head comments, to no avail, of course: "Não sei . . . como o povo desta rua se lembra de carnaval. Só sendo mesmo para esquecer a desgraça" (p. 95). But a return to ancestral rhythms and frank

Rêgo also saw the nonwhite woman in "Dionysiac terms" (see Ramos, *Sociologia Brasileria*, pp. 196–97).

[34] For the novelist's basically conservative point of view in the matter of social change, see Gregory Rabassa, *O Negro na Ficção Brasileira*, trans. Ana Maria Martins (Rio de Janeiro, 1965), p. 167. Cf. Castello, *José Lins do Rêgo*, pp. 158–59.

sensuality may also occasion less happy thoughts of the past: "O canto do maracatu era triste. Os negros se entristeciam com aqueles lamentos de prisioneiros, de algemados, de negros gemendo para Deus, rogando aos céus" (p. 106).

Aside from such illusive moments, the black in *O Moleque Ricardo* is the most alienated member of the proletariat. His spontaneity and mysticism render him unfit for modern urban society, and so the reader finds the frequent expressions of nostalgia for the rural past which have been noted. As in Jorge de Lima's poems, the future is problematic and points to social agitation between rich and poor, the lighter and the darker. Basically, for the poet as well as the novelist, the Afro-Brazilian appears as an object rather than a subject. There is little if any revelation of what the black experience might be with regard to the Negro's own human condition in a society which considers him, albeit benevolently, as a theme of historical and anthropological significance. Aside from the characteristics of sensuality, suffering, rhythmic spontaneity, and exotic mysticism, the black presence in the works of both men is bereft of the vital pulse of autonomous life. For this reason, then, such critics as Gilberto Freyre are in the main quite correct in affirming that a genuine Afro-Brazilian literature is nonexistent. Certainly, what the reader finds here is the "Afro" world seen from the outside. But to point to cultural and racial assimilation as the reason for such a lack is to simplify the matter. Rather, it would seem that such a literary expression could be possible only if the objectivized Negro became a subject. A true Afro-Brazilian art form would then be a vehicle whereby the black would focus on himself and his perspective rather than be portrayed in terms of "them" and "their" culture. It would, in short, be the expression of a group experience which, up to the present, has been examined but has not examined either itself or its place in Brazilian society.[35]

Jorge de Lima provides several valuable insights into what many of his supporters have failed to notice. In writing of the black presence in 1929, he stated: "O problema do negro foi assim resolvido sexualmente. O Americano do norte vai resolvê-lo de outro modo.

---

[35] For the distinction between the Negro as an "object" or "problem" and rarely, if ever, as a "subject" in Brazilian culture, I am indebted to Ramos, *Sociologia Brasileira*, pp. 147–50.

Vamos ver se resolve! . . . Resolvemos os nossos problemar mais sérios não os resolvendo."[36] The paradox expresses the elusive character of Brazilian racial assimilation, which seems to imply on the one hand that all races are equally good, but on the other hand hastens to add that mixture has led to the gradual disappearance of the black. The population is thus described as becoming "whitened"; no one ever says "mulattoized."

Rangel Bandeira is perhaps the only critic who scores this ambiguity in Jorge de Lima, but even he asks: "Será possível admitir-se que o autor mais significativo da poesia afro-brasileira . . . jamais tenha compreendido o sentimento da raça negra? Não, não pode ser. Nisso devemos lutar contra a evidência intrínsica."[37] And the perplexed critic provides an explanation by appealing to the poet's generally contradictory nature, which thus leads him to espouse the validity of an "Afro" culture while at the same time showing a definite white bias.

Jorge de Lima himself, however, provides a surprising admission which apparently has escaped Rangel Bandeira's attention. In an autobiographical sketch the poet writes: "[Before going to Bahia] eu desconhecia o negro como muito brasileiro desconhece, como mesmo o negro desconhece. E eu tinha que ver o negro. Vi efetivamente o negro."[38] The result is the descriptive rather than the empathetic rendering of the black world noted above, a rendering perhaps more genuine than a tourist's point of view but certainly no more profound than the case study of the anthropologist or the sociologist. And, in an observation which apparently has yet to be mentioned by any critic, the author of *Poemas Negros* unknowingly refutes the views of his colleagues of the regionalist *Manifesto* who, like Lins do Rêgo and Gilberto Freyre, believe that a real Afro-Brazilian poetry is impossible. In a discussion of works based on social themes, the poet concludes with the observation that such literature is invariably artificial and external in tone. A genuinely social literature will evolve, he affirms, only when "o operário ou o intelectual proletarizado puderem escrever suas vidas, fixar no

---

36 Quoted in Rangel Bandeira, *Jorge de Lima*, pp. 53–54.

37 *Ibid.*, p. 69.

38 In "Auto-retrato" in *Obra Completa*, p. 145. It is curious that the poet should distinguish between the black and the (average) Brazilian.

papel . . . suas rebeldias triunfantes" (p. 71). For the same reason, one may conjecture, his own view of the black and that of other respected writers likewise fails to ring true. One might paraphrase his comment and say that an Afro-Brazilian literature in the fullest sense of the word is possible only when the Brazilian nonwhite expresses himself as an aspect of a social panorama now rather than consenting to wait until he becomes tomorrow's rarely acknowledged ancestor.[39]

In conclusion, it must be admitted that the black presence in Brazilian literature owes much to the modernist movement, with both Jorge de Lima and José Lins do Rêgo as conspicuous contributors to a clearer understanding of traditional Brazilian society. No writer before them succeeded in attracting national and even international attention to the Afro-Brazilian culture of the northeast, a culture ignored by previous generations even when not looked upon as an embarrassment or maligned by the occasional black or mulatto writer who identified with prevailing middle-class values.[40] However, their perspective is both ethnocentric and inadequate for the present. One could hardly expect more in view of their creative point of departure: a nostalgic recollection of the Negro as part of the paternalistic world of a vanishing plantation culture.

[39] In his article "Alejo Carpentier: Dos Visiones del Negro, Dos Conceptos de la Novela," *Hispania*, 55 (1972), 34–44, Pedro M. Barreda-Tomás convincingly argues that the stereotype Negro (humble, sensual, a telluric force, and the like) need not be *all* that a white novelist can achieve and finds more creditable creation in Carpentier's later novels. For a contrary view—personal experience as a *sine qua non* for literary portrayal—see Addison Gayle, Jr., *The Black Situation* (New York, 1970), especially pp. 164–97.

[40] The classic example in Brazilian letters is the black Cruz e Sousa. See Morães, *Três Fases de Poesia*, pp. 67–70.

Native and Foreign Influences in Contemporary Mexican Fiction: A Search for Identity

Luis Leal

It is not uncommon to find that critics of Mexican fiction divide writers into two groups: those dedicated to the treatment of native subject matter and those writing under the influence of foreign literatures who are not necessarily interested in national themes. This separation is natural, as there has been a constant struggle between the two groups, but while the struggle between nationalist and cosmopolitan critics, and sometimes even among writers, can actually be documented, literary works in themselves are not purely native or cosmopolitan. This does not rule out the fact, however, that in all of those works one or the other tendency predominates. Mexican fiction, like the nation itself, is the result of a synthesis of native and foreign influences. In order to better understand the forces that have molded contemporary Mexican fiction it is necessary to trace briefly the development of this synthesis. Although the following remarks deal with fiction only, the same could be said of other genres.

Among the Mexican works of fiction mentioned by nationalist critics as representative of a native novel we find José Joaquín Fernández de Lizardi's *El Periquillo Sarniento* (1816), Luis G. Inclán's *Astucia* (1865), Manuel Payno's *Los bandidos de Río Frío* (1889–91), and José Tomás de Cuellar's *La linterna mágica* (1889–

92) .[1] Critics are unanimous in considering these novels as the most representative of a national trend in Mexican fiction. A typical criticism is that of a twentieth-century national novelist, Mariano Azuela, who said about them, "Lo que nos atrae de Fernández de Lizardi, de Inclán, de Payno, y de Facundo, no es su literatura, sino el mexicanismo que rezuman sus libros, lo auténticamente nacional, cuando lo auténticamente literario está muy lejos todavía en la novela."[2] Azuela considered *El Periquillo Sarniento* as essentially limited to what is Mexican because "nosotros somos los únicos capacitados para encontrar lo que de íntimamente nacional hay de ella."[3] Of Payno's novel he said, "El mexicanismo de Payno rezuma por todos los poros de su novela."[4] Cuéllar he considered to be the most original novelist, as he never wrote, Azuela tells us, after the manner of any other writer.[5]

And yet, in spite of the emphasis that critics give to the national elements in Lizardi's novel, the form used is the picaresque, of Spanish origin; the philosophical ideas are those of the French thinkers of the eighteenth century,[6] and some of Periquillo's adventures are similar to those of Gil Blas de Santillana, Lesage's hero.

Astucia is perhaps the most Mexican novel. John S. Brushwood has this to say about it: "The language of the people is present to an even greater extent than in *El Periquillo Sarniento*, and description of rural customs appears to be accurate enough. . . . All these qualities evoke strong identification on the part of the Mexican reader who finds familiar things that are distinctively Mexican."[7] These

---

[1] For a complete survey of the origins of the national novel, see Doris King Arjona and Carlos Vázquez Arjona, "Apuntes sobre los orígenes del nacionalismo en la novela mexicana," *Revue Hispanique*, 81, part 2 (1933), 440–55 .

[2] Mariano Azuela, *Cien años de novela mexicana* (Mexico City: Botas, 1947), p. 47.

[3] *Ibid.*, p. 49.

[4] *Ibid.*, p. 84.

[5] *Ibid.*, p. 103.

[6] See Jefferson Rea Spell, "The Intellectual Background of Fernández de Lizardi as Reflected in *El Periquillo Sarniento*," *PMLA*, 71 (June 1956), 414–32; Bernabé Godoy, *Corrientes culturales que definen al "Periquillo"* (Guadalajara: Editorial Navegación Poética, 1938). For what the critics had to say about Lizardi's novel, see Alfonso Reyes' essay, *"El Periquillo Sarniento* y la crítica mexicana," in *Obras completas de Alfonso Reyes*, vol. 4 (Mexico City: Fondo de Cultura Económica, 1956), pp. 169–78.

[7] John S. Brushwood, *Mexico in its Novel* (Austin: University of Texas Press, 1966), p. 92.

observations are true if we think of the contents of the novel and not about its form, where Inclán follows that of Dumas' famous *The Three Musketeers*. "The structure and ethics of the gang," says Brushwood, "appear to a non-Mexican to be as Dumasesque as they are rural Mexican."[8] It is not necessary to be a non-Mexican to detect these similarities between *Astucia* and *The Three Musketeers*, a novel well known throughout Mexico. Azuela mentions the resemblance and extends it to include other novels. "Once our hero has joined the gang of smuggling cowboys," he says, "he is to receive a new baptism in a ceremony that makes us laugh, for it is the most indiscreet borrowing of the scene in *The Three Musketeers* where they use the well known 'one for all and all for one.' And the same thing happens in the scene where they watch over the arms in the inn's well, taken from Don Quijote."[9] Azuela forgives Inclán these "innocent plagiarisms" because later in the novel they do not appear. Nevertheless, it is interesting to observe that the influence of the French popular novel was so pervasive that it reached such national novelists as Inclán. The same influence can be detected in Payno's novel, *Los bandidos de Río Frío*. In Cúellar, on the other hand, the influence that predominates is that of the Spanish *costumbristas*.

Among the realists and naturalists, French influence is even more pronounced. Federico Gamboa's *Santa* (1903) reflects the influence of Zola's *Nana*, and his *Reconquista* that of *L'Œuvre*.[10] The realist López Portillo y Rojas, on the other hand, fell under the influence of the Spanish regional novelists, such as Pereda and Alarcón. Manuel Pedro González tells us that some critics have tried to compare López Portillo y Rojas with Dickens. "Más," he says, "le debe a los novelistas finiseculares españoles, y en particular a Pereda, que al famoso narrador británico. Por lo que a *Fuertes y débiles* respecta, recuerda vagamente *I promessi sposi*, de Manzoni. . . ."[11] Dickens'

---

[8] *Ibid.*, p. 93.

[9] *Cien años de novela mexicana*, p. 64. The translation is mine, as are all others in this study unless otherwise indicated.

[10] See R. J. Niess, "Zola's *L'Œuvre* and *Reconquista* of Gamboa," *PMLA*, 61, no. 2 (1946), 577–83. Also see Seymour Menton, "Influencias extranjeras en la obra de Federico Gamboa," *Armas y Letras*, 2nd ser., 1 (July–September 1958), 35–50.

[11] Manuel Pedro González, *Trayectoria de la novela en México* (Mexico City: Botas, 1951), p. 67.

influence, if not present in López Portillo y Rojas, can be detected in one of his contemporaries, the short-story writer Ángel de Campo, famous under the pseudonym *Micrós*. His treatment of the poor, especially children, reminds one of Dickens. His friend, the novelist Federico Gamboa, observed that *Micrós* is a direct descendant of Charles Dickens and Alphonse Daudet.[12]

The influence of foreign literatures is even more decisive among the writers known as the *modernistas*, and especially in Manuel Gutiérrez Nájera, Amado Nervo, and José Juan Tablada. A precursor of this group of writers was Justo Sierra, who in 1868 began to publish in the principal newspapers of Mexico City a series of stories and legends dealing with non-Mexican subjects. With these tales Sierra prepared the way for the *modernistas*, who in the 1880's rejected the nationalist credo and again turned to Europe, and even the United States, for inspiration. The influence of French fiction reached its peak during the era of Don Porfirio Díaz (1877–1910). In the short period between 1887 and 1896 in only one newspaper, *El Siglo XIX*, there appeared no fewer than 255 short stories translated from the French.

Manuel Gutiérrez Nájera, the creator of the *modernista* short story, had published in 1883 a slender volume, *Cuentos frágiles*, of importance because with it he initiated a new trend in Spanish American narrative prose, characterized by its interest in the creation of an artistic work and not in the depiction of a national consciousness or reflection of a national way of life. He was, of course, severely criticized by the nationalists, and one critic, himself a poet, even said that Nájera "dio la espalda al españolismo; se afrancesó."[13] In 1885 Nájera had discussed the problem of foreign and native influences in Mexican literature as well as the treatment of non-Mexican subject matter. To him, national literature was a misnomer: "Desde luego, declaro que no estoy conforme con el nombre de literatura nacional." Instead of *literatura nacional* he proposed the use of the term *literatura propia*, as the word *nacional* should be reserved for that literature written to keep, revive, or extol the

---

12 Federico Gamboa, *La novela en México* (Mexico City. Eusebio Gómez de la Puente, Editor, 1914), p. 24.

13 Luis G. Urbina, *La vida literaria en México* (Mexico City: Imprenta Sáez Hermanos, 1917), p. 221.

patriotic spirit of the people. The use of native subject matter is not enough to declare the work dealing with it as national. He takes the critic Pimentel to task for declaring that the poem "Turco" by Carpio was not a Mexican poem. But, he argued, "tampoco es una poesía turca, porque . . . los turcos no hablan como el turco de Carpio. . . . Ese turco es mexicano, es Carpio cuando era joven." Neither, Nájera goes on to say, is the language in which a work is written sufficient to declare it as belonging to a certain country: "Yo he escrito en francés articulos y poesías, para no escribirlos en galicismo: sin embargo, no aspiro a que se me cuente entre los poetas y pensadores franceses. La *Divina comedia* del Dante es un poema italiano, porque su autor era de Italia: nada más." More important, Nájera rejected the advice of Altamirano, who in 1868 had told young authors to write about Mexican subjects. "Hoy," Nájera said, "no puede pedirse al literato que sólo describa los lugares de su patria y sólo cante las hazañas de sus héroes nacionales. El literato viaja, el literato está en comunicación íntima con las civilizaciones antiguas y con todo el mundo moderno. . . . Lo que se exige a un poeta, por ejemplo, para considerarlo como gran poeta en la literatura propia, es lisa y llanamente que sea un gran poeta, es decir, que la luz que despida sea suya y no refleja."[14]

The other great *modernista* poet, Amado Nervo, also admired French culture. He tells us: "Se va especialmente de América a París, porque aquí se nos predica constantemente que en París hay muchas cosas nuevas para nosotros."[15] The themes we find in Nervo's poetry and short stories are representative of the period; the influences come from France, ancient Greece, and the Orient. Very few of his short stories deal with Mexican themes. On the other hand, his writings reflect a preoccupation with the problems of Europe, especially France. Even Mariano Azuela, who later became known as the novelist of the revolution, began writing under the influence of the French realists and naturalists. His novels are

[14] Manuel Gutiérrez Nájera, "Literatura propia y literatura nacional," in *Obras*, vol. 1, *Crítica literaria* (Mexico City: UNAM, 1959), pp. 84–86. This essay first appeared in *El Partido Liberal*, 2 August 1885.

[15] *Obras completas de Amado Nervo*, vol. 4, *El éxodo y las flores del camino* (Madrid: Biblioteca Nueva, 1927), p. 51.

a good example of the change brought about by the revolution of 1910. His first four novels, written between 1907 and 1909, still reflect the influence of the French novelists. Speaking about the writing of his first novel, Azuela tells us: "Estudiaba quinto año de medicina [in Guadalajara] empapado más que en la patología y en la terapéutica, en las novelas realistas de Francia y España, entonces en su apogeo. *Sor Filomena* de Edmundo de Goncourt me había seducido con sus admirables retablos de la vida de los estudiantes de medicina, en su internado en los hospitales de París. ¿Quién de nosotros no soñaba con el Barrio Latino que nos habían hecho familiar Murger y tantos otros poetas y novelistas franceses? Número obligado en nuestro programa de médicos jóvenes recién titulados era el viaje a Europa, con permanencia preferente en París."[16] One must remember that during that period of Mexican history the works of French poets and novelists, even those of inferior quality, were translated into Spanish and published in every newspaper and magazine. If a Mexican novelist wanted to sell his books, he had to imitate the French writers, as the public was used to reading this type of literature. About this problem, Azuela comments: "Escribí *María Luisa* [his first novel] hace cincuenta y tres años. En ese tiempo la escuela realista estaba en su apogeo: dominaban en Francia Flaubert, los Goncourt, Zola, Daudet, Maupassant, y los estudiantes nos avorazábamos con estas novelas como con las de Galdós, Pereda y Valera. La influencia de los románticos no acababa aún de borrarse. . . . La inmensa mayoría de los lectores seguía gustando la literatura de Víctor Hugo, de Jorge Sand y de Eugenio Sue, muy lejos todavía de las complicaciones psicológicas que ahora hasta los peluqueros exigen."[17]

Why did Mexican writers imitate the French authors? Although the problem is much more complex than it appears to be, and although we recognize the dangers of generalizing, we may say that during the Díaz period of government writers were trying to adapt themselves to a new philosophy and to a new way of life that had been brought about by the break with the past that took place

---

[16] Mariano Azuela, *Obras completas*, vol. 3 (Mexico City: Fondo de Cultura Económica, 1960), pp. 1012–13.
[17] *Ibid.*, p. 1025.

(among the intellectuals and the political leaders) during the period of reform under Juárez. Having rejected the Spanish tradition, and unable to go back to an Indian heritage, they had to turn to France, whose culture, which had been introduced by Maximilian and Carlota during the 1860's, was familiar to them. By imitating the French writers who were in the forefront of literary development in Europe, Mexican authors could also demonstrate their intellectual independence from Spain, which they had not done up to that time. The *modernistas* ignored local influences, and their works, although written in elegant style, reflected French life and tastes. They had been able to emancipate themselves from their Spanish masters only to fall under the influence of the French.

The predominant influence of French culture in Mexico came to an end around 1906, the year that a group of young intellectuals founded the Society of Lectures and edited the review *Savia Moderna* to voice their dissatisfaction with the official doctrine, French positivism, and the exclusive acceptance of French thought. Among these young men we find the names of such well-known writers as Alfonso Reyes, José Vasconcelos, Antonio Caso, and the Dominican Pedro Henríquez Ureña. This new generation rejected the ideas of the *científicos*, as the positivists under Díaz were called, and declared freedom of thought and expression. They believed that other philosophers, besides Comte, should be studied, and therefore they introduced the ideas of James, Bergson, and Boutroux, whose systems are based on freedom of thought and inquiry. This group, which organized itself under the name Ateneo de la Juventud, was able to influence Minister of Education Justo Sierra, who in 1908 made a speech rejecting positivism as an official philosophy.

Alfonso Reyes is the best example of how beneficial foreign influences can be when they are assimilated and given original expression. In the writings of this distinguished man of letters, often called "el mexicano universal," we find the influence of all world literatures. In his numerous essays one never fails to detect the presence of the great thinkers from all countries and all ages. No subject matter, no theme, no area of knowledge was strange to him. An excellent example of his adaptation of universal subject matter is the dramatic poem *Ifigenia cruel* (1924), in which Reyes uses the tragic story of Iphigenia to suggest personal experiences and historical events that occurred during the Mexican Revolution when his father, General Bernardo Reyes, was assassinated. Due to his long absence from Mexico, and to his preference for non-Mexican subject matter, he was criticized for supposedly forgetting the land of his birth. Luis Garrido defended him with these words:

> El nacionalismo de un escritor no se finca en la cantidad de cuartillas que ha dedicado a los asuntos y cosas del patrio solar. . . . Desde su juventud fijó su posición al respecto con estas palabras: 'En nuestra literatura nacional—particularmente me contraigo aquí a la novela—, el color local y la imitación de la vida han producido un resultado funesto a todas luces: no hallaréis, o la hallaréis difícilmente, novela nacional en que no se describa esta festividad, la más vulgar de todas, la menos sugestiva de todas: un 15 de septiembre en la noche.' Con esto Reyes quiere ponernos en guardia contra alardes de falso nacionalismo, de las mistificaciones y de los pastiches. . . . Nuestro poeta y ensayista, a pesar de su larga ausencia del país, nunca postergó los valores nacionales que conocía, y a su regreso no dejó de interesarse por el espectáculo del México de hoy.[18]

Pedro Henríquez Ureña, who was influential with this group of Mexican writers, represents a new tendency in Latin American letters and criticism. He advised young writers to read not only Spanish and French authors, but also English, North American, and German ones, not for the purpose of imitating them, but to learn new ways of writing. He thought that the writer should strive for a synthesis of foreign and native elements, as well as a synthesis of learned and current literary trends and revolutionary and conservative ideas. In his famous essay "El descontento y la promesa," he says: "Los inquietos de ahora se quejan de que los antepasados hayan vivido atentos a Europa, nutriéndose de imitación, sin ojos para el mundo que los rodeaba. . . . Existieron, sí, existen todavía los europeizantes, los que llegan a abandonar el español para escribir en francés, o, por lo menos, escribiendo en nuestro propio idioma ajustan a moldes franceses su estilo y hasta piden a Francia sus ideas y sus asuntos. O los hispanizantes, enfermos de locura gramatical,

---

18 Luis Garrido, *Alfonso Reyes* (Mexico City: Imp. Universitaria, 1954), pp. 58–59. For a study of Reyes' interest in classical literatures, see Ingemar During, "Alfonso Reyes, helenista," in *Dos estudios sobre Alfonso Reyes* (Madrid: Insula, 1962).

hipnotizados por toda cosa de España que no haya sido trasplantada a estos suelos."[19] He goes on to show that the influence of foreign cultures prevailed in Imperial Rome, in the Middle Ages, and during the Renaissance. He ends by saying that Spanish American literature is the result of a synthesis of native and foreign elements: "Al expresarnos había en nosotros, junto a la porción sola, nuestra, hija de nuestra vida, a veces con herencia indígena, otra porción sustancial, aunque sólo fuere el marco, que recibimos de España. Voy mas lejos: no sólo escribimos el idioma de Castilla, sino que pertenecemos a la romania, la familia románica que constituye todavía una comunidad, una unidad de cultura descendiente de la que Roma organizó bajo su potestad; pertenecemos—según la repetida frase de Sarmiento—al Imperio Romano."[20]

This synthesis of which Henríquez Ureña speaks did not take place in the Mexican novel during the period of the Mexican Revolution, that is, between 1915 and 1940. As a matter of fact, there were two well-defined schools: the novelists of the revolution on the one hand and the postmodernists and vanguardists on the other.

In the field of the novel, the first great work that is a direct result of the revolution is Mariano Azuela's *Los de abajo*, first published in November, 1915, precisely one hundred years after *El Periquillo Sarniento*. If Lizardi's work revived a lost form, the picaresque romance, Azuela's initiated another, the novel of the Mexican Revolution, the first body of Mexican literature to have an impact outside the country. The book is significant not only for its theme but also for its form. Azuela abandoned the techniques of the European novelists he had used in earlier novels and created a new form, genuinely Mexican and admirably adapted to give expression to the theme of social turmoil.

Other novelists of the revolution (Guzmán, López y Fuentes, Muñoz, Magdaleno, and so on) were also inspired by the social and political events they had witnessed and drew upon those events to write their fiction. These novels and short stories reflect Mexican society, contain descriptions of actual events, have characters that

---

[19] Pedro Henríquez Ureña, "El descontento y la promesa," in *Ensayos en busca de nuestra expresión* (Buenos Aires: Editorial Raigal, 1952), p. 39. This essay was first published in *La Nación* (Buenos Aires), 29 August 1926.

[20] *Ibid.*, pp. 47–48.

are often historical, and display a style that is the opposite of that of the *modernistas*. It reflects the speech of the people; it is obsessed neither with purity of language, as were the works of the nineteenth-century realists, nor with the use of a syntax patterned after that of the French models, as in *modernista* prose.

We must not think, however, that the novelists of the revolution were the only active writers during this period. Another current was the one represented by the group known as the *colonialistas*, whose origin can be traced to the studies of colonial architecture undertaken by Jesús T. Acevedo. The best representative of this group is Artemio de Valle-Arizpe, who discovered a rich source of material in the writings of the chroniclers and historians of the colonial period. In his novels and short stories he re-creates the atmosphere of colonial Mexico in a style which reflects the taste of the period.

Both the novelists of the revolution and the *colonialistas* made use of nationalistic themes and subject matter. Not all the writers of the period, however, followed in their steps. The *contemporáneos*, a group of writers active between 1915 and 1930, believed that it was possible to reflect Mexican reality without writing about national themes. In their works foreign influences do not disappear. There is a great difference, however, between the *modernistas* and the *vanguardistas*, represented in Mexico by the *contemporáneos* and the *estridentistas*. The *contemporáneos* (among whom we find the well-known names of Xavier Villaurrutia, Jaime Torres Bodet, Bernardo Ortiz de Montellano, and José Martínez Sotomayor, to mention those who wrote fiction) tried to express the Mexican spirit through its universal features and by adapting, not only imitating, suitable literary modes regardless of their origin. Commenting upon the influence of the Mexican Revolution on literature and the arts, Ortiz de Montellano observed: "Como señalamos—dice—, los beneficios, la influencia de la revolución mexicana en el arte debemos buscarla más que en los frutos inmediatos que arrancan del árbol de los hechos nuestros novelistas, en la semilla que un nuevo sentido de los valores espirituales, con vistas al tono verdadero de la sensibilidad mexicana, a la cultura y a las ideas universales, pueden aportar sus obras."[21]

21 Quoted by Merlin H. Forster in "La revista *Contemporáneos* ¿Hacia una me-

The fiction of the vanguardists did not have an impact beyond national frontiers, as the social novels previously had; neither can it be said that their fiction was popular inside the country, as was their poetry. The influence of Azuela and Guzmán was the one that predominated until the 1940's, when once more fiction writers were influenced by foreign novelists, this time not only those from Europe, but those from the United States as well. But the whole process was different. The novel that appeared during this decade is not a simple imitation of foreign forms, as had been the case with the realists, who disregarded the Mexican narrative tradition. And yet the novelists of the revolution, who still dominated the literary scene, could not be brushed aside. What actually took place was a blending of narrative techniques—national ones and those coming from foreign sources. The novel that was produced did not lose its Mexican identity, since it did not break entirely with tradition. The influence of the national novelists is evident in the selection of themes, in the creation of backgrounds, and in the techniques of characterization. But the influence of the European and North American novel is also evident in the treatment of themes, in the form, and in the introduction of new points of view. Of the North American novelists the most obvious influence has been that of Faulkner, Dos Passos, and Hemingway. Of the English, that of Joyce, Woolf, and Huxley. Of the French, that of Robbe-Grillet and Nathalie Sarraute. The application of new techniques to the development of Mexican subject matter has produced an original novel that has become universal without losing its national identity. The novelists who have contributed most to the development of this new novel are José Revueltas, Agustín Yáñez, Juan Rulfo, Carlos Fuentes, Juan José Arreola, Salvador Elizondo, José Agustín, José Emilio Pacheco, Gustavo Sainz, and Fernando del Paso.

In 1943 Revueltas published *El luto humano*, the first novel written by a Mexican author in which an attempt is made to apply modern novelistic techniques. Although in some respects it shows the influence of Azuela, Guzmán, and López y Fuentes, in others that

xicanidad universal?" *Hispanófila*, 17 (1963), 117–22; quotation on p. 122. For a discussion of this problem, see also John S. Brushwood, "*Contemporáneos* and the Limits of Art," *Romance Notes*, 5 (1964), 1–5.

of William Faulkner predominates.[22] This novel represents a contribution to the development of Mexican fiction because Revueltas, without abandoning Mexican subject matter, tried to solve the problems of narrative technique. Some critics may object that Revueltas' novel fails to attain an artistic form because of the direct presentation of the novelist's political ideas. This could not be said of Agustín Yáñez' novel *Al filo del agua*, which appeared in 1947 and represents perhaps the most ambitious undertaking in the field of the novel by a Mexican writer. It brings together several trends that had been present in Mexican fiction; it is a work of art that is, at the same time, national and universal, artistic and social. If some critics consider *Al filo del agua* to be a novel of the revolution, it is because in it we find the best explanation of why the revolution took place. The novelist selected a dramatic moment not only in the life of the characters, but also in the history of Mexico. The unfolding of the novel is parallel to the unfolding of Mexican history. The causes to which the author attributes the revolution are not stated explicitly in the novel; the reader himself has to reach the conclusions from the actions of the characters.

When the French translation of *Al filo del agua* appeared in 1961, Octavio Paz made the following observations, which we quote at length because they touch directly upon the subject of native versus foreign influences in literature:

> Yáñez es uno de los escritores mexicanos que con mayor decisión se han enfrentado a un conflicto (falso a mi juicio), que desde hace años preocupa a los hispanoamericanos: la pretendida oposición entre el universalismo (o cosmopolitismo) de la literatura moderna y la realidad local. ¿Se puede ser moderno sin dejar de ser de su tierra? La obra de Joyce, el más irlandés de los irlandeses (hasta en sus fobias), el más cosmopolita de los modernos (hasta convertir a Dublín en Babel), cancela la disputa. . . . El nombre de Joyce no es una intrusión accidental; vino a mi memoria porque, si no me equivoco, fue un ejemplo decisivo para Agustín Yañez. Digo ejemplo y no influencia, aunque haya sido lo uno y lo otro, porque lo de-

---

22 The influence of Faulkner on Revueltas has been studied by James E. Irby in *La influencia de William Faulkner en cuatro narradores hispanoamericanos* (Mexico City: UNAM, 1957), pp. 40–131. Revueltas' novel was translated into English by H. R. Hays under the title *The Stone Knife* (New York: Reynal and Hitchcock, 1947).

terminante no fue la asimilación de ciertos procedimientos sino la actitud ante la realidad: tradición católica y realismo descarnado; gusto por los fastos del lenguaje y por los laberintos de la conciencia; avidez de los sentidos y sabor de ceniza en los labios; y en fin, cierta ferocidad amorosa ante el lugar natal.[23]

Another decisive example, not mentioned by Paz, is that of John Dos Passos. Yáñez himself has confessed, "Me propuse aplicar [in *Al filo del agua*] a un pueblo pequeño la técnica que Dos Passos emplea en *Manhattan Transfer* para describir la gran ciudad."[24] At the same time, Yáñez has spoken about the influence of Mexican fiction writers. When the critic Emmanuel Carballo asked him, "¿Cree usted que los novelistas [Mexican] de ahora estén respaldados por una tradición?" Yáñez answered, "Buena parte de la novela actual tiene rasgos comunes con el modo de narrar de *Micrós* y de Rabasa, y estos rasgos pueden remontarse a narradores anteriores." He went on to say that one of the characteristics of the Mexican novel is "la visión superada de una realidad precisa. A este respecto, piénsese en Lizardi."[25]

In an effort to give their novels a national tonality, writers, according to Yáñez, usually abuse the language. "Algunos novelistas llegan al empleo de barbarismos, que no creo son necesarios para escribir una novela de este tipo. Lo que más importa son las formas sintácticas. Refiriéndome a ellas le diré que me parece muy feliz la manera de novelar de Juan Rulfo. Una de sus características mexicanas estriba en los valores sintácticos, más que en la deformación aislada de los vocablos. Siempre he sostenido, y he tratado de practicar, esa fisonomía idiomática nacional con puntos de apoyo en la sintaxis y no en la deformación del idioma."[26]

If the national elements in Rulfo's fiction (short stories in *El llano en llamas*, 1953, and the novel *Pedro Páramo*, 1955) are to be found in the use of language, the structures reveal the influence of

[23] Octavio Paz, "Novela y provincia: Agustín Yáñez," in *Puertas al campo* (Mexico City: UNAM, 1966), pp. 142–47; quotation on p. 144.

[24] Emmanuel Carballo, "Agustín Yáñez (1904)," in *Diecinueve protagonistas de la literatura mexicana del siglo XX* (Mexico City: Empresas Editoriales, 1965), pp. 281–324; quotation on p. 291.

[25] *Ibid.*, p. 304.

[26] *Ibid.*, p. 303.

Faulkner as well as other foreign novelists.[27] To be sure, Rulfo's knowledge of European and North American fiction is well known. He reads and admires the North Americans Dos Passos and Hemingway, the Russians Andreyev and Korolenko, the Scandinavians Lagerlöf, Bjørnson, Hamsun, Sillanpää, and Laxness,[28] the Brazilian Guimerães Rosa,[29] and, of course, the new Spanish-American novelists, not to speak of the Mexicans Azuela, Rojas González, Campos Alatorre, Yáñez, and Efrén Hernández. Octavio Paz tells us that *Pedro Páramo* makes him think of the novels *The Plumed Serpent* by D. H. Lawrence and *Under the Volcano* by Malcolm Lowry, both having Mexican settings. "Juan Rulfo," says Paz, "es el único novelista mexicano que nos ha dado una imágen—no una descripción—de nuestro paisaje. Como en el caso de Lawrence y Lowry, no nos ha entregado un documento fotográfico o una pintura impresionista sino que sus intuiciones y obsesiones personales han encarnado en la piedra, el polvo, el pirú. Su visión de este mundo es, en realidad, visión de otro mundo."[30]

Rulfo's language, as Yáñez says, gives his fiction a national tone; yet his style is poetic, and in *Pedro Páramo*, by means of this poetic style, Rulfo is able to give life to a dead town, a town that has been choked to death by the local *cacique*, Pedro Páramo. The transitions between the scenes are not carried out by formal linking elements, but, like the stanzas in a poem, the scenes are juxtaposed, united only by the central theme and lyrical motifs, which Rulfo can use with great effectiveness. The novel, a mixture of realism and fantasy which may be called magic realism, has been created through the use of images which, although poetic, are structured in a language that is characteristic of the countryside.

[27] For a study of the influence of Faulkner on Rulfo, see Irby, *Influencia de William Faulkner*, pp. 132–63.

[28] Rulfo speaks about these and other European and American novelists in his interview with Luis Harss. See the latter's book *Los nuestros* (Buenos Aires: Sudamericana, 1966), pp. 334–35, translated into English by Barbara Dohmann as *Into the Mainstream: Conversations with Latin-American Writers* (New York: Harper & Row, 1967).

[29] See the interview with Rulfo published in the *Jornal do Brasil*, 25 September 1971.

[30] Octavio Paz, "Paisaje y novela en México," in *Corriente alterna* (Mexico City: Siglo XXI, 1967), pp. 16–18; quotation on p. 18. This book by Paz has been translated into English by Helen R. Lane as *Alternating Current* (New York: Viking Press, 1972).

Rulfo's works reflect cosmopolitan influences; still, his stories are often cited as examples of a truly national literature and contrasted to those of Juan José Arreola, whose books *Varia invención* (1949), *Confabulario* (1952), and *Palindroma* (1971) present a definite cosmopolitan orientation. In 1954 Emmanuel Carballo, comparing the fictions of Arreola and Rulfo, commented:

> Ahora que el nacionalismo en el arte se ha entregado a golpe de demagogia y de ineptos enfoques, confundiéndose muchas veces con el folklore y otras con una baja patriotería, ha nacido una nueva regla para enjuiciar los productos literarios. Una obra es buena—se juzga ante todo—no por el hecho de realizar valores estéticos sino por ser eminentemente mexicana. Se ha trastocado la azotea con los cimientos. La mexicanidad como cualquier nacionalismo bien entendido no es una preocupación consciente, una finalidad, sino una manera de ser y de actuar en la vida. El escritor que en realidad lo es no se evade de su circunstancia, por el contrario al expresarse la expresa. Igualmente se puede ser mexicano por alusión que por omisión. Y esto es lo que muchos lectores y críticos no se han dado cuenta al comentar a Arreola. Los pone fuera de pista que sus cuentos rara vez traten asuntos mexicanos. Su nacionalismo no reside en la anécdota sino en la manera de tratarla: es más un nacionalismo de reacciones que de acciones.[31]

The criticism of the nationalists doubtless affected Arreola, who made up his mind to write about Mexico. The result was the excellent novel *La feria* (1962), in which he demonstrates his deep understanding of Mexico. In the novel we see not only the external aspects of Mexican culture, such as popular celebrations, but also the psychology, ways of thinking, and general attitudes of the people.

Carlos Fuentes, in spite of the Mexican subject matter used in his most important novels, has also come under the fire of nationalist critics, but for another reason: they criticize him for lack of originality. One of his Mexican critics even accuses him of plagiarism: "Como todos saben, *La región más transparente* es el producto de una serie de 'expropiaciones' . . . Si externa o formalmente la novela de Fuentes es un pastiche, una falsa y revuelta imagen de las formas

---

[31] Emmanuel Carballo, "Arreola y Rulfo cuentistas," *Revista Universidad de México*, 8, no. 7 (March 1954), 28–29, 32; quotation on p. 29.

y las técnicas de Joyce, Dos Passos, Baroja, Cela, etc., esto para mí
tiene una importancia secundaria. . . . En cuanto al contenido de
la novela del señor Fuentes, la cosa sí es grave [ya que] a lo largo de
La región más transparente va exponiendo las tesis—sin perdonar ni
una sola—de *El laberinto de la soledad* como si fueran suyas."[32] It is
of course unreasonable to demand the acknowledgment of the ideas
expressed by fictitious characters in a novel. But what is of interest in
the above is the fact that the writer thinks that Fuentes imitated in
form the novels of English, American, and Spanish novelists. The
same idea is voiced by another critic, Manuel Pedro González, who
says about Fuentes' second novel, *La muerte de Artemio Cruz*
(1962): "Lo innegable es que ambos, Joyce y Lowry, están palmaria-
mente presentes en *La muerte de Artemio Cruz*, si bien la emulación
de Joyce se me antoja más frecuente y literal que la de Lowry."[33]

It is true that Fuentes' first novel is experimental, but it is not,
as suggested by the nationalistic critics, a slavish imitation of foreign
forms. In it the author tries to give expression to the spirit of Mexico
City, the region where the air is clear, a metaphor used ironically.
The structure of the novel is built up through the accumulation of
scenes in Mexico City, but instead of passing, as in *Al filo del agua*
and *Pedro Páramo*, from the mind of one character to that of another, the reader is transported from one social group to another.
In order to integrate the diverse elements, Fuentes makes use of a
mythical character, Ixca Cienfuegos, who moves from group to
group with great ease. But it is the city that really comes to life, leaving the reader a sense of it being the real protagonist. According to
Joseph Sommers, *La región más transparente*, by comparison with
Al filo del agua and *Pedro Páramo*, "is considerably more complex
in modes of narration, in stylistic development, and in conscious
assimilation of influences from European and American literature.
Many of the techniques employed, already familiar in other litera-

[32] Eulogio Cervantes, "Carlos Fuentes y el plagiarismo," *Excélsior*, 30 August 1961.
It is interesting to note that this critic objects to the borrowing of subject matter but
not forms. *La región más transparente*, Carlos Fuentes' first novel, published in Mexico
by the Fondo de Cultura Económica in 1958, has been translated into English by Sam
Hileman as *Where the Air is Clear* (New York: Obolensky, 1960).

[33] Manuel Pedro González, "La novela hispanoamericana en el contexto de la internacional," in *Coloquio sobre la novela hispanoamericana* (Mexico City: Fondo de
Cultura Económica, 1967), pp. 37–109; quotation on pp. 91–92.

tures, were new to Mexico—especially such a large number of innovations within the covers of one novel."[34]

In *La muerte de Artemio Cruz* Fuentes integrates the elements of the novel much better by creating a central character, Artemio Cruz, who, on his deathbed at the age of 71, reviews his entire life. All the scenes in the novel have one purpose: to show how this self-made man has survived and how he has become selfish, arrogant, and hard to the point of despising his own family, his best friends, and his own country.

The novels of Fuentes' last period (*Zona sagrada*, 1967; *Cambio de piel*, 1967; *Cumpleaños*, 1969) are criticized not only by the nationalists but also by the younger novelists, over whom his influence seems to be waning. The young writers do not criticize him for his imitation of foreign novelists, but because his books no longer provide them with a model. A representative of the younger generation of novelists, José Agustín, had this to say about Fuentes' *Cumpleaños*, whose action takes place in London, whose characters are European, and whose theme is reincarnation:

> La novela no interesa desde un punto de vista anecdótico, porque sólo existe una trama diluida en palabras que obvian conceptos; es aburrida en cuanto a su proposición filosófica, porque sus intenciones están platicadas, obviadas; todo es gratis: no existe el proceso que conduzca al fin: el incesante fluir; está mal vigilada desde un punto de vista riguroso de lenguaje (necesario, pues elimina paja y aprehende major al lector para que éste colabore activamente) . . . Lo terrible del caso es que el desarrollo de *Cumpleaños* a la larga va en contra de lo que propugna Fuentes: no hay una pluralidad sin fronteras', sino una onda limitadísima: sitúa las bases de su esencia en unas palabras a la larga previsibles (su mayor intensidad está en el monólogo pedantísimo, pero interesantísimo, del viejo, traducido por Nuncia).[35]

The above criticism by Agustín is revealing because it demonstrates the attitude of the young novelists when they face a literary

---

[34] Joseph Sommers, *After the Storm* (Albuquerque: University of New Mexico Press, 1968), p. 111. A study of literary influences on this novel appears on pp. 127–43. The names of Joyce, Huxley, Faulkner, Dos Passos, Arreola, Lawrence, Paz, and Samuel Ramos are mentioned.

[35] José Agustín, "Happy Reincarnation to You," *La vida literaria*, 1, no. 2 (March 1970), 12–13.

work. They are no longer interested in the problem of influences or imitations, Mexican or foreign; the thing that matters to them is whether the work has any literary merit. They do not reject *Cumpleaños* because the subject matter is not Mexican, but because it lacks not only thematic depth but also density in the world it presents, and most important of all, because it offers no linguistic or philosophical ambiguity. Criticism based on the degree of Mexicanism contained in the novel has been abandoned in favor of an aesthetic evaluation of the work. That *Cumpleaños* is so different from Fuentes' previous novels perhaps can be attributed to the fact that the author wanted to demonstrate the Latin American novelist's independence from the national scene. In his book on the new Spanish American novel he says: "Los latinoamericanos son hoy contemporáneos de todos los hombres. Y pueden, contradictoria, justa y hasta trágicamente, ser universales escribiendo con el lenguaje de los hombres de Perú, Argentina o México. Porque, vencida la universalidad ficticia de ciertas razas, ciertas clases, ciertas banderas, ciertas naciones, el escritor y el hombre advierten su común *generación* de las estructuras universales del lenguaje."[36]

As an example of the cosmopolitanism obtained by the Latin American novelists, Fuentes mentions José Emilio Pacheco's novel *Morirás lejos* (1967), in which we find a theme, according to Fuentes, "que tradicionalmente hubiera parecido vedado para un novelista latinoamericano."[37] Fuentes is right in pointing out that the theme of Pacheco's novel had not appeared before in Spanish American fiction. No Latin American novelist had ever attempted to write about the extermination of the Jewish people by the Nazis in the concentration camps or about the destruction of Jerusalem by Titus' Roman legions. But it is also true that no novelist anywhere had attempted to synchronize the two events from a contemporary point of view, as was done by Pacheco in his novel. The action, which takes place in the minds of the characters living in Mexico City, is of interest not because it gives the novel a Mexican setting but because in the process it makes the capital of Mexico part of the international scene, both in space and time.

[36] Carlos Fuentes, *La nueva novela hispanoamericana* (Mexico City: Joaquín Moritz, 1969), p. 32.
[37] *Ibid.*, p. 33.

This trend toward the treatment of universal themes had also been attempted by Salvador Elizondo in the novels *Farabeuf* (1965) and *El hipogeo secreto* (1968) and in the collections of short stories *Narda o el verano* (1966) and *El retrato de Zoe y otras mentiras* (1969). With *Farabeuf* Elizondo introduced the antinovel into Mexican literature—antinovel in the sense that *Farabeuf* is not an adventure story or a character or psychological study. While it is true that Elizondo is an avid reader of universal literature,[38] the subject matter of *Farabeuf* was inspired by a Chinese photograph, and the form was modeled on the French *nouveau roman*. In his autobiography he tells us: "Una experiencia singular vino a poner un acento todavía más desconcertante en mi vida; un hecho que en resumidas cuentas fue el origen de una obra que emprendí algunos meses después y que se vería publicada con el título de *Farabeuf, o La Crónica de un Instante*. Este acontecimiento fue mi conocimiento, a través de *Les Larmes d'Eros* de Bataille, de una fotografía realizada a principios de este siglo y que representaba la ejecución de un suplicio chino."[39] A literary influence, that of Ezra Pound, completed Elizondo's introduction to Chinese culture. "Mi lectura exhaustiva y apasionada de Ezra Pound," he says, "me había encaminado, también, hacia el descubrimiento de ciertos aspectos de la cultura china que tendían a complementar esa otra inquietud, más profunda, que acerca de este pueblo maravilloso había despertado en mí la foto del suplicado."[40]

For Elizondo the most important aspect of narrative technique is what he calls "la escritura" (the writing itself), through which the author is able to apprehend vital experiences. Not all contemporary Mexican novelists, however, belong to this school. Opposed to narrators like Elizondo who give great importance to language and style there is another group called "la Onda" (the Wave), a movement initiated in 1964 by José Agustín with the novel *La tumba*. The narrative of these young writers is characterized by the interest demonstrated in the latest manifestations of the anticulture, the culture of young people, be they of Mexico, the United States, or

---

[38] See his *Cuaderno de escritura* (Guanajuato: Universidad de Guanajuato, 1969).
[39] Emmanuel Carballo, ed., *Salvador Elizondo* (Mexico City: Empresas Editoriales, 1966), pp. 43–45.
[40] *Ibid.*, p. 45.

Europe, who reflect in their fiction a desire to adapt to the latest trends and to depend less on tradition. Their fiction is characterized by the rejection of anything that is solemn, by the use of the language of adolescents, by the use of a special typography—for example, the substitution of the final period by a diagonal line—and by the many references to the new culture and rock music. Their social attitude is that of rejection of the culture of the older generation and especially that of the middle class. In short, it is a narrative that rejects and denounces anything that has to do with the established way of life.

Examples of this fiction, mostly influenced by young novelists of the United States, are the works of José Agustín (novels *La tumba*, 1964; *De perfil*, 1966; and *Abolición de la propiedad*, 1969; and short stories in *Inventando que sueño*, 1968); Gustavo Sainz, who became well known in 1965 with the novel *Gazapo*; Margarita Dalton, whose novel *Larga sinfonía en D y había una vez . . .* (1968) is set in London, whose characters are young people under the influence of drugs, and whose narrator is hard to distinguish from those of North American novelists; Héctor Manjarrez, whose novel *Acto propicitorio* (1970) has Mexican and North American characters and an international scene (New York, London) ; and Parménides García Saldaña, who, in the novel *Pasto verde* (1968), makes fun not only of the bourgeois decadent society but also of the adolescents themselves, who cannot escape their frozen environment. In his collection of short stories, *El rey criollo* (1970), we find some, like "Good Bye Belinda," inspired by the Rolling Stones' song "Under My Thumb," that reflect the total conquest of Mexican youth by popular art forms of the United States. Other novelists belonging to "la Onda" are Manuel Farill, Xorge del Campo, Jorge Aguilar Mora, Orlando Ortiz, Humberto Guzmán, and Elsa Cross.[41]

The influence of other art forms and of modern technology can best be observed in the fiction of Agustín and Sainz. In his third book, *Inventando que sueño* (1968), José Agustín experiments with form. The six stories are united in a dramatic structure: six acts, the first and last separated by an interlude and a promenade. The

---

[41] See Margo Glantz's two anthologies, *Narrativa joven de México* (Mexico City: Siglo XXI, 1969) and *Onda y escritura en México: Jóvenes de 20 a 33* (Mexico City: Siglo XXI, 1971).

last act, "Juego de los puntos de vista; amor del bueno," has the form of a television script, with a list of characters, technical instructions, and even canned applause. In this last act the author foreshadows the structure of his next novel, *Abolición de la propiedad* (1969), in which we find, besides the dramatic form, two worlds—the world of the two principal characters and the world reproduced by the machines, in this case the tape recorder, the movie projectors, the slides, the closed-circuit television, and the monitors. The protagonists, Norma and Everio, surrounded by machines, almost become a part of that mechanized world. In an interview published in 1966, Agustín made these observations about the novel as a literary form:

> Un género artístico no se extingue, sino que se renueva cons-tantemente. Entonces podemos hablar en cierta manera de la extinción de las formas más caducas de novelar, pero jamás de la novela en sí. La novela se vuelve a dar con nuevas características de acuerdo con la época que se está viviendo. Entonces no podemos hacer literatura joyceana o a la manera de Proust o de Musil porque ellos ya vienen a ser verdaderamente clásicos, aunque estén cerca en el tiempo; desde el momento en que son clásicos hay que romper con ellos, pero tomando los mejor de ellos para poder adaptarlo a las necesidades estéticas, sociales, políticas, de la época.[42]

In the development of Gustavo Sainz as a novelist we see a parallel with that of José Agustín. In his first novel, *Gazapo* (1965), he focuses upon the world of the adolescent in Mexico City as Agustín had done in *La tumba*. But in his next novel, *Obsesivos días circulares* (1969), Sainz develops a universal theme. The author himself has explained how the change occurred: "Pretendía describir el insólito mundo de la adolescencia. Durante mucho tiempo sentí necesidad de retenerlo, aferrándome a él como suelen hacerlo algunas señoras a contar sus enfermedades. . . . Nuevas lecturas, cine, otras amistades, modificaron mi punto de vista sobre la literatur‾ y sobre lo que puede contarse en una novela. Escribo de sensaciones, sole-

---

[42] Federico Campbell, "Entrevista con José Agustín," *Excélsior*, 31 July 1966, "Diorama de la cultura" section, 1.

dad, opresión, todo lo que puede fatigar muchos de nuestros días."[43]

In *Obsesivos días circulares* the element of time is of prime importance. The action lasts as long as it takes the narrator to read the novel *Ulysses* by James Joyce. The structure of the novel is temporal: that of a plane flight, ending when the plane lands at the airport of Acapulco. The protagonist, who travels with Papá la Oca's gunmen and who suspects that they are going to kill him, takes refuge in the automatic repetition of a phrase of Cantinflas which has a peculiar singsong rhythm: "From generation to generation, the generations degenerate with greater degeneration." The type in which the phrase is written becomes larger and larger, until on the last page of the novel there is only a part of an enormous letter *g*, the first letter of the word *generation*. Sainz writes with an interior fire. In order to create a new rhythm, he takes advantage of lexical, syntactic, and typographical innovations, such as the omission of quotation marks from direct discourse. His speech thus becomes one with the narrative element. All this is done with the purpose of expressing himself without the conventions used by the traditional novelists. In a recent interview, Sainz said about *Obsesivos días circulares*: "La novela está contada en varios planos de lenguaje, en diversas tensiones, y aún más, en algo que yo llamo 'texturas.' Esto es, un dibujo que sobre la página hacen la velocidad de la prosa o el uso de portugués o latin, y sobre le mente también, un dibujo que el tono narrativo hace en nosotros. La suma de éstos integra la estructura de la novela en un sentido muy epidérmico, pero bastante legible ya también. Digamos que lo primero que dice *Obsesivos días circulares*, lo dice desde (o con) su estructura."[44]

Have the novelists belonging to the movement "la Onda" been excessively influenced by American culture? Another young novelist, Alberto Dallal, in his review of García Saldaña's book *El rey criollo*, has raised that question. He asks: "¿No convendría analizar la influencia de la problemática juvenil norteamericana (drogas, libertad sexual, oposición a lo establecido, etcétera) en términos de

[43] Rafael Rodríguez Castañeda, "Gustavo Sainz: La literatura, zona franca de la mentira," *Excélsior*, 22 November 1970, "Diorama de la cultura" section, 12–13.

[44] Graciela Mendoza, "Entrevista con Gustavo Sainz," *El Nacional*, 8 February 1970, "Revista mexicana de cultura" section, 3.

una realidad juvenil mexicana que por razones históricas (econó-
micas, políticas y sociales) no puede asimilar automáticamente, ni
mucho menos aplicar toda una gama de valores sin los peligros del
colonialismo y su propio vacío social?"[45] This question remains to
be answered. But this is a task for the sociologist and not for the
critic of fiction. What the critic can tell us is that in the novels and
short stories of the writers of "la Onda" the influence of North
American culture is the one that predominates.[46]

Not all fiction writers, however, belong to the two groups under
discussion: those represented by Elizondo and Agustín. Among the
writers who have taken a more independent stand, who have not
fallen totally under the influence of foreign writers but who, on
the other hand, are not rabid nationalists, we find, among others,
the names of Fernando del Paso, Juan Tovar, René Avilés Fabila,
and Mauricio González de la Garza. The novel *José Trigo* (1966)
by Fernando del Paso is the most ambitious work of fiction published in Mexico since *La región más transparente*. In *José Trigo*,
as in Fuentes' novel, we find the history of Mexico City from its
origins to the year 1960 and, in addition, that of the national rail-
ways. In the chapters entitled "Cronologías" we see the gradual but
always violent development of the legendary suburb of Tlatelolco,
the scene of a frightful tragedy on October 2, 1968, when a student
protest meeting was fired upon by army and police troops and hun-
dreds of students were killed. José Trigo, the protagonist, is, like
Ixca Cienfuegos in Fuentes' novel, a mythical character who can be
identified with the community of Nonoalco-Tlatelolco, with the
Toltec gods, and with the city of Mexico. The work partakes of the
characteristics of the new Latin American novel in that it is written
in an ambiguous and, at times, ironic style; although it presents a
tragic sense of life, it is, at the same time, mythical; the characters
are archetypal but also real; the social protest is energetic but also
humane. The novel's structure, which reflects an interest in the
creation of a new form rooted in the past, is that of an Aztec pyramid;
half the chapters are enumerated in an ascending order, and the

[45] *El Nacional*, 10 March 1971, "Revista mexicana de cultura" section, 6.
[46] For an example of the influence of American popular culture upon this group,
see José Agustín's *La nueva música clásica* (Mexico City: Instituto Nacional de la
Juventud, 1968), in which he demonstrates a penetrating understanding of American
popular music.

other half in a descending order; the latter have the same titles as the former. *José Trigo*, because of its Mexican subject matter, characters, and theme on the one hand and its experimental form based on Mexican images on the other, can be considered as one of the most significant novels written by a young writer. It is, in short, a synthesis of the Mexican novel from Azuela to Fuentes.

That del Paso should have written in 1966 a novel about Tlatelolco seems to be an act enveloped with prophetic significance, for it is precisely what happened at Tlatelolco in 1968 that has inspired fiction writers to return once more to the treatment of Mexican subject matter. And it was Octavio Paz, in his book *Postdata* (1970), who was the first to analyze the significance of the incident from the point of view of its causes and consequences. It is also revealing that the third essay in Paz's book should be a "Crítica de la pirámide," in which Paz says, "La pirámide es una imagen del mundo; a su vez, esa imagen del mundo es una proyección de la sociedad humana"[47]—words that could very well be used to analyze del Paso's novel.

The events that took place in Tlatelolco that night of October 2, 1968 (a date which, according to Paz, put an end to a period in Mexican history), mark the appearance of a new consciousness in the Mexican writer. They ask themselves if cosmopolitanism has been a simple mask with which an attempt has been made to cover up a past little understood but nevertheless latent. In the same essay Paz says: "México-Tenochtitlán ha desaparecido y ante su cuerpo caído lo que me preocupa no es un problema de interpretación histórica sino que no podamos contemplar frente a frente al muerto: su fantasma nos habita. Por eso creo que la crítica de México y de su historia—una crítica que se asemeja a la terapéutica de los psicoanalistas—debe inicarse por un examen de lo que significó y significa todavía la visión azteca del mundo."[48]

Following Paz's advice, young writers are beginning to examine the past and to ask themselves questions about the meaning of Tlatelolco. René Avilés Fabila, in his novel *El gran solitario de palacio*

---

47 Octavio Paz, *Postdata* (Mexico City: Siglo XXI, 1970), pp. 110–11, translated into English by Lysander Kemp as *The Other Mexico: Critique of the Pyramid* (New York: Grove Press, 1972). See in this volume Orrantia's analysis of del Paso's novel.

48 *Ibid.*, p. 127.

(1971), presents on a tragic plane the 1968 conflict between the students and the government and on a satirical one the system of government in Mexico, which he describes as a dictatorship by a president who every six years has his face lifted in order to keep on ruling. With this novel Avilés Fabila abandons the techniques and subject matter of the writers of "la Onda," with whom he was formerly identified. In the introductory remarks to his novel, in reference to his contemporaries, he says:

> Otros [narradores] son Juan Vicente Melo, Fernando del Paso, Vicente Leñero, José Emilio Pacheco, Juan García Ponce, José Agustín, Juan Tovar, Jorge Ibargüengoitia. Hay otros, sólo que por su edad y por la estrechez de sus obras, dudo que logren transponer las fronteras nacionales, salvo por accidente. José Agustín y Gustavo Sainz, más conocido el segundo, pero muchísimo más importante el primero por sus facultades creadoras, inauguraron la corriente de la literatura de adolescentes—influenciados por Salinger—que ha prendido entre los escritores que tienen menos de vienticinco años y que ahora son un verdadero problemón, sobre todo para los que ya están hartos de que los personajes citen a los Beatles y hablen *slang*.[49]

The killings at Tlatelolco moved the young writers to identify themselves with the protest group called "el Movimiento." It also awakened in them a consciousness of Mexico's past, literary as well as historical. One of these young novelists, Juan Tovar, expressed that idea with these words:

> Alguien dijo que los nuevos escritores mexicanos estaban abiertos a más influencias que antes, que tenían más raíces en la literatura universal o algo así. Esto es cierto, más o menos; por ejemplo, todo el mundo te habla de Sontag, Joyce, Robbe-Grillet . . . Lo que quería decir es que hay una inquietud por extender raíces y nutrirse de todas partes, pero se están olvidando varias partes fundamentales. Incluso entre escritores nacionales; ya Revueltas está teniendo la valoración que merece, pero como que a Azuela todavía se le hace el feo y como que no es justo.[50]

49 René Avilés Fabila, *El solitario de palacio* (Buenos Aires: Fabril Editora, 1971), p. 11.
50 Jesús Luis Benítez, "Entrevista con Juan Tovar," *El Nacional*, 10 May 1970, "Revista mexicana de cultura" section, 2.

Tlatelolco also affected older writers, who have composed novels on the subject. One of these is Luis Spota, whose novel *La plaza*, published in February of 1972, has been a best seller. In it a group of parents whose sons and daughters died at Tlatelolco kidnap, judge, and execute the culprit, allegedly one of the highest officials but not directly named. This novel is not very far removed from another political novel written to protest a killing: Martín Luis Guzmán's *La sombra del caudillo* (1929). Both are based on political events documented by historians and the press; however, in Guzmán's novel, because of the style, an aesthetic distance is established that is lacking in Spota. But they are similar in their treatment of the assassination of a group of persons for political reasons as well as their desire to expose the events.[51]

The fact that young men interested in "el Movimiento," well-established novelists like Spota, and essayists like Paz have been deeply affected by the events of 1968 at Tlatelolco indicates the profound effect that the incident has had not only on fiction writers but also on all intellectuals in general, regardless of the point along the political spectrum at which they may find themselves. Before 1968 the tendency in the world of letters was not the preoccupation with national problems or a national destiny; writers were, first of all, engrossed with the problem of integrating Mexican literature into a world literature, that is, the problem of attaining an international identity. The young men did not want to be identified as followers of causes essentially Mexican or accused of writing under the influence of the national authors. They wanted Mexican literature to be considered as a contribution to world literature. They were not interested in writing exclusively for a Mexican public or even the Spanish-speaking countries. They wanted their works to be immediately translated, read, and commented upon by readers in the United States and the non-Spanish-speaking countries of Europe. The influence upon these writers did not come from the Mexican authors (with the possible exception of those more world oriented like Reyes, Paz, Fuentes, and Arreola), but from Borges

---

51 Another novel about Tlatelolco is that of Luis González de Alba, *Los días y los años* (Mexico City: Ediciones ERA, 1971), told from the point of view of some of the students who were imprisoned because they participated in the demonstrations against the government.

and Cortázar among the Latin Americans and from all the foreign writers, especially those of the United States. With few exceptions the novels of these new Mexican writers had the characteristics of literary works without frontiers, of universal works. The characteristics of the national novel, and even more so those of the regional novel, had disappeared.

After 1968, however, a dramatic change occurred—a change that manifested itself not only in narrative fiction but also in the essay and even in poetry. The main preoccupation of the writer now is to unravel the true significance of the new Mexico. This concern is found in Octavio Paz's *Postdata* and Carlos Fuentes' *Tiempo mexicano* (1971), in the poetry of Montes de Oca, and in the latest novels and short stories. It is significant that the events of Tlatelolco occurred in the Square of the Three Cultures. Carlos Fuentes says that Mexico is a country with powerful cultural reserves that can be everything—"indio, mestizo, occidental, sin abocarse a la fatalidad, sino creando la libertad, de sus tres grandes herencias."[52] And the same thing could be said about its fiction—that it is, at the same time, traditional and innovative, national and cosmopolitan, Mexican and universal.

[52] Carlos Fuentes, *Tiempo mexicano* (Mexico City: Joaquín Mortiz, 1971), p. 42.

The Function of Myth
in Fernando del Paso's *José Trigo*

Dagoberto Orrantia

Alejo Carpentier, in an essay which has become indispensable for readers of the new Spanish American novel, has pointed out one of the major challenges which modern novelistic form presents to the American writer: "inscribir la fisonomía de sus ciudades en la literatura universal"; "revelar una ciudad y establecer sus relaciones posibles—por afinidades o contrastes—con lo universal."[1]

This important challenge is being met through the continued efforts of a number of Spanish American novelists. Marechal's *Adán Buenosayres* set an early example of daring experimentation that was continued in Fuentes' *La región más transparente*, which, as Rodríguez Monegal has noted,[2] offered a synthetic vision of Mexico City. In 1966, the year of publication of that fundamental inscription of the Cuban world which is Lezama's *Paradiso*, the young Mexican writer Fernando del Paso brought out his first novel, a work that was recognized as "la novela más ambiciosa que se haya publicado en México desde *La región más transparente*."[3] *José Trigo* details his peculiar vision of Mexico City and represents an-

---

[1] *Tientos y diferencias*, 2d ed., enl. (Montevideo: Arca, 1970), pp. 15, 19.

[2] "The New Novelists," *Encounter*, 25 (September 1965), 100.

[3] Luis Leal, "La nueva narrativa mexicana," *Nueva narrativa hispanoamericana*, 2, no. 1 (January 1972), 92. Del Paso was born in Mexico City in 1935. He studied at the National University, and he was a fellow at the Centro Mexicano de Escritores during 1964 and 1965. Prior to his first novel, he published a brief collection of poems, *Sonetos de lo diario* (Mexico City: Cuadernos del Unicornio, 1958).

other step toward the realization of Carpentier's injunction: "Hay que fijar la fisonomía de las ciudades como fijó Joyce la de Dublín."[4]

Like *Ulysses* or *Paradiso*, del Paso's novel is a work of dazzling complexity which in its various readings may never be completely unraveled by its critics. Taking as a base the reality of a country in all its ramifications, as do the novels of Joyce and Lezama, it is possible to attempt a reading of *José Trigo* beginning with one of its most fundamental aspects—the use of mythology, a code which leads inevitably to a consideration of the past, the foundation of the collective space envisioned in the novel. In this particular case, the author chooses one of the most significant ancient sites of Mexico: the Nonoalco-Tlatelolco section of Mexico City, which even in the present continues to be one of the places where Mexican destiny is being acted out.

The anonymous narrator, who arrives at Nonoalco-Tlatelolco sometime in the 1960's in search of the character José Trigo, finds a place where the past persists and flows into the future, diluting the present. "The year of José Trigo,"[5] 1960, marks one of the many sad and unfortunate epochs endured by the people of Nonoalco-Tlatelolco. As he searches for José Trigo, the narrator awakens a sleeping sea of words which pour forth from the mouths of five characters, bringing to life a past which is constantly referred to a mythological realm. They tell the narrator, "La madrecita Buenaventura lo espera, a usted y a todo el que quiera que le cuente una historia, la historia de un hombre que se llame José Trigo o José Trigo, da lo mismo porque lo que vale es la historia de los hombres" (p. 11). The mother figure Buenaventura then opens her "baúl mundo" (p. 19) to the narrator, and when she pauses three railroad workers and an old carpenter, "los cuatro dioses" (p. 263), begin to speak. From the freight car where the old woman lives, "el lugar del eterno olvido" (p. 264), the world of the railroad workers and their women unfolds to reveal their past, their present, and their future.

Del Paso organizes this enormous body of interrelated meanings in a pyramidal design which encloses in three separate phases his

---

[4] *Tientos y diferencias*, p. 16.

[5] *José Trigo*, 3d ed. (Mexico City: Siglo XXI, 1969), p. 503. Hereafter, references to this edition are incorporated into the text.

all-encompassing view of the Mexican world. The novel is set out
in two large sections, the first ascending from chapters 1 through 9
and the second descending from chapters 9 through 1. The two
parts are connected by an intermediate section entitled "El
Puente."[6] Octavio Paz has already taken note of the significance of
this image:

> Arquetipo arcaico del mundo, metáfora geométrica del cosmos,
> la pirámide mesoamericana culmina en un espacio magnético: la
> plataforma-santuario. Es el eje del universo, el sitio en que se
> cruzan los cuatro puntos cardinales, el centro del cuadrilátero:
> el fin y el principio del movimiento. Una inmovilidad en la que
> se acaba y se reengrendra la danza del cosmos. Tiempo petrificado,
> los cuatro lados de la pirámide representan los cuatro soles o edades
> del mundo y sus escaleras son sus días, meses, años, siglos. Arriba,
> en la plataforma: el lugar del nacimiento del quinto sol, la era
> nahua y azteca. Un edificio hecho de tiempo: lo que fue, lo que será,
> lo que está siendo. Espacio, la plataforma-santuario es el lugar de
> aparición de los dioses y el altar del sacrificio: punto de conver-
> gencia entre el mundo humano y el divino; tiempo, es el centro
> del movimiento, el fin y el principio de las eras: presente eterno
> de los dioses.[7]

The formal disposition of the novel shapes the concrete setting
of the story. The Nonoalco-Tlatelolco section of the city, where the
railroad workers who act as the protagonists of the novel live, is set
up in two camps, the West and the East. These are, respectively, the
titles of the ascending and the descending segments. The Bridge of
Nonoalco divides the two camps and intersects perpendicularly the
Street of the Chrysanthemum, the thoroughfare that runs the length
of Nonoalco-Tlatelolco. In an interview published soon after he
finished writing the novel, del Paso, referring to the significance of
spatial arrangement in the plot, made this observation: "Me gustaría hacer notar una coincidencia de carácter toponímico que
contribuye, así lo siento, a la magia del libro: la calle de los cam-
pamentos es Crisantema, que quiere decir 'flor de oro,' y que no

---

[6] José Luis Martínez, "*José Trigo* de Fernando del Paso," *Revista de la Universidad de México*, 22, no. 8 (April 1968), 6.
[7] *Posdata* (Mexico City: Siglo XXI, 1970), p. 111.

es sino una rama dorada que como muérdago se enlaza a Fresno,
Naranjo, Ciprés, etc. (las calles perpendiculares), enlazando asimis-
mo las leyendas del mundo."[8]

The central plot of the novel, which takes as a framing device the
search for José Trigo, has to do with the railroad strike declared
against the national railroad company in 1960. This plot is set
around two principal characters, Luciano and Manuel Angel. Luciano, the union representative in his shop, encourages and directs
the strike. Manuel Angel, a worker who has been bribed by the
authorities to discredit the movement, tries to tempt Luciano, but
when he fails he resorts to sabotage. The workers are blamed for the
destruction of certain installations, and Luciano is forced to flee
to the eastern camp. When he learns that the movement is failing
without him, he reappears only to be assassinated by Manuel Angel.
The defiant workers punish some of the traitors, but their uprising
causes the intervention of government troops who dissolve the strike.

These two central figures in the novel can be clearly identified
with the creative gods in Aztec mythology: Luciano with Quetzalcoatl and Manuel Angel with Tezcatlipoca. The plot therefore reflects the myth of the battle between the two divine powers.[9] This
reflection, as del Paso indicated in the interview referred to above,
is a coincidence of a historical nature; that is, the confluence of the
historical and the imaginary planes grows out of the perspective
which the narrator adopts to tell the story. It is by means of an analysis of that perspective that it is possible to approach an understanding of the function of myth in *José Trigo*.

The homology Luciano : Quetzalcoatl :: Manuel Angel : Tezcatlipoca is a kind of parallelism which can be extended to include
the majority of the characters in the novel. For example, Eduviges,
the wife of Manuel Angel and later José Trigo's mistress, and the
object of Todolosantos' desire, can be identified with Xochiquetzal,
the goddess of love and of flowers. The same identification is possible with María Patrocinio, Luciano's wife, and with the second

8 Juan Carvajal, "*José Trigo* de Fernando del Paso," *La cultura en México*, no. 225
(8 June 1966), 3.

9 Miguel León-Portilla, *Pre-Columbian Literatures of Mexico* (Norman: University
of Oklahoma Press, 1969), pp. 31–32.

wife of Manuel Angel, Genoveva, who at the same time can be connected with Aphrodite. The old man Todolosantos is identified with Huehueteotl, the old god, and with Xiuhtecuhtli, god of fire, with whom it is also possible to identify Atanasio, Manuel Angel's father-in-law. "El albino," Buenaventura's youngest son and Luciano's uncle, is Xolotl, the double-faced.[10] Eduviges' parents can be identified with Tlaloc and Chalchiuhtlicue, the rain gods. Buenaventura, the character who is richest in mythical associations, is located in the center of the novel and atop the pyramid. She is identified with the goddess of creation and with the goddesses of fertility, most especially with Tlazolteotl, who represents mother earth and is the goddess of sin and confession, "the eater of filth"—that is, "she who eats the sins of men, leaving them cleansed." Alfonso Caso explains that this symbolic devouring is "el rito de la confesión que se practica ante los sacerdotes de Tlazolteotl."[11] It is precisely this rite of confession which is the generating force of the novel.

The symbolic homology between the characters of the novel and the gods is repeated, then, in the perspective from which the novel is narrated; the rite of confession is directed to the goddess Tlazolteotl-Buenaventura in the same way that the novel is directed toward the reader. That confession, however, must be complete in order to be effective, and it is for this reason that the novelist must inevitably be obliged to exhaust the theme and the form of the novel and to use completely the possibilities of language and structure. Because of this, *José Trigo*, again like *Ulysses* or *Paradiso*, is a novel which can be characterized by its attempt to create a total reality.

On the level of plot, myth operates in *José Trigo* as the constituent of the two second terms of the homology. Nonetheless, the analysis at that level cannot go beyond the task of identifying the characters of the novel in their relationships with the mythological gods; it seems apparent that on that level myth does not come into play in its fullest sense. It is necessary, therefore, to consider the

10 Jesús Flores Sevilla, "*José Trigo:* Un mito sobre Nonoalco-Tlatelolco," *Hojas de crítica, Suplemento de la Revista de la Universidad de México*, no. 16 (January–February 1970), 6.

11 Alfonso Caso, *El pueblo del sol* (Mexico City: Fondo de Cultura Económica, 1953), p. 75.

mythological element in its relationship to narrative perspective, that is, to consider the narrative as discourse.[12]

When the narrator takes his place within the story and surrounds himself with the characters who are a functioning part of the plot, the perspective of the narration goes through a transformation which operates on the narrator himself; in his very telling of the story, he becomes one of the participants. The novel begins in the first person: "El me vio llegar desde lejos, en el amanecer de un once de enero de un año bisiesto de hace muchos años" (p. 5). It is brought to a close from the same point of view: "Porque todo esto, y esto es un decir, fue la mañana, la tarde, la noche en que soñé o creí soñar que buscaba a José Trigo por cielo y por tierra: bajo todos los cielos habidos, sobre todas las tierras por haber" (p. 536). This point of view puts the narrator within the world he is narrating, but still without giving him the status of narrator within the mythological perspective. That quality is conferred upon him only after he enters Buenaventura's boxcar. The alternation of first- and second-person points of view, which also occurs in the first pages of the novel, is sustained on the same narrative plane; the narrator addresses a person in *tú* with perfect awareness that he is speaking to himself from within the narrated world: "Y entonces tú, tú que buscas a José Trigo, tú que quieres saber quién es y tú que no sabes quién es la madrecita Buenaventura, tú preguntas '¿La madrecita Buenaventura?'" (p. 10). The narrator walks toward the East along the tracks of the Street of the Chrysanthemum; when he arrives at the boxcar he becomes part of the rite in which Buenaventura is officiating. Also present are the four men who along with her know the story of José Trigo. The narrator then joins the collective confession:

> Manzanas incircuncisas, rosario, jaula, zancos: con éstas y otras palabras que sacó de su baúl mundo, comenzó la madrecita Buenaventura la historia siempre trunca o aún no comenzada, y siempre detenida en los momentos en que la realidad y el sueño se confundían: realidad de su mundo llanero y bajuno de atorrantes y descamisados, y sueño de mi mundo de piedras manantías que

[12] Tzvetan Todorov, "Las categorías del relato literario," *Análisis estructural del relato*, trans. Beatriz Dorriots (Buenos Aires: Tiempo Contemporáneo, 1970), p. 174.

brillan al sol de la mañana cuando José Trigo, largo o languruto, desgarbado o desgarbilado, camina por las vías y se aleja del furgón de la Eduviges mientras ella multiplica su reflejo en sus ojos baña-dos de lágrimas y no por él, sino:

"Porque yo lo único que hice fue llorar como una idiota, deján-dolo ir, dejando que se llevara con él mi vergüenza y mi amargura."

Y esto sucedió, según Anselmo:

—Por ahi de mayo.

Y según Bernabé, Guadalupe y don Pedro el carpintero:

—Apenas cuando llegó, al tercer día.

O sea, cuando apenas los ferrocarrileros iniciaban la lucha por el aumento de salarios.

Porque también esto hay que contarlo: lo de Luciano, lo de la huelga, las bayonetas, el automóvil azul. [P. 19]

The narrator becomes, in turn, a confessor. This shift in perspec-tive produces a reality which deforms and makes relative its com-ponents; the shift leads to an interpretation and not merely to a presentation of the elements of the fictitious reality. That interpre-tation comes through as a formulation from the perspective of legend and myth which is, as Mario Vargas Llosa has defined it, "ese nivel de lo real que tiende a exagerar los datos de lo real obje-tivo."[13]

In his study of myth in a short story by Gabriel García Márquez, Vargas Llosa has isolated three formal devices whose appearance is simultaneous with the appearance of mythical perspective: exag-geration, enumeration, and language with the capacity to deform.[14] A brief analysis of these devices as they are used in *José Trigo* will help to show that myth functions in the novel as the creator of a perspective for the narrative process.

Vargas Llosa comments on the device of exaggeration in the fol-lowing way: "Desde la perspectiva mítico-legendaria, todos los componentes de la realidad ficticia sufren cambios cuantitativos. Aumentan, se alargan en el tiempo y se extienden en el espacio, sus propiedades se proyectan a un nivel de excepcionalidad, se poten-cian hasta un límite extremo. Seres, situaciones, objetos se vuelven

---

13 Mario Vargas Llosa, *García Márquez: Historia de un deicidio*, 2d ed. (Barcelona: Barral Editores, 1971), p. 400.

14 "Los funerales de la Mamá Grande," in *ibid.*, p. 402.

únicos, incomparables y paradigmáticos."[15] This technique is used decisively in *José Trigo*, as can be seen in the following examples. Buenaventura as a young woman "era más linda que todos los ángeles de todas las jerarquías, órdenes y coros celestiales," and as an old woman she is "más fea que la bruja del candilejo" (p. 386). When her great-grandmother was born "ocurre una aurora boreal" (p. 149), and she herself, carried a month beyond term, was born "en una noche en la que llueven las andromeidas" (p. 151). It is said of the old man Todolosantos, who has a different name each day, that when he was born "su dedo meñique era más grueso que los lomos de su padre" (p. 382). The night Buenaventura met Santos "ocurrió una cristofanía" (p. 151). When the old man drives his grandson Luciano out of the camp he withdraws into himself and never speaks again (p. 146). Luciano's face appears to be "tan grande como el mundo" (p. 29), and his walk through the camps is "un recorrido cosmogónico y metafísico" (p. 322). In their pilgrimage to the volcano of Colima, Buenaventura, her husband, and the children "pasaron por lugares por los que nadie había pasado antes" (p. 97).

The narrator sits in Buenaventura's boxcar while he listens to the narratives of the five characters. Before arriving, however, he observes the world of Nonoalco-Tlatelolco and gives us his vision of that objective reality; he communicates what he sees and hears around him. But when he joins in the rite of confession, he, too, becomes a source for the story. The shift allows the mythical perspective to come into play. The narrator takes his tone from a latent mythology in things, characters, situations, and the actions of characters; as his own narrative becomes an act on the same level as that of the other characters, he can modify objective reality by viewing it from a mythological perspective where the presence of a chronology of events and a linear narrative (as in the two fifth chapters and in the sections entitled "Cronologías") does not reduce the scope of that perspective.

The device of enumeration produces an exhaustive catalogue of objects, situations, and actions which give the narrative a peculiar cadence, "un ritmo encantatorio."[16] Such an accumulation causes

---

[15] *Ibid.*, p. 403.
[16] *Ibid.*, p. 406. Nora Dottori, in *"José Trigo*: El terror a la historia," *Nueva Novela*

a change which at times is only rhythmic, as, for example, when the narrator enumerates what he saw on his arrival: "Góndolas que llevan arena, grava y piedras . . . polvo de balasto, de herrumbre, de hollín, de tierra y hierbas . . . miré furgones, miré rieles y locomotoras y palomas, ratas, patos, bodegas, perros, niños mamones, almacenes, humilladeros y entronques, hombres de uniformes azules y mujeres panzonas, mendigos picosos de viruelas, árboles secos y cementerios de armones y bateas abandonadas . . . mendigos, borrachos, factores y patieros . . . carpinteros y herreros y cobreros y soldadores y electricistas y paileros y lavadores de calderas" (pp. 6–8). Here, Casimiro speaks to his daughter Eduviges: "Niña, niñita mía, cabeza de tepeguaje, collar de alondras, piedrita fina, corazón de teyolote, ojos de vidrio extraño, desorejadita, sangre de machigüis, chuparrosa . . . tu nahual es un perro. Tu nahual es un huehuenche con cabeza de iscatón. Tu nahual es un cacomixtle, tu nahual es un tencuán. Tu nahual es un chichime. Tu nahual es un cencuate" (pp. 81–82).

On the day of the blessing of the animals, the rebel camp hears "rebuznos, cacareos, mugidos y estufidos . . . ululaciones, balidos, graznidos, roznidos, cloqueos y bramidos" (pp. 100–2). The trains pass through "lugares de saltaciones y besamanos, charreadas, jaripeos y novilladas, solemnidades y relaciones, jolgorios y sanjuaneadas, kermeses, torneos, tauromaquias, verbenas y luminarias" (p. 224); their passengers are "hombres y mujeres de todas las razas, negros o blancos, huicholes, babispes, chochopopolocas, tarahumaras, acafes . . ." (p. 223), and they travel with "velices y valijas, maletas, petacas con flejes, cartoneras, arzones, bujetas, escriños y portamanteos . . . neceseres, mochilas, capoteros, carrieles y fiambreras" (p. 224).

The device of enumeration is also employed to effect a different and more significant alteration in the discourse. This occurs when qualities and objects—the abstract and the concrete—are named in combination with set phrases. When this happens, as Vargas Llosa points out, "lo concreto adquiere, por contagio rítmico, una apariencia abstracta y retórica, lo abstracto un semblante concreto y

---

Latinoamericana, vol. 1 (Buenos Aires: Paidós, 1969), pp. 265–67, considers the device of enumeration from another point of view.

retórico, y el nivel retórico se contagia de rasgos concretos y abstrac-
tos a la vez" (p. 408). This combination occurs in passages like the
following:

> Con sombras y montañas, cielos y fábricas, y trenes cargados de abe-
> jas y carmín, y peluquerías y palabras las más bellas de la tierra,
> del orbe, del tutilimundi, del universo girasol, llameante, furgón,
> campamentos, sudor, horizonte y descarrilamiento, me contaron
> como te cuento a José Trigo. [P. 29]

> [Hablaron de] contribuciones para el sindicato, adicionales y
> retroactivas; exención de impuestos prediales; los componentes de
> la comunidad rielera; fotobotones, novatadas . . . bandos; ceses;
> derogación del draconiano Artículo 145 del Código Penal Federal,
> contra el cual la emprendieron; posibilidad de pozos artesianos
> en los campamentos; miopía de las autoridades; remuneraciones;
> gestación del movimiento y purgas para depurarlo y dignificarlo
> en forma básica; estúpidos estupros que deturpan; salida de divi-
> sas; bagatelas confidenciales; conquistas; candorosos candidatos
> pasivos y estacionarios; alabanzas mutuas; relaciones obrero-
> patronales; faenas taurinas; anexionarse a; confederaciones. [Pp.
> 178-79]

Exaggeration and enumeration are the formal techniques which
produce, by means of imbalance and repetition, a language which
has the capacity to deform. The result is a texture of meanings
which modify reality and transform history into myth. In *José
Trigo*, Fernando del Paso first unfolds a history, the history of
Nonoalco-Tlatelolco and the development of the national railroads
viewed in the context of the social conflicts they precipitated. The
history of the participants in those conflicts, the railroad workers,
takes us back to the Cristero revolt, in which they also participated.
Myth takes this history beyond its explicit chronology. It provides
a transcendence over the temporal, identifying the ephemeral existence of men with the eternal life of the gods but at the same time—
and herein is found the basic function of myth in the novel—endow-
ing the narrative with a perspective which transforms its discourse
into a perfect embodiment of word and object.

Four Contemporary Mexican Poets: Marco Antonio Montes de Oca, Gabriel Zaid, José Emilio Pacheco, Homero Aridjis

Merlin H. Forster

In one of his *coloquios espirituales*, the sixteenth-century Mexican playwright Fernán González de Eslava has a character make this disparaging remark about poets and poetry: "Poco ganarás á poeta, que hay más que estiércol; busca otro oficio; más te valdrá hacer adobes un día, que cuantos sonetos hicieres en un año. . . ."[1] Although Eslava's pungent image of a poetic dungheap has been often repeated, it is apparent that his admonition was not taken to heart, even in his own day. One commentator has numbered over three hundred poets and versifiers who competed in a late-sixteenth-century *certamen*,[2] and while literary styles have changes since that time, the characteristic abundance and exuberance of Mexican poetry have not. The works of Nezahualcóyotl, Bernardo de Balbuena, Sor Juana Inés de la Cruz, Manuel Acuña, Salvador Díaz Mirón, Manuel Gutiérrez Nájera, Amado Nervo, and Octavio Paz are promontories in a poetic geography which began to take shape even before the arrival of the Spanish in the New World.

Mexican poetry shows no signs of decline in the twentieth cen-

---

[1] "Coloquio diez y seis, del bosque divino" (jornada segunda), *Coloquios espirituales y sacramentales* (Mexico City: Díaz de León, 1877), p. 229.

[2] Francisco Pimentel, *Historia crítica de la literatura y de las ciencias en México desde la conquista hasta nuestros días* (Mexico City: Lib. la Enseñanza, 1885), p. 51.

tury. Mexico City was one of the chief centers of literary activity during the modernist period, and it was a Mexican, Enrique González Martínez, whose sonnet recommended in 1911 that the wise owl take the place of the beautiful modernist swan. Each subsequent decade has represented another step forward, and one can appreciate the perceptivity of Octavio Paz's kinetic title *Poesía en movimiento* for an anthology of recent Mexican poetry.[3]

There are three fundamental points of reference for the development of that poetry during the twentieth century. The first has to do with the decade immediately following modernism—the turbulent revolutionary period of political and social upheaval which brought Mexico sharply into the twentieth century. González Martínez was a stabilizing influence during those years and, in fact, well into the 1950's. His poetry was traditional in form, but his sober dedication to the literary and intellectual life was an example which was not lost on aspiring poets who followed. The influence of José Juan Tablada was of a different sort. Tablada was the personification of an insatiable search for novelty, as is seen, for example, in his adaptation of the Japasese *haiku* and the visual forms of Apollinaire. The slightly younger Ramón López Velarde was important for his novel depiction of the Mexican countryside and his striking use of language and imagery.

A second dimension is formed by the group which followed the postmodernists, a group which is now generally referred to as the Contemporáneos. Perhaps the most imposing figure here is that of Carlos Pellicer, whose colorful and exuberant verses form a connecting link between López Velarde and subsequent poets. However, the polished meditations of José Gorostiza on the anguished metaphysical realities of life and death and the hallucinatory subterranean worlds of Xavier Villaurrutia are also important influences. The intensely visual and even patriotic verses of Pellicer and the equally intense internalized poetry of Gorostiza and Villaurrutia express an unresolved duality which can still be seen in Mexican life and culture.

A third determining presence is that of Octavio Paz, who is influential both as a poet and as an accomplished essayist on literature and culture. As a poet Paz is the epitome of an endless search for

[3] *Poesía en movimiento: México, 1915–1966* (Mexico City: Siglo XXI, 1966).

meaning and identity, a search which began with conventional words and images and has developed toward open and visual forms. Paz is a watershed rather than a promontory; all recent developments flow from him, and the intricacies of his concepts and techniques have left an indelible impression on those who follow.

The four poets to be considered here come essentially from the 1960's. It is no longer accurate to call them young poets, since each has passed a little beyond the magic age of thirty years. In each case, however, recently lost youth is compensated for in a poetic production which is sizable enough to allow serious study and in a maturity which makes such study meaningful.

Montes de Oca

Marco Antonio Montes de Oca, born in 1932 in Mexico City, is the oldest of the four and has by far the most imposing production.[4] He is a central figure in recent Mexican poetry and in many ways has a role which is comparable to that of Carlos Pellicer in an earlier generation. His literary expression is almost entirely in verse form, in contrast to that of many other poets among his contemporaries who also utilize prose fiction and the essay in order to express their ideas. He shows a rhetorical brilliance which is also reminiscent of Pellicer as well as a tendency to see in multiple external details the complexities and profundities of existence.

In a fairly early poem, "Vísperas," the sound of the evening vesper bells is reason for flourishing hope:

Cuando la radiante asunción de la noche inaugura las chispas
que el poder de su alquimia convertirá en planetas,
nacen seres propicios madurando en conchas tornasoles,
mínimas creaturas alimentándose con un rocío que
    ellas mismas inventan.
Aparece el conejo que poda con afelpadas tijeras
el silencio pacífico y loable

4 *Ruina de la infame Babilonia* (Mexico City: Medio Siglo, 1953); *Contrapunto de la fe* (Mexico City: Los Presentes, 1955); *Pliego de testimonios* (Mexico City: Metáfora, 1956); *Delante de la luz cantan los pájaros* (Mexico City: Fondo de Cultura Económica, 1959); *Cantos al sol que no se alcanza* (Mexico City: Pájaro Cascabel, 1964); *Vendimia del juglar* (Mexico City: Joaquín Mortiz, 1965); *Las fuentes legendarias* (Mexico City: Joaquín Mortiz, 1966); *Pedir el fuego* (Mexico City: Joaquín Mortiz, 1968); *Poesía reunida* (Mexico City: Fondo de Cultura Económica, 1971).

y se graba sobre el valle luciente y recién llovido
el súbito paso que sobre la llama no nos quema
y sobre el agua sí nos humedece.
¿Serán éstos los albores de la fiesta,
las colmadas primicias que apenas nacidas
ya desfallecen, aniquiladas por la dorada combustión
de un júbilo sin límites?
¿Y este primer vagido de la campana flamante y recién nacida
será la señal que aguarda el prodigio,
para irrumpir con dulce río estival,
sobre los muros de jade salado que levanta el mar,
sobre esta llanura desmantelada de todo verdor
y que hoy, por la primera vez,
arponean sin compasión los destellos de la dicha?

[*Delante de la luz cantan los pájaros*, p. 114]

The first lines of the poem describe the peaceful descent of night on the countryside, in which a mysterious alchemist's touch lights the fireflies as constellations in the night sky and the striking image of a rabbit prunes and punctuates the scene with the scissorslike shape of its ears. Two extended interrogations form the last part of the poem and change it from a description to an abstract progression. Several words and images (*albores, primicias, júbilo*) suggest that a new hope is about to burst forth, taking as a signal the limpidness of the vesper bells. This jubilant hope becomes as incandescent as combustion and summer and bids in its ardor to reverse and overcome the approaching night. The violent final image, in which the glimmers of hope become harpooners in merciless attack on the shadowy forms of a darkened valley-sea, provides a vivid connection with the descriptive earlier lines while expressing a surging hope against the barriers that restrain it.

A second example is reminiscent of Huidobro's theories of creationism in its expression of life and nature through language:

E

Se agrieta el labio nace la palabra
Surge un otoño de hojas verdes y perpetuas
Aquí es allá el norte ya no existe
Vamos en viaje todos
La isla avienta contra el aire su ancla milenaria

Solas se dicen las palabras
Pálidos rubíes que manan de la plena bonanza
Arados de luz sobre las aguas
Unitarias palabras semejantes
A una selva que se vuelva un árbol
Un mismo árbol creciendo
Como un solitario y fabuloso perchero para pájaros

Hay que apilarlas como pesos de fuego
Pagar con ellas por el milagro que conceden
O echarlas a volar como una baraja de cantáridas
Bajo la piel de ciertos ciegos

Se agrieta el labio nace la palabra
Viajamos por una ventana erizada de sonrisas
El castor hunde su diente minucioso en pilares de ceniza
Caminan las palabras por la calle torturada
Que va desde la garganta al infinito
Marchan las palabras en perfecta disciplina
Hacia la gorjeante emboscada de sí mismas

Ellas nos comunican o nos matan
Denodadas palabras
Llaves maestras de los pechos
Que también abren la caja fuerte y porosa de las piedras
Ellas nos comunican o nos matan
Y suben por la noche los tejados
En que autómatas orean sus camisas de lámina

Se agrieta el labio nace la palabra
El cielo agita su collar sonoro sus brazaletes de campanas
Corremos montados en el ciervo que perseguimos
Aquí es allá
Traspasamos la estallante hornaza
Que mueve rizos de mármol en la cornisa
Hemos llegado
Por una rendija en el misterio
Al corazón de la palabra hemos llegado

                              [*Cantos al sol que no se alcanza*, pp. 20–21]

The superficial form of the poem is striking. There is no strophic
nor metrical consistency, and a certain fluidity is heightened by a
lack of punctuation throughout. At the same time, there is a counter-
motion produced by insistent capitalization, as if each verse were

unconnected to those contiguous to it. These metrical and syntactical orderings carry a sense of vertigo into the conceptual structuring of the poem ("Aquí es allá el norte ya no existe").

The repeated beginning line suggests that expressive language, like precious stones from the earth, is born in the fissures and ruptures of human experience. The word springs from the cracked lips which formed it, and in some mysterious way it takes on independent existence. Words are daring personages who carry with them the keys of understanding and who have powers of communication or destruction. There is a consistent circular motion in the poem which carries us ultimately, as if through a vortex and the heat of a jeweler's fire, to the heart of understanding. Words create the oneness of man's world, and for a brief moment we glimpse infinity in the disciplined perfection of organized language.

A later poem is "Ala," in which the poet perceives the world around him in terms of winged forms from nature and mythology:

> Ala que me ayudas a darle nombre a cada yerba,
> Sólo cataplasma que tolera el cielo herido,
> Ala capaz de abofetear el interior de una pagoda
> Y de hacerla estallar en miles de mosaicos rotos;
> Ala en desorden,
> Vivo abanico para las estrellas
> Siempre sentadas en su gran temperatura;
> Ala pacífica, retén de innominadas claridades,
> Ala que todo lo visitas sin robarte nada,
> Ala religiosa
> Ala magnífica,
> Parasol de seda en los insectos insolados,
> Brazo irisado de los ángeles y querubines
> Que aún se conservan en servicio activo;
> Ala iracunda que arrancas centrales alaridos
> Cuando tropiezas con un arpa;
> Ala espléndida
> Ala repintada con dos manos de escarcha:
> Ahora estás en mi puño,
> No en calidad de prisionera,
> Sino enrollada como un florero
> Donde amanecen con salud gemela,
> El mito y la certeza.
>
> [*Vendimia del juglar*, p. 44]

The poem is characteristically irregular in form, with no visible systems of rhythm or rhyme. The theme is the heightened awareness of the natural world, brought about through created or real winged forms. The title of the poem suggests a single abstraction for these forms, an abstraction which in the poem permits personification and a familiar *tú* relationship. Wings have force and strength; they are the insect's silken medium of flight; they allow a vision of stars and celestial clarities and are the means of locomotion for such divine creatures as angels and cherubim. The poet connects all of these possibilities in his rapid succession of images, finally to hold in his hand the distillation of all he perceives. The wings are at rest, and the poet sees in them a bipartite reality: the multiple certainties of the physical world and the traditional beauties of the mythological and religious one.

Montes de Oca's poetry overflows conventional limits. His themes —love, death, the cycles and seasons of nature, the unexpected beauties of the natural world—express the richness of a mythical search for the meaning of existence. His images, brilliant and at times almost overpowering in their continuous flow, come in large part from nature, but often take on a magical quality. The poetic forms are open and ebullient and tend toward long compositions with widely varying stanzas and line lengths. Montes de Oca's poetic style disdains restraint and contemplation in favor of verbal brilliance and power.

Zaid

Gabriel Zaid was born in Monterrey, Nuevo León, in 1934. He has published two collections of poetry and is esteemed as well for his essays and literary criticism. His most recent work is an anthology of Mexican poetry which appeared in 1971.[5]

In contrast to Montes de Oca, Zaid is notable for restraint and brevity in his poems. He uses some of the same themes, such as love, death, the beauty of a woman, and the ultimate meanings of life and existence; however, he does not take himself or his surroundings

---

[5] *Seguimiento* (Mexico City: Fondo de Cultura Económica, 1964); *Campo nudista* (Mexico City: Joaquín Mortiz, 1969); *Ómnibus de poesía mexicana* (Mexico City: Siglo XXI, 1971).

nearly as seriously, and while his language and imagery are careful, they do not appear consciously worked. He is often colloquial, even crude, in his choice of words, and he pokes irreverent fun at some treasured conventionalities.

The composition "Templo," which appears in heptasyllabic quatrains, is a description of the evening and night:

> Y ya la tarde en ruinas
> no se sostiene apenas
> de tan augusta luz
> erigida en columnas.
>
> Y ya el anochecer
> del aire, picotea
> la eternidad, vencida
> de pájaros voraces.
>
> ¿Y qué se hará la senda
> que te iba dejando,
> migas de mí, poemas,
> pistas para encontrarnos?
>
> [*Seguimiento*, p. 24]

The afternoon and evening are in ruins, with the direction of the poem a descending one. In a metaphor suggesting the cruelty and subjugation of a pecking order, nightfall overcomes eternity and the poet is forced to reflect on his own destruction. The paths which he has constructed toward others, a poetic Hansel attempting to mark his way with bread crumbs against the voracious birds of the night, are doomed to be blotted out.

"Marcha Fabulosa" is a mocking commentary on things as they are:

> Un brazo nada más no es cosa mala
> si ves que el otro se convierte en ala.
>
> Y para qué dos pies, no es cosa buena,
> si a cuatro viva el alma suena.
>
> Tener mil pares de ojos para ver-
> te-ver-te-ver-te-ver.
>
> Y dos espaldas para tanta gente
> que sueña, pero sigue la corriente.
>
> [*Campo nudista*, p. 13]

The obvious conventionality of the rhymed hendecasyllabic couplets supports the theme of the poem. Human form—two arms, two feet, two shoulders—has no real meaning; nevertheless, while we may dream of freedom, we are forced to accept the limitations which have been placed upon us. The third couplet, which breaks slightly the rhythmic pattern, is the fulcrum point of the poem. A thousand pairs of eyes would not change things or make us see any better, and the insistent repetitions of the couplet underscore that impossibility.

It is possible to see in this poem a second and rather different interpretation. The title suggests that it could be a description of a couple walking, perhaps holding hands and swinging their other arms as if they were wings. The sound of footsteps, made either by one person or by two, is sufficient to produce a sense of pleasant introspection. In that moment of emotion it would be desirable to have a thousand pairs of eyes to see, and the insistent verb-object repetition extends toward that number. In the final stanza the two people, still within their own world, turn their backs on others who stream past them, each caught up as well in his own individual dream.

In "Homero en Cuernavaca," the poet reflects on the essential ugliness and stupidity of the human race:

> ¿Qué le hubiera costado a Dios
> que todas fueran unos mangos?
> Así cada uno tendría el suyo
> y nunca hubiera ardido Troya.
>
> Pero si todas fueran bonitas
> y todos inteligentes,
> ¿quién cuidaría la tienda
> de la Historia?
>
> [*Campo nudista*, p. 27]

God could have given grace and beauty to everyone and thus have avoided a lot of trouble, theorizes the poet in the first quatrain. (His colloquial use of the term *mango* to mean here a person of desirable physical beauty increases the sharpness of the idea.) If that were the case there would be no history as we know it, and the poet suggests that human events will continue to be determined by homely and stupid people.

One final example is entitled "Balística Celestial." Here the poet combines the squeaking of the matrimonial bed and the nine-month term of pregnancy into a kind of celestial music box which needs to be wound so that conception will occur at the propitious moment:

> Miraron el reloj,
> las tablas astrológicas
> y el mapa del cielo
> nueve lunas después
>
> Sincronizadamente
> le fueron dando cuerda
> a la cama: una caja
> de música de las esferas.
> [*Campo nudista*, p. 33]

Pacheco

José Emilio Pacheco, born in Mexico City in 1939, has already published four collections of poems.[6] In addition, he is a successful novelist and short story writer, literary critic, translator, and anthologist.

Pacheco's poetry tends toward brevity and an economy of language, as does that of Zaid, but he is much more introspective and metaphysical. Pacheco is troubled by the cyclic flow of time and the impossibility of recapturing prior experience, and his thematic use of physical love and poetic creation serve to heighten this anguished sense. The poet probes deep beneath the surface, often in unconventional forms and with brilliant images, in order to reach the essential meanings of life and experience.

In "La enredadera," time and lineages are solidified in the climbing vine which fastens itself against a wall:

> Verde o azul, fruto del muro, crece;
> divide cielo y tierra.
> Con los años
> se va haciendo más rígida, más verde,

---

[6] *Los elementos de la noche* (Mexico City: UNAM, 1963); *El resposo del fuego* (Mexico City: Fondo de Cultura Económica, 1966); *No me preguntes cómo pasa el tiempo* (Mexico City: Joaquín Mortiz, 1969); *Irás y no volverás* (Mexico City: Fondo de Cultura Económica, 1973).

costumbre de la piedra cuerpo ávido
de entrelazadas puntas que se tocan,
llevan la misma savia, son una breve planta
y también son un bosque;
son los años
que se anudan y rompen;
son los días
del color del incendio;
son el viento
que a través del otoño
toca el mundo,
las oscuras
raíces de la muerte
y el linaje
de sombra que se alzó en la enredadera.

[*Los elementos de la noche*, p. 23]

The single stanza and the varied line lengths of the poem suggest both the vine itself and its multiple components. The vine lives and grows, and with its intricate structure and varying colors it becomes a point of reference between earth and sky. At the same time, the insistent references to temporal and seasonal cycles underscore sharply the destructive effect which the passage of time has on all that it touches. The poet sees himself, his lineage, his life, and his death in the contradictory substance and fragility of the climbing vine.

The poem "Sangre y humo alimentan las hogueras . . ." contemplates the cyclic destruction of man and his world in symbolic fires which are fed by the blood of sacrifices:

Sangre y humo alimentan las hogueras
Nada mella el fulgor. Y las montañas
reblandecen los siglos, se incorporan,
desbaratan su ritmo, son de nuevo
piedra,
          mudez de piedra,
                    testimonio
de que nada hubo aquí; de que los hombres
como piedra tambien
                    se tornan viento.
Ser de viento espectral, ya sin aullido,

aunque busque su fin, aunque ya nada
pueda retroceder. El tiempo es polvo;
sólo la tierra da su fruto amargo,
el feroz remolino que suspende
cuanto el hombre erigío. Quedan las flores
y su orgullo de círculo, tan necias
que intentan renacer, darse al aroma
y nuevamente en piedra convertirse.

[*El reposo del fuego*, pp. 21–22]

The poem is presented in unrhymed hendacasyllables which gain somewhat in complexity from spatial arrangements and from a series of insistent run-on lines. The cyclic patterning of the theme suggests to begin with the violent human sacrifices of the Aztecs. Nothing lasting is achieved, however, and in the same way that the natural landscape of the world changes with time, man also becomes nothing more than a whisper of wind. Time crumbles at the touch, as do the structures which are erected by man. Only the shorter cycles of the flowers of the field make a stupid attempt to move against the inevitably destructive effects of time.

In "To Grow Old" age is a caricature of youth which develops gradually with each wrinkle and furrow:

Sobre tu rostro
                crecerá otra cara
de cada surco en que la edad
                                madura
y luego se consume y
                te enmascara
y hace que brote
                tu caricatura

[*No me preguntes cómo pasa el tiempo*, p. 37]

The poem has the tone of a cruel joke in which the unusual spatial arrangements and the insistent plays on rhymes add to the charade. The cyclic process of aging ultimately hides a reality which was once visible: the wrinkled mask of old age is planted in the smooth face of youth, grows in its deepening furrows, and finally matures in death.

The passage of time shapes "No me preguntes cómo pasa el tiempo":

A nuestra antigua casa llega el invierno
y pasan por el aire las bandadas que emigran.
Luego renacerá la primavera,
revivirán las flores que sembraste.
Pero nosotros
ya nunca más veremos
ese dulce paraje que fue nuestro.
[*No me preguntes cómo pasa el tiempo*, p. 45]

In form and tone the poem is reminiscent of the ancient Nahua lyrics. A past experience is remembered in terms of the changing seasons, and images suggest the successive beauties of passing time: flights of migratory birds which signal the oncoming winter; flowers which are a part of spring. Although the seasons return unfailingly, the past cannot be relived, and the sweetness of a distant love cannot be tasted a second time.

One final example, "Preguntas sobre los cerdos, e imprecaciones de los mismos," comes from a series of poems in the bestiary tradition:

¿Por qué todos sus nombres son injurias?:
puerco marrano cerdo cochino chancho.
Viven de la inmundicia, comen, tragan
(porque serán comidos y tragados).
De hinojos y de bruces roe el desprecio
por su aspecto risible, su lujuria,
sus temores de obsceno propietario.
Nadie llora al morir más lastimero
interminablemente repitiendo:
y pensar que para esto me cebaron,
qué marranos qué cerdos qué cochinos.
[*No me preguntes cómo pasa el tiempo*, p. 88]

The pig is endowed with human qualities and becomes an Orwellian representation of man. He is known by a series of uncomplimentary names, lives from the swill of the earth, and has mannerisms and actions which make him despicable. The pig screams as he is taken to the slaughterhouse, and his curses against those responsible for his death turn the force of the poem back toward human society. Man has invented the names for the pig, consumes the flesh of the filth eater, and can himself be indicted by the same terms with which he expresses his disgust for an unclean animal far beneath his level.

Aridjis

The youngest of the four poets is Homero Aridjis, who was born in Michoacán in 1940. He already has nine collections of poems in print and gives every indication of continuing in the same prolific manner.[7]

Aridjis' poems are varied in form. Some are short, with unusual structures and dispositions on the printed page, and others, often in the form of prose poems, are discursive and more conventional. His themes are also varied. He has a number of poems which are descriptions of nature, occasionally even with a hint of a romantic fascination with its power. "Viene el río bajo la lluvia" is an example:

> Viene el rió bajo la lluvia
>
> pasa entre árboles
> cada gota lo abre
>
> relámpagos hermosos
> señalan el curso de sus aguas
>
> su inmensidad es íntima
>
> pesadamente se mueve
> hacia la ciudad
> que deja atrás sin irse
>
> solo es divino
>
> [*Los espacios azules*, p. 50]

The mysteries and complexities of poetic creation are of concern to Aridjis, as the poem "Te hago nacer en mí" shows:

[7] *La musa roja* (Mexico City: privately published, 1958); *Los ojos desdoblados* (Mexico City: La Palabra, 1960); *La difícil ceremonia* (Mexico City: Pájaro Cascabel, 1963); *Antes del reino* (Mexico City: Ediciones ERA, 1963); *Mirándola dormir* (Mexico City: Joaquín Mortiz, 1964); *Perséfone* (Mexico City: Joaquín Mortiz, 1967); *Los espacios azules* (Mexico City: Joaquín Mortiz, 1968); *Ajedrez-navegaciones* (Mexico City: Siglo XXI, 1969); *El poeta niño* (Mexico City: Fondo de Cultura Económica, 1971).

Te hago nacer en mí
a cada instante,
eres una creación continua
como el tiempo en mis manos.
Primero te me diste inasequible
en una complejidad total,
pero tus equilibrios de geómetra
desmenuzaron el evento
y has persistido con tus leyes,
alzándote sobre mi universo
en una órbita perfecta.
Ya no esperes el eclipse,
está sembrado un momento
y un poema.

[*Los ojos desdoblados*, p. 18]

Poetry here is personified and takes on female form, which allows the poet to express familiarity and desire. Poetry surrenders herself, however, in accordance with her own complexity and mysterious laws, and the poet is aware of these things only as an inferior being who contemplates celestial spheres from a distance. Creation does take place, nonetheless, in those few moments when all forces are in accord.

Aridjis' most frquent theme is love—in particular, physical love. The following passage from his long prose poem "Perséfone" expresses this insistent concentration:

Ante el deseo de inmovilizar lo amado que se fuga, uno pone sobre la mesa sus mejores palabras y sus mejores noches; uno oficia el amor en torno de los cuerpos; uno germina en las posibilidades, para volver al punto de partida, después de bosquejar el porvenir. Uno entrega a lo vano pensamientos y errores; uno pasa; uno piensa.

[*Perséfone*, p. 16]

In "La mujer va desnuda bajo cada mirada . . ." the act of love is a moment of joy and communion, but one which does not prevent man from wandering the earth in his unhappiness:

La mujer va desnuda bajo cada mirada
y el hombre la adivina

como una sola carne bajo la luz se sienten
en su viviente dicha

su comunión es consagrada
y ofrecen su sangre para beber de ella

el amor está en sus caras
y el hombre sobre la tierra es desdichado
[*Los espacios azules*, p. 68]

The same bittersweet complexity is expressed in "Viajo por la enorme variedad de la mujer creada . . .":

Viajo por la enorme variedad de la mujer creada
por baños y templos como solemnes ruinas

por el silencio de tu cuerpo después del amor
por seres que despiertos en el sueño hablan de la creación

caminos de luz llevan al ser al borde de sus propios ojos
en siglos como pozos el ser amado cae
la carne   abierta bajo el sol   sufre de azul que pasa
[*Los espacios azules*, p. 103]

In this poem love's passion has subsided and the poet allows himself to wander in meditation. He walks, almost in a dream state, among imagined women in the baths and temples of antiquity, and at the same time he is aware of the silent body of his lover. His own eyes become bottomless wells, into whose depths the beloved person falls. The connection to physical reality remains sharply visible, however, and the last line of the poem, with its unusual divisions, represents that final and painful awareness. Again, love is an inseparable combination of joy and pain.

Conclusions

I have considered briefly four different voices in recent Mexican poetry and should now like to encompass them within a single perspective and place them clearly in the ongoing process of Mexican poetry.

First, there is in all four a fundamental involvement with the ultimate meanings and problems of human existence. The expression of beauty, both natural and created, is fundamental for each poet, and each has an awareness of the mythological and even the magical as a part of life. Love is represented in contradictory terms by Aridjis, Pacheco is painfully aware of cyclic time and transistory human experience, and Zaid takes a half-serious, half-sardonic view of all he surveys. Montes de Oca maintains a unique positive response to many of these concerns; for him there is hope, love, beauty in nature, and poetic creation. On a more concrete level, each of the four expresses a preoccupation with moral problems in contemporary society. Debasing cruelty, the futility of war, the depersonalizing effects of materialism, pervasive stupidity, and so on, are the objects of poignant denunciations.

Each in his own terms, these four poets evidence the verbal brilliance which is a part of the Mexican poetic tradition. Each is aware of the expressive qualities of language, and consequently each consciously shapes the elements of his poems. There are some differences in technique and form, to be sure. Montes de Oca piles image on image in an unending flow, and Zaid and Pacheco choose to be much more austere in their words and images. Aridjis stands somewhere in between, using imagery and language with considerable exuberance but at the same time with a sense of balance and control.

Finally, all four use at one time or another the theme of complex poetic creation. The muse is personified, and they express a familiar but contradictory relationship with her. Poetry is a taxing and often impossible mistress, and she is satisfied fitfully and imperfectly even by those who give themselves passionately to her.

The assessment of the individual and combined contributions to the development of Mexican poetry of the four poets is more difficult. They are obviously a part of a developing tradition and consequently are forced to search for originality against a background which includes modernism, López Velarde, Tablada, the Contemporáneos, and Octavio Paz. Montes de Oca has evolved an overly rich style which, together with his sustained rhetorical brilliance, makes his production impressive in terms of variety and extent. He is important as a latter-day Pellicer linking old with new, but in the midst of his abundance he is often insubstantial. Zaid is brief by comparison, not only in total extent but also in the customary length of his individual poems. His earlier works are particularly reminiscent of Paz and others, but they are nonetheless preparation for the brusque and sometimes enigmatic short poems which represent the more mature Zaid. Pacheco is also very much indebted to Paz and others in his earlier works, but in his more recent collections he has been able to express with great penetration and polish the eternal problems of man's existence. Aridjis is abundant and sensual, and in many ways he is reminiscent in his earlier poetry of Pellicer and even of Montes de Oca. However, he very often attains an exuberant expression tempered by control and profundity.

Taken together, these four voices represent strong individuality with both successes and failures, and collectively they do a great deal to advance the cause of Mexican poetic expression. They are not slavish imitators of a recent or distant past, but rather use a rich legacy to express the committed Mexican humanism which is a product of their peculiar circumstances. They are rhetorical and at the same time aware of social justice; they are metaphysical and at the same time very much a part of the technological culture of the present moment; they admire and attempt to express beauty and at the same time see ugliness and degradation in much about them.

Montes de Oca, Zaid, Pacheco, and Aridjis are by no means the only figures of distinction among the younger poets of Mexico. They are important voices, however, and they typify the strengths and weaknesses of this recent segment in their country's poetic tradition. They represent, as one might well expect, substantial achievement, occasional failure, and considerable hope for the future.

Jenaro Prieto:
The Man and His Work

Thomas C. Meehan

The decades from 1920 to 1940, following the decline of modernism, were characterized by intense experimentation in literary style throughout Spanish America. This was especially true of poetry, but the daring changes and innovations wrought in the language of that genre also carried over into prose fiction. Novelistic style became increasingly more imaginative and personalized as artists sought to project their unique visions of reality. *Modernismo*'s "art for art's sake" dictum undoubtedly had made writers more conscious of their role as linguistic craftsmen. Max Henríquez Ureña has isolated the one attitude implicitly shared by all *modernistas*: their firm commitment to "trabajar el lenguaje con arte."[1] An intense preoccupation with language thus became one of the most distinguishing features of the *modernista* movement and an important part of the artistic heritage it bequeathed to the next literary generation. The enriched prose creations of José Martí, Manuel Gutiérrez Nájera, Rubén Darío, Enrique Larreta, Leopoldo Lugones, and José Enrique Rodó attest to this new awareness of the expressive potential of both narrative and discursive prose.

A second characteristic of modernism was its tendency to assimilate the stylistic discoveries and techniques of European, especially French, movements such as Parnassianism, symbolism, and impressionism and to apply them to the presentation of exotic and, slightly

---

[1] *Breve historia del modernismo*, 2d ed. (Mexico City, 1962), pp. 19, 34.

later, to native or American scenes and themes. Succeeding generations of writers were not inclined to forget the artistic lessons taught by their *modernista* mentors or to relinquish the latters' hard-won victories over language. While they abandoned modernist *preciosité* and that movement's fascination with the exotic in favor of expression of autochthonous realities, the best of the *postmodernista* and *vanguardista* prose writers remained conscious stylists. Their reaction to *modernismo* is characterized not by an extreme shift of emphasis back to an exclusive concern with content at the expense of form, but rather by a felicitous striking of a balance, a more finished unity of the twin literary components of form and content. They now possessed the ability not only to tell a substantial and meaningful story, but to tell it well. Octavio Corvalán correctly observes: "Esta continuidad esencial del modernismo fue la más grande y benéfica herencia que dejó la generación finisecular. Los poetas modernistas enseñaron a escribir a los novelistas hispanoamericanos del presente siglo. Desde *La gloria de don Ramiro* hasta *Los pasos perdidos* hay constantes testimonios de esta herencia."[2]

Perhaps the most outstanding example of that blend of a native theme and an essentially foreign but carefully wrought style in the Spanish American novel of the twenties is the gaucho novel *Don Segundo Sombra* (1926) by the Argentine Ricardo Güiraldes (1886–1927). Güiraldes brought to bear upon his River Plate reality a refined sensibility born of his familiarity with certain tendencies in late nineteenth- and early twentieth-century French literature. In an earlier poetic work, *El cencerro de cristal* (1915), Güiraldes had written: "La forma obedece a lo que el sujeto le dicta desde su significado interior."[3] Corvalán emphasizes that in the expression of this aesthetic ideal Güiraldes evinces his debt to impressionism, but that equally noteworthy in this quotation is the author's focus on form,[4] that abiding *voluntad de estilo* which places Güiraldes in the forefront of the prose writers who followed in the wake of *modernismo* and profited from its influence.

One of the problems the artist encountered in composing *Don*

---

[2] *Modernismo y vanguardia: Coordenadas de la literatura hispanoamericana del siglo XX* (New York, 1967), p. 15.
[3] Cited by Corvalán in *ibid.*, p. 85.
[4] *Ibid.*

Segundo Sombra was the creation of a literary language he intuitively felt was necessary. The same critic clarifies the novelist's procedure: "Güiraldes construyó un estilo en el cual el idioma suena lo bastante natural para parecer auténtico, pero trabajado en la forja más sofisticada de los impresionistas europeos. El ideal artístico de Güiraldes [expressed in *El cencerro de cristal*] se cumplió en *Don Segundo Sombra*: expresar su visión interior de las cosas; dictar la forma desde dentro."[5] Güiraldes' achievements in capturing the fleeting essence of the moment, the changing nuances in light and color, his occasional nominal phrases, and his faithful registering of sensory perceptions clearly point to an impressionistic aesthetic whose formula is not that of the realist—"La realidad tal como *es*"—but that of the impressionist—"La realidad tal como la percibo *yo*." The Argentine reality depicted in *Don Segundo Sombra* is strained and filtered through the sensory network and consciousness of a highly perceptive *yo*. Rich in imagery, daring metaphors and similes, and striking points of view, the work reveals linguistic awareness and tension of the highest degree.

Critics consistently emphasize the binary structure of Güiraldes' masterpiece, thereby referring not only to his treatment of a native theme with foreign stylistic methods but also to the duality of the work's language itself. In narrative and descriptive passages, despite the impressionistic quality of the narrator-protagonist's perceptions, the overall effect remains genuine as a result of a simple but inventive procedure: innovative imagery abounds, but each metaphor and simile is firmly anchored in the natural phenomena of the Argentine *pampa*. Secondly, in the dialogue sequences, which are admittedly quite stylized, the conversations of the gaucho personages miraculously retain the authenticity and spirit of the *pampa* inhabitants' speech . Güiraldes and others were discovering and demonstrating that the realities of America could be more artistically expressed by eclectically drawing upon foreign though well-assimilated narrative and descriptive modes. Changes with profound implications were subtly taking place within the traditional.[6]

[5] *Ibid.*, p. 86.

[6] In this regard, it is relevant to note a curious discussion of Argentine literature which takes place among a group of personages in the pages of Ernesto Sábato's latest novel. Referring to the *europeísmo* of Güiraldes' famous work, one character remarks: "—Bueno, sí. En algún sentido y por momentos, *Don Segundo Sombra* parecería haber

The importation of stylistic techniques and their application to Spanish American subjects and themes was a trend which continued unabated throughout the 1920's and 1930's with intensified borrowings from the latest fashionable vanguardist schools and movements of Europe such as expressionism, futurism, cubism, and surrealism. The literary language of the times became experimental, bizarre, playful, and audacious in conception and at times humorous in tone. It was studded with pyrotechnic imagery which often disregarded reason and logic completely in its expressive efforts to penetrate beneath surfaces, to record the inner, psychic life of man, and to perceive, from differing and extraordinary perspectives, previously unexplored dimensions of reality.

Imaginative language was, of course, only one means of responding literarily to contemporary intellectual and artistic currents. The traditional, chronologically constructed story would be broken and fragmented. The familiar, "realistic," cause-and-effect relationships of linear plot structure would give way to more subtle approaches involving associative thought patterns, the use of symbol, myth, leitmotif, parallels, and contrastive procedures which demanded increasingly greater reader participation in the creative act. Shifting and multiple points of view and character-narrators (not infrequently unreliable ones) would replace the omniscient author-god of nineteenth-century fictional worlds who had conveniently explained everything for his trusting, passive readers. An additional important contribution was the creation and application of novelistic equivalents of cinematographic techniques and transpositions from the other arts, especially painting and music. Finally, one would need to take into account the influence of the superb models of narrative art provided for Spanish American writers by the giants of twentieth-century occidental prose fiction: Proust, Joyce, Kafka, Virginia Woolf, Dos Passos, Hemingway, and, above all, William Faulkner. A long period of gestation ultimately led, in the post–World War II period, to the birth of the Spanish American "new novel" and that genre's complete maturity in our own days.

---

sido escrito por un francés que hubiese vivido en la pampa. Pero mire, Martín, observe que he dicho 'en algún sentido,' 'por momentos.' . . . Lo que significa que esa novela no podría haber sido hecha por un francés. Creo que es esencialmente argentina . . ." (*Sobre héroes y tumbas*, 9th ed. [Buenos Aires: Sudamericana, 1969], pp. 175–76).

Only recently, however, have researchers begun to identify the important precursors of this flowing of the Spanish American novel "into the mainstream" of world fiction. One significant case in point, by way of brief example, is the reawakened interest in Roberto Arlt (1900–42), an Argentine writer whose work of the late twenties and thirties is now being reevaluated in terms of its spiritual and aesthetic affinities with the writings of Borges[7] and Julio Cortázar. In a rejection of linguistic embellishment which was to be echoed by Cortázar three decades later, Arlt wrote, in the prologue to *Los lanzallamas* (1931): "Hoy, entre los ruidos de un edificio social que se desmorona inevitablemente, no es posible pensar en bordados."[8] Yet, despite Arlt's disdain for literary "embroidery," it has been claimed that few Argentine writers have achieved more forceful expressiveness in their style than Roberto Arlt.[9] Indeed, the same critic hails the author of *Los siete locos* (1929) as "at least the best" if not the first of the vanguardist novelists.[10]

Jenaro Prieto (1889–1946)

In the same year that saw the appearance of *Don Segundo Sombra* and Arlt's caustic *El juguete rabioso*, across the Andes, in far-flung and somewhat isolated Chile, another now-forgotten talent was quietly at work. Jenaro Prieto, one of the earliest stylistic innovators of twentieth-century Chilean prose fiction, published his first novel, *Un muerto de mal criterio*.

Jenaro Prieto Letelier was born in Santiago, Chile, on August 5, 1889, the eldest of the many children of Jenaro Prieto Hurtado and María Letelier. His great-grandfather, José Joaquín Prieto, had been a president of Chile.[11] The author's earliest childhood mem-

---

7 See the striking thematic similarities Corvalán perceives in the fiction of Arlt and Borges in *Modernismo y vanguardia*, p. 197.

8 Cited by Corvalán in *ibid.*, p. 192.

9 "Desde *El juguete rabioso* la habilidad narrativa y la riqueza expresiva de Arlt han ido en constante superación, y a pesar de su queja de que 'no es posible pensar en bordados,' hay pocos escritores argentinos que le aventajen en eficacia estilística. Los 'bordados' a que se refiere son los meros adornos de la prosa invertebrada que se dio en llamar artística y que sólo era artificio. Cuando el furor o el desaliento lo asaltan, Arlt no produce elocuencia sino estilo; tenso, gráfico, conciso" (*ibid.*, p. 197).

10 *Ibid.*, p. 189.

11 Biographical information, unless otherwise indicated, is based upon José Luis González González, "P. El humorista Jenaro Prieto," *Memoria de Prueba* for the

ories are recorded in an unfinished autobiographical novel, *La casa vieja*, posthumously published in 1957. Jenaro completed his primary and secondary education under the direction of French priests at the Colegio de los Sagrados Corazones in Santiago, where, with classmates, he collaborated in publishing a clandestine magazine which poked fun at the authoritarian atmosphere of the school. This early journalistic activity and satire significantly foreshadowed the direction his future life would take. Even then, Prieto's satirical and humorous bent was being formed, for, in an article composed many years later for the newspaper *El Diario Ilustrado*, he looked back on his mischief as an adolescent fledgling reporter and recalled that every issue of the student magazine was devoured by public opinion, "que siempre ha gozado más con una tomadura de pelo a la autoridad. . . . "[12] It is probable that the author's first contacts with European artistic currents also date from these formative years in a French *colegio*.

In 1912 Prieto received a law degree from the University of Chile. The title of his *memoria de prueba*, "El hipnotismo ante el derecho," is noteworthy not only for its farsighted theme but also for its revelation of the writer's early personal orientation toward the unusual, dark, hidden recesses of the human mind and the potentially creative products of those areas. Such interests would later manifest themselves artistically in his novel *El socio* (1928). With the exception of a brief and insignificant sojourn in politics and a protracted, well-paid position with the Caja de Crédito Hipotecario, to whose organ, *La Información*, he contributed numerous articles, Prieto never practiced the legal profession. With little interest in and no real vocation for law, he had embarked upon that career only to please his father; he was soon disillusioned by most forms of human justice, and, as a result, he hid his law degree where none might see it. However, his knowledge of jurisprudence later would provide him with the central situation for his first novel, *Un muerto de mal criterio* (1926). The law and related fields such as politics

---

degree of Profesor de Estado en la Asignatura de Castellano, Facultad de Filosofía y Educación, Instituto Pedagógico, University of Chile, Santiago, 1949. See also the *Diccionario de la literatura latinoamericana*, vol. 2, *Chile* (Washington: Pan American Union, Letters Section, 1958), pp. 161–63.

[12] See "El arresto de un ministro" (September 1929), anthologized in *Con sordina*, 6th ed. (Santiago: Nascimento, 1931), p. 218.

and economics always served him well, but almost exclusively as the frequent targets of his editorial satire and humor.

The years 1912 and 1913 were transitional ones for Jenaro Prieto. He married Doña Elvira Vial, abandoned law, and began to dabble in business and the stock market, activities which would partially occupy his attention for many years. A friend of the author recounts how a fortuitous meeting changed the course of the young man's destiny:

> He had already taken the preliminary steps toward becoming full-fledged proprietor of a creamery, when he met by chance on the street an uncle of his who was part-owner of *El Diario Ilustrado,* a paper which at that time boasted a circulation greater than that of the other Santiago dailies put together. This uncle, Don Joaquín, proposed to him that he join the editorial staff of his paper, payment to be made on the basis of so much for each article. Jenaro accepted the offer with enthusiasm, and began writing about every-day happenings, giving up with alacrity all idea of his creamery. It is an amusing coincidence that the word *lechero* (milkman) is applied in Chile to a man enjoying good fortune; when a person has good luck, it is said of him that *anda con leche*. He entered his journalistic career, then, *con toda la leche* (with all good luck).[13]

Prieto's first article, for which he received ten pesos, bears the date April 10, 1913. The beard which he would wear throughout his days also appeared the same year, as if to give the new man of letters a somewhat bohemian, yet, paradoxically, also slightly Franciscan image.

For the remaining thirty-three years of his life (1913–46), Jenaro Prieto was associated, as coeditor (secretario de redacción), with the conservative Catholic newspaper *El Diario Ilustrado.* From its founding in 1902 this daily had maintained norms of journalistic excellence and promoted *belles lettres* in its Sunday literary supplement. Approximately three to five days each week, Prieto composed short, pithy editorials consisting of sometimes serious, sometimes witty and satirical commentaries on all aspects of the passing scene in Chile: character types; customs; petty vices; urban, national, and

---

[13] Januario Espinosa, "Jenaro Prieto—Humorist," *Chile: A Monthly Survey of Chilean Affairs,* 9, no. 56 (December 1930), 190.

international affairs; history; economics; the theater; literature and art; clothing fashions; and, above all, politics. He also drew cartoons of familiar public personalities and clever sketches of imaginary beings to illustrate his articles. The pieces occasionally included original verses penned by the author. Each morning, thousands of *santiaguinos* eagerly sought in the pages of *El Diario Ilustrado* his most familiar by-line, a simple "P.," and they read with equal avidness his thoughtful essays as well as the lampoons of the life they saw around them. Ideological supporters and adversaries alike enjoyed his column, sometimes titled "Al pasar." It is paradoxical that although Prieto's political opponents, the liberals, were pulverized by his irony and humor with alarming regularity, he apparently was a man without enemies. The reason was that he attacked ideas, not people; his satire was tempered by compassion, and his tone was never cruel, malicious, or personal.

Another significant facet of Jenaro Prieto's profile was his passionate, lifelong interest in the plastic arts, especially painting. He was a talented amateur landscape painter, and, upon his death, he left numerous canvases. Proud of his paintings, Prieto frequently lamented the fact that he had not pursued his avocation more seriously. When an interviewer once queried him about what he would have liked to become had he not been a journalist, he responded without hesitation: "¿Qué hubiera querido ser yo? . . . Pintor, si hubiera sido rico." He associated with the famous group of Chilean poets, artists, novelists, and intellectuals known as "Los Diez" and was an intimate friend of their acknowledged leader, Pedro Prado, the author of *Alsino* (1920) and *Un juez rural* (1924).

Prieto's career as painter can be partially traced in the short-lived but beautiful *Pacífico Magazine* (1914–21), edited by Alberto Edwards and Joaquín Díaz Garcés. One of Prieto's paintings, "Cementerio," adorns the cover of the January, 1917, number, and another picture, entitled "Caserones Coloniales," may be seen in the December, 1918, issue (No. 72, page 574). Other Prieto paintings appear in various issues of the magazine. The author participated in at least three art exhibitions: one with Manuel Magallanes Moure, Rafael Valdés, and Pedro Ovalle. In November, 1916, he exhibited his work with that of the professional painter Alfredo Araya; the exhibition was apparently quite successful, since both artists sold all their canvases. The third exposition of the artist's paintings, exhibited with those of Manuel Magallanes, Luis Strozzi, and Alfredo Araya, was in May, 1919.

Prieto's interest in sculpture manifests itself in a five-page article appearing in the October, 1918, issue of *Pacífico Magazine*.[14] Titled "El brazo de Laocoonte," the essay is a disquisition on the famous classical statue and the finding of its long-lost right arm in 1906 by the German archaeologist Louis Pollak. More noteworthy, however, is the Chilean writer's broad knowledge of classical art and renaissance art history which becomes abundantly apparent to the reader despite the article's brevity.

The pages of *Pacífico Magazine* (No. 76, April, 1919) also highlight another facet of Prieto's artistic bent—his skill at drawing and sketching. He participated in a "Concurso de dibujantes" (pp. 403–10) in response to the editors' efforts to find a temporary replacement for their regular illustrator, Pedro Subercasseux, who was traveling in Europe. Each contestant was requested to illustrate six scenes of *El sepulcro acusador*, a *novela folletín* by Diego Zamora. The *Pacífico Magazine* piece describing the contest includes several of Prieto's original drawings, the dramatic effects of which elicited praise from the professional judges. However, they also faulted the artist for his tendency to exaggerate and distort facial expressions. These basic techniques of the cartoonist and the satirist, exaggeration and distortion, are constantly brought to bear in the sketches and caricatures of himself which illustrate Prieto's journalistic articles and may also be seen, to a certain extent, in the literary style of his novels.

Prieto's interest in and practice of the plastic arts demonstrates a fundamental fact concerning his creative imagination. It tended to be intense, highly visual, and, despite the contradiction, kinetic. It is not surprising, therefore, that one writer, basing her remarks on a personal interview with Prieto, should record this revealing piece of information concerning his childhood: "Era un niño preocupado, nervioso y muy imaginativo. *Padecía alucinaciones, veía*

---

[14] González attests also to having seen, in the author's home, "un precioso márbrit [sic], —vidrio coloreado,— que representa en relieve una carabela ágil y esbelta; también vi bustos de cristos y cabezas hechos por sus manos. Y a decir verdad que las tenía afortunadas" ("P. El humorista," p. 52).

todos los objetos dobles y movibles. Una vez, escuchando un cuento, vió un animal enorme que cruzaba la pieza. Nunca había tenido un sobresalto tan angustioso como aquella fantasía. Sufría espantos inmotivados, su alegría era rara y deprimente."[15] These dimensions of his creative talents manifest themselves much more clearly in the style of his major novel, *El socio*, than in his tranquil landscape paintings.

From all accounts, Jenaro Prieto was a shy, unimposing individual; yet just beneath his serene, almost beatific surface lurked a whimsical, pixyish sense of humor which endeared him to innumerable friends and acquaintances. His self-effacing, ready wit is exemplified by the following anecdote. Once, when Prieto was informed that a Swiss Franciscan missionary had included the French translation of his masterpiece, *El socio*, among the books he took to the Orient, without hesitation the author quipped: "Entonces, bien mereció que lo mandaran allí. Con razón sus superiores lo tienen por allá desterrado."[16] His legendary generosity was a frequent source of mirth among his friends, who were often obliged to lend him money to pay for his transportation home after he had given his last peso to some needy beggar. Because of his great compassion and understanding, he was often pressed into service as the confidant of numerous people, many of them complete strangers. When teased by colleagues for his readiness to listen to others' troubles, he responded wittily: "Yo no sé si es mi barba franciscana la que provoca las confidencias o si he errado mi vocación, porque como confesor no habría tenido precio." His gracious personality won him admirers abroad also. Manuel Vega, one of Prieto's associates on the editorial staff of *El Diario Ilustrado*, recalls a visit in 1935 to Alberto Gerchunoff in the offices of *La Nación* in Buenos Aires; after personal greetings were exchanged, the Argentine writer immediately inquired of Vega: "¿Qué es de ese magnífico ejemplar humano que se llama Jenaro Prieto?"

Although his newspaper column was often censored, and he was repeatedly imprisoned during the dictatorship of General Carlos

---

[15] Julia García Games, *Como los he visto yo* (Santiago, 1930), p. 100, italics mine. The essay entitled "Jenaro Prieto Letelier," pp. 97–107, is one of several in this book which includes useful information about distinguished Chilean artists and intellectuals of the times.

[16] González, "P. El humorista," p. 104.

Ibáñez del Campo (1927–31), Prieto never considered his persecution as anything extraordinary or himself as particularly brave or heroic. When he would disappear for several days at a time during this period, his friends surmised that he was either in jail or hiding out from the authorities. No vengeful, recriminatory tone appears in Jenaro's writings after the downfall of Ibáñez, although the author did immediately bring out a volume of articles which had been previously forbidden publication in *El Diario Ilustrado*. Entitled *Con sordina*, the book's second edition was sold out in four days, a tribute to the author's fame and popularity. The personification of humility, Prieto always minimized his own importance and role in affairs. The fame and prestige which *El socio* brought were a constant source of embarrassment to him.

Prieto's frequent criticism of the political scene ultimately led him to take an active part in politics. In the first free elections held after Ibáñez's downfall, the eminent journalist won and from 1932 to 1936 held a congressional seat as conservative representative of Santiago. His unpretentious but original electoral campaign, waged in the pages of *El Diario*, consisted of cartoons of himself showing his gaunt, bearded face with the ever-present pipe in his mouth; the simple motto below exhorted the voter: "Hágame la cruz y llegaré al Congreso." Once elected, however, he seldom participated in legislative debates. His innate shyness and humility, his fear of crowds, and his detached humorist's personality may partially explain, of course, his disinterest in parliamentary procedures.[17] Just as certain, however, is the journalist's realization that his forte was more the written than the spoken word. Jenaro remained an alert bystander, a penetrating observer of the folly he frequently witnessed. The drama, pageantry, and pettiness of the Chilean national congress provided the reporter in Prieto with material for countless editorial pieces.

In 1934, Senator Giovanni Gentile, director of the Instituto Interuniversitario de Cultura de Italia, invited Prieto, on behalf of the Italian government, to deliver a series of lectures on the history,

---

17 González points out that an essential ingredient of humor is its unexpectedness ("*lo inesperado*"): "En la Cámara, ante el público que aguardaba burlas y latigazos de sus labios, no supo reaccionar. La actitud de espera destruía en su esencia lo inesperado" (*ibid.*, p. 73).

life, and culture of Chile in several Italian cities, including Rome, Florence, Turin, Genoa, and Naples. Prieto was sufficiently fluent in Italian to deliver his talks in that language. A man easily disoriented even in his native Santiago, Jenaro frequently got lost in the labyrinthine streets of Rome, which he explored with great interest and curiosity. From March to August of that year the author toured most of Italy by automobile and visited northern Spain, France, and Switzerland. Heralded in the land of Dante by the Italian translation of his masterpiece, *El socio*, the Chilean was warmly received in intellectual circles, wherein he became familiar with the work of writers such as Bontempelli, Papini, Moretti, Sofía Alerano, authoress of *Una Donna*, and Corrado Alvaro, author of the war novel *20 Anni*. The same year that Prieto visited Italy, the renowned Italian dramatist Luigi Pirandello won the Nobel Prize for Literature, and Jenaro dedicated an essay of tribute to that author, whose influence many critics have seen in *El socio*. Some of Prieto's impressions of Europe, and one of his lectures, "El Nuevo Descubrimiento de América," appeared in the pages of *El Diario Ilustrado* after his return to Chile. At the same time he regretted having to decline a similar invitation tendered by the German government to speak in a cultural center in Hamburg; he felt obliged to refuse not for political reasons but because of his inability to speak German.

Prieto had two favorite forms of relaxation, both of which manifest themselves in *El socio*. He was a superb horseman; among his enjoyable pastimes were the long horseback rides he took along the seashore or through the Chilean countryside around El Convento, his *fundo* near the town of Llolleo. The ocean also held a special attraction for Jenaro. He was familiar with many forms of marine life—rare fish, algae, etc.—and could identify many types of ships, sailing boats, and other vessels from great distances. In addition to sitting on the beach and sketching sailboats, fish, and various forms of underwater life, Prieto, a powerful swimmer, loved to swim in the ocean. He spent many enjoyable holidays at the Chilean seaside resort of Viña del Mar, near Valparaíso. When caught up in the hectic urban activities of Santiago and the noisy routine of the newspaper office, he longed for the calm and peace of the ocean and occasionally remarked: "No quisiera tener sino una casita en la costa, leer y pintar." Final rest was nearer than he suspected.

Two months before he died, symptoms such as slurred speech, dizziness, and temporary paralysis warned Prieto that he was seriously ill and obliged him to undergo extensive medical treatment. Although he had requested retirement several times before, but continued working at the request of friends and employers, he now withdrew from his editorial duties at *El Diario Ilustrado*. Having no terror of death, he made light of it. To friends who offered words of encouragement with remarks about his "good appearance," he would humorously reply, "Están tocando la segunda seña, compañero." His beloved friend and colleague Lautaro García was advised: "Lauta, anda preparándome la necrología. Me gustaría saber cómo vas a salir del paso." His only fear was "making the long trip alone": "Morirse no es nada: lo terrible es emprender ese viaje, el más apasionante y desconocido; solo, sin tener con quien comentar las incidencias y descubrimientos que en él se hagan y aún con el peligro de encontrarse con algún otro viajero cuyo idioma desconozcamos y con el cual no podríamos entendernos."

On the afternoon before his death Jenaro composed, in an almost illegible hand, his pitiful final farewell to his colleagues of *El Diario Ilustrado*, which he addressed to its editor-in-chief, Don Luis A. Silva. His note appears on the front page of the newspaper's issue of March 8, 1946, and reads as follows:

> Querido Lucho:
> Daría cualquier cosa por no tener que escribirte estas líneas. Sé que ni tú, ni Fernando Varas, ni Jorge ni los treinta compañeros con que he vivido tres cuartas partes de mi vida, necesitan de ellas para comprender con cuánta pena pongo punto final a una tarea que forma parte de mi vida misma, y que todas las frases de agradecimiento al Diario mismo y a los innumerables compañeros que me dieron su amistad abonarán un ápice a la deuda de afecto con que me alejo de esta casa.
> Con la esperanza de evitar este paso, me he sometido a tratamiento médico, he afrontado pelotillas e inyecciones y he acatado la generosa insistencia del Diario al oponerse una y otra vez la jubilación.
> Me resistía a "entregar la pala", como dicen los huasos.

Cuando cada mañana al leer el diario se ve a los viejos colegas ocupar su puesto de combate con el mismo brío que veinte años antes, la ausencia de la fila, por forzada que sea, parece una deserción.

Por desgracia los años han pasado y no puedo decir que soy el mismo del año veinte.

¡Quien sabe si es para mejor! Hay algo más lamentable que los años y es no darse cuenta de ellos. Corre el riesgo de que si uno no lo nota, lo noten los lectores. En estas condiciones, no me queda más recurso que la jubilación.

That night Prieto finished a film script, and, while riding in a car with friends around the grounds of El Convento, he absent-mindedly lit up his pipe against the strict orders of his doctor. When cautioned by his alarmed friends that he was only deceiving himself, he replied calmly, "Para los días que me quedan ya de vivir. . . ." He had often said, "Hay que morirse de una enfermedad limpia." Jenaro Prieto Letelier died of a cerebral hemorrhage on March 5, 1946, at El Convento, surrounded by his family and loved ones. His death occasioned a dignified outpouring of grief and expressions of condolences in the Santiago press, and for years afterwards the anniversary of his demise was marked by nostalgic homages and anecdotes concerning the artist and the man by his friend Lautaro García and other colleagues and associates. The author's existence has been summarized in the following manner: "Y así, su vida se diluyó entre cuadros, negocios, política, periodismo, teatro y literatura. Cientas fueron las telas pintadas por él, y miles los artículos humorísticos escritos sobre los más variados temas. . . ."[18]

The Work of Jenaro Prieto

Prieto was tremendously prolific. Even during the darkest years of the waning Ibáñez dictatorship, "P.," "L.," or "Juan Peralta" (three of his by-lines) published more than 150 articles. Prieto's wife, Doña Elvira Vial, collected approximately a thousand columns produced from 1912 to 1918 and about an additional thousand written from 1928 to 1946.[19] It is not surprising, therefore, that Prieto's

[18] *Ibid.*, pp. 42–43.
[19] *Ibid.*

contribution to novelistic prose was limited, for it was severely and lamentably curtailed by this assiduous and lifelong journalistic activity which absorbed his time and sapped his energies. Nevertheless, in addition to their intrinsic value, his almost daily newspaper columns gave him a well-deserved renown which insured instant recognition of the author and sympathetic reception of his literary works upon their appearance. In the midst of a busy career and family life, Prieto did find time to write three novels: *Un muerto de mal criterio*, *El socio*, and the somewhat autobiographical but regrettably unfinished *La casa vieja*, published posthumously in 1957 with a brief prologue by the author's close friend Lautaro García.

One other incomplete work of fiction is reported to have been salvaged by Prieto's widow. From among the numerous drafts, plans for stories and articles, sketches, and other works found on the writer's cluttered worktable after his death, Doña Elvira Vial "patiently compiled and put together" a story bearing the title *Así pasó el Diablo*. Although publication was promised and seemed imminent in 1949, the piece has remained unpublished, as nearly as can be ascertained. The plot of *Así pasó el Diablo* has been synthesized in the following manner:

> Mefistófeles, el mismo que rejuveneciera a Fausto, a cambio de su alma, y saliera chasqueado, ha estado inactivo en el Infierno. . . . Satanás le encarga sembrar cizaña en el villorrio andino "San José de las Pataguas," pueblo rutinario y de pecar mezquino. . . . Baja a la tierra y sus artimañas no surten efecto: nadie cree en él. Decide, entonces, atacar a fondo y ofrece oro a un ambicioso, rejuvenecimiento y virilidad a un mustio solterón, y amor a una viuda no resignada con su suerte. . . . Se enreda la madeja en tal forma que el pueblito se convierte en un infierno, pero todo sale contrario a Mefistófeles, que, derrotado otra vez, se vuelve mohino a su antro de fuego.[20]

It is unclear whether this work would have been a novel or a short story, but the phrase "Se enreda la madeja en tal forma que el pueblito se convierte en un infierno . . ." would lead one to suppose

[20] *Ibid.*, p. 93.

a more lengthy tale of the supernatural cut of *Un muerto de mal criterio.*

During his lifetime, Prieto also issued two anthologies of his newspaper columns under the titles *Pluma en ristre* (1925) and *Con sordina* (1931). Nine years after the artist's death, Fernando Castillo Infante brought out a third volume of Prieto's vignettes of Chilean life with the title *Humo de pipa* (1955). The title is that of one of the included selections, but it is also an allusion to an object intimately associated with Prieto, a personal possession which became a kind of trademark, leitmotif, or insignia of the man—his *cachimba.* Jenaro was seldom seen without this pipe with its smoke curling about his beard and his gaunt, roguish features. (In *El socio,* the imaginary English business partner, Mr. Walter Davis, is always envisioned by his creator, Julián Pardo, with a Sherlock Holmes type of pipe.)

Taken as a whole, the three volumes of journalistic pieces chart the internal history of Chile during approximately three decades of stormy national existence and provide penetrating, original insights into multiple facets of Chilean life of the times. In style, tone, diversity of subject matter, and general approach, the pieces would remind any American newspaper reader of the humorous, ironical, allusive editorials of Art Buchwald. Although each consecutive volume contains some duplication, each book, in a sense, corresponds to one of three very general political periods into which the thirty years (1915–45) may be divided; indeed, the first two collections appeared, significantly, just upon termination of the first two eras in question.

Pluma en ristre, which covers roughly the years 1915–25, contains a prologue by the author of *El roto* (1920), the famous Chilean novelist Joaquín Edwards Bello. The volume is divided into two parts: the first contains light, humorous articles on a variety of subjects written by Prieto from 1913 to 1920; the second, more important part is titled "Alessandri" and consists exclusively of satirical pieces composed during the first presidency (1920–26) of Arturo Alessandri.[21] This section of *Pluma en ristre* is introduced by the following words of the author:

---

[21] For further information on this controversial political figure, consult the *Columbia Encyclopedia,* 3d ed., s.v. "Alessandri, Arturo."

ALESSANDRI

Bajo este nombre que durante varios años ha llenado las columnas de la prensa, he querido reunir en un capítulo unos veinte o treinta artículos arrancados a la campaña más tenaz, accidentada e infructuosa de mi vida periodística.

Supla su falta de interés, el de la época en que fueron escritos.

Época tragi-cómica de extrañas perturbaciones sociales y políticas, violentos cambios de gobierno, censura de la prensa, motines militares, deportaciones, dictaduras, y personajes de opereta, acaso no merezca ni siquiera el fallo adusto y justiciero de la historia.

A falta de él, vengan, por ahora, estos artículos que, si son más deleznables, serán en todo caso más benévolos, como que fueron escritos tratando de mirar siempre los hombres y los sucesos por el lado menos triste. . . .[22]

Con sordina covers the period 1925–31, which takes in the short-lived presidency of Emiliano Figueroa Larraín (January–May, 1927) and the military dictatorship of Colonel Carlos Ibáñez del Campo (May, 1927–July, 1931). In addition to articles of a non-political nature, it contains many pieces which Prieto was unable to publish in *El Diario Ilustrado* because of severe press censorship under the oppressive Ibáñez regime. Jenaro held these columns in readiness and rushed the volume into print immediately upon the fall of the dictator. *Con sordina,* whose title ("muffled" or "muted") calls attention to the censored quality of its contents, not surprisingly went through several editions very rapidly, for the Santiago reading public was eager to see what their leading wit had to say about Ibáñez. Prieto did not disappoint his readers, because in those years he had conceived his imaginary counterpart of Chile, which he named "Tontilandia" ("Foolish Land"), with its capital, "Cretinópolis," humorous place names reminiscent of the fantasy lands of Lilliput, Brobdingnag, and so on created by another earlier satirist, Jonathan Swift, similarly to unmask and lampoon the follies of mankind. In his prologue to *Con sordina,* entitled "Alegre historia de un tiempo triste," C. Silva Vildósola comments that future historians might find it difficult to believe some of the grim, at times absurd incidents of those unhappy years: "Por eso conviene

---

[22] Jenaro Prieto, *Pluma en ristre,* 2d ed. (Santiago: Imprenta Chile, 1925), p. 173.

dejar un testimonio, y es el objeto de estas líneas, de que el maravilloso viaje al país de Tontilandia, los capítulos más ingeniosos y
de más honda sátira del libro de Jenaro Prieto, son una descripción
exacta, fotográfica, de la vida en Chile en esos tiempos."[23] The
volume also contains a wide variety of articles ranging in subject
from Proust to the new talking movies. As Silva Vildósola concludes:

> No cabe duda: cuando alguien, en veinte o treinta años más,
> quiera saber lo que fueron ciertas formas de gobierno y las modas
> de en que las mujeres lo recortaban todo, melenas y faldas, y las
> ventas a plazo, y las doctrinas políticas de los señores Edwards
> Matte, y los superávit y los rotarios que declararon miembro de su
> corporación a Arturo Prat, cuando todo esto parezca fantasía, algún
> sabio escarbador hallará este libro y en él la revelación de una
> época. Como los precisos objetos de uso diario acumulados en la
> tumba de Tut-Ank-Amon han servido para escribir la vida privada
> de este Faraón, así estos artículos permitirán escribir la historia
> íntima de Chile.[24]

Humo de pipa includes representative articles from the last fifteen
years of Prieto's journalistic career which take in Arturo Alessandri's second presidency (1932–38) and the years of the leftist "Frente
Popular" (1938–44). An additional attractive feature of this volume,
from a literary point of view, is the inclusion of a number of satirical
pieces on vanguardist poetry and others on Prieto's now distinguished compatriot Pablo Neruda, whose communist candidacy
for the senate seat representing Tarapacá and Antofagasta Jenaro
good-naturedly opposed in "Un candidato que aúlla."[25] Further
entries on "Tontilandia" now apply to governments and political
figures that succeeded the Ibáñez regime.

A little-known fact is that Prieto also wrote light dramatic pieces.
He laughed at the totally unsuccessful results and the inconsequen-
tial literary value of his now-forgotten theatrical ventures: ". . . yo
también he sido autor teatral . . . y de los peores del país."[26] His
sainete, El cuarto poder, written and produced around 1917, he

[23] *Con sordina*, p. 6.
[24] *Ibid.*, pp. 8–9.
[25] See Jenaro Prieto, *Humo de pipa* (Santiago: Editorial del Pacífico, 1955), pp.
257–59.
[26] "Recuerdos de un estreno," *Con sordina*, p. 291.

humorously judged as a "calamidad nacional."[27] He later collaborated in the composition of a musical review, *Claveles y albahacas*, which consisted of comical Chilean *cuadros de costumbres*. The more successful run enjoyed by the latter piece at the *Teatro de la Comedia* in Santiago prompted Prieto to write another three-act comedy, *Se necesita un suicida*, which premiered at the same theatre on December 1, 1932. Daniel de la Vega, writing in *El Mercurio* (December 2, 1932), lauded especially Prieto's first act, his comical plot, and his able manipulation of character. The audience applauded until the author appeared onstage to take a bow. Prieto's friend and colleague Lautaro García deserves credit for a somewhat more reserved and objective review of the play in *El Diario Ilustrado* (December 2, 1932). García was aware of his friend's theatrical inexperience and stated that Prieto's dramatic humor needed to be elevated by "intenciones trascendentales"—in short, that the author should attempt more serious theatre. Upon his death, Prieto left another unpublished and unperformed three-act comedy titled *El Hermano Silvestre*.

In the final years of his life, Prieto turned his talents to the related art of motion pictures. Desirous of helping the fledgling Chilean film industry, he remained unsure of the applicability of the humorist's stock in trade, spontaneity and incongruity, to a form requiring other techniques such as deliberation, continuity, and consistency of situation. He lived to see very few of his film efforts brought to fruition. Prieto collaborated with Luis Hiriart on the film version of *Fedora* by the French dramatist Victorien Sardou (1831–1908) and with Armando Hinojosa on the screen adaptations of several other literary works. The former movie was produced by an Argentine company. Upon his death, Prieto left two film scripts finished, a few others in various stages of completion, and several only planned or roughly sketched. One of the completed film stories was *La batalla de Julepe* for Chile Films; the other, whose title is reminiscent of the denouement of *El socio*, is called *Un crimen casi perfecto*. Early death truncated the development of what might have been another interesting side of Prieto's multifaceted talent.

---

27 *Ibid.*, and "Carta de un suicida," *El Diario Ilustrado*, 29 November 1932.

Two of four attempts by foreign companies to film Prieto's own masterpiece, *El socio*, were successful. The author saw neither of them. A highly acclaimed Italian version was produced before World War II, but it was never shown in Chile. At the time of Prieto's death, a Mexican adaptation was in production. An English version was withdrawn when the company holding the film rights declared that the essence and spirit of the novel had been completely distorted in the transposition from one art form to the other. *Mr. Davis, mon associé*, a French enterprise, was cancelled because of the death, during filming, of the starring actor. As if to reaffirm the timeless and universal relevance of the theme of Prieto's novel, man's greed and duplicity, a new play based upon *El socio* is, at the moment of this writing, enjoying a very successful run on the Madrid boards.[28]

In this sketch of Jenaro Prieto's life and work, what emerges most clearly is the portrait of a man of numerous talents and interests: lawyer, businessman, stockbroker, politician, landscape artist, art historian, journalist, humorist, novelist, lecturer, literary and theater critic, dramatist, film scriptwriter, and others. All these forms of human endeavor occupied the attention of this multifaceted Chilean during his brief, fifty-six year life. Jenaro Prieto will be primarily remembered, however, as a humorous journalist and as the creator of *El socio*. If he had written only this novel, his place in the history of the Spanish American novel would be assured.

Jenaro Prieto's Place in Chilean Prose Fiction

Chile has one of the richest novelistic traditions in Spanish America, perhaps second only (in quantity) to those of Mexico and Argentina. The Chilean novel, throughout much of its history, has shown a dual profile: (1) the native, traditionalist, and regionalist; and (2) the foreign, innovative, and universalist. Historians and critics of Chile's novel have concerned themselves with the native versus the foreign and universalizing tendencies. At times there has occurred a fusion of the two tendencies, what might be termed "change within the traditional." The first major figure in Chilean prose fiction,

---

[28] Juan Ignacio Luca de Tena's *El rey de las finanzas*. I am presently at work on a study of the relationship of play and novel.

Alberto Blest Gana (1830–1920), author of *Martín Rivas* (1862),
set out to become the "Chilean Balzac" by novelizing his nation's
total society as did the great writer of France. Blest Gana recorded
that *infrahistoria*, of which Unamuno spoke, in works of fiction
with Chilean scenes and characters to which the author applied the
canons of a literary realism acquired through his familiarity with
French and Spanish literature.[29]

Early in our century opposition arose between the respective
advocates of regionalism and universalism. This dichotomy became
the hallmark of the Chilean novel of that period, and it was to remain its keynote for almost half a century. As Fernando Alegría
has indicated, regionalism emerged triumphant from the nineteenth century but held sway among the generation of the centenary
(1910) only until Chilean men of letters discovered the Russian
novel and became aware of "la necesidad de conferir universalismo
a la literatura criolla." The relevance, at this point, of the eminent
Chilean critic's further remarks merits their being quoted at length:

Se reconocen las limitaciones del cuadro de costumbre y se siente
el ansia de incorporar al pueblo chileno al drama de una humani-
dad que revisa, en circunstancias fatales, los valores éticos tradi-
cionales. . . . Surge en Chile una Colonia Tolstoyana. En ella,
entre otros, se agrupan tres novelistas de innegable valía: Augusto
d'Halmar, Pedro Prado y Fernando Santiván. En la obra de estos
escritores aparece con meridiana claridad el conflicto esencial que
ha de transformarse en seña característica de la novela chilena de
comienzos del siglo XX. Nos referimos a una antinomia entre lo
regional y lo universal, o, para decirlo en términos de una nomen-
clatura literaria, entre el realismo y el imaginismo. Por una parte,
esa obra demuestra que nuestros novelistas buscan un estilo nacional y lo buscan en la anécdota típica, como si la temática pudiera
imponer la individualidad del estilo; y, por otra, se esfuerzan en
captar esencias filosóficas a través del símbolo o la parábola o la
alegoría.[30]

<hr/>

[29] "En su juventud tuvo la ambición de ser el 'Balzac chileno,' como Gálvez y
Ocantos quisieron serlo en Argentina. En él es muy fuerte la influencia de *Negro y
rojo* de Stendhal y de Fouillet, autor de *La novela de un joven pobre*" (Orlando
Gómez-Gil, *Historia crítica de la literatura hispanoamericana* [New York, 1968], pp.
362–63).
[30] Fernando Alegría, *Literatura chilena del siglo XX*, 2d ed. (Santiago, 1967), pp.
57–58.

In a statement strongly reminiscent of our earlier observations concerning native and foreign elements in the style of Ricardo Güiraldes and other *postmodernistas*, Alegría concludes with a revealing and important comment on the language of these writers: "El lenguaje mismo parece ser una extraña mezcla de barbarismo y de la quintaesencia modernista que ya había impuesto Rubén Darío.[31]

The debate between regionalists and universalists, renewed with regularity, polarized Chilean authors into two groups: those who sought to establish ever closer literary ties with the land and to exploit to the fullest autochthonous reality, and others who were weary of traditional, regionalist themes and the outmoded, nineteenth-century approaches and techniques of *costumbrismo*, with its relentless search for and portrayal of the "typical" and the superficially picturesque. The latter faction advocated stylistic innovation and exploration of zones of human existence disregarded by their adversaries—the fantastic, the obscure, the irrational, and the subconsciousness of man. The very year of publication of Prieto's *El socio*, 1928, saw these contending forces, now called *criollismo* and *imaginismo*, reengaged in polemic in the pages of an important literary journal of the times, *Letras*. The struggle was later rejoined in *Indice*.[32] In 1954 the perennial argument was taken up once again by the well-known critic Alone, paladin of the *imaginistas*, and the respected novelist and *cuentista* Mariano Latorre (1886–1955), who championed the cause of *criollismo*.

Employing the chronological and generational schemes respectively provided by two distinguished Chilean scholars, we may now situate Jenaro Prieto within the literary scene of the period from 1920 to 1940.[33] As Fernando Alegría has substantiated, the first two decades of the twentieth century were characterized by that antinomy in Chilean prose fiction, adumbrated above, between the regionalists and universalists of the so-called *mundonovista* generation. Although elements of both orientations can be found in the

---

[31] *Ibid.*

[32] See Cedomil Goić, "La novela chilena actual: Tendencias y generaciones," in *Estudios de lengua y literatura como humanidades: Homenaje a Juan Uribe Echevarría* (Santiago, 1969), p. 38. First published in *Anales de la Universidad de Chile*, 118 (no. 119, 3rd semester, 1960), 250–58.

[33] The following is based primarily on Alegría, *Literatura chilena del siglo XX*, pp. 60–68.

work of each of the two groups, the former were most clearly represented by the *cuentista* Baldomero Lillo (1867–1933), whose numerous short stories, collected in the volumes titled *Sub-Terra* (1904) and *Sub-Sole* (1907), initiated what Alegría calls "realismo proletario"; the latter found their most resonant voices in Pedro Prado (1886–1952), Eduardo Barrios (1884–1963), Augusto d'Halmar (1880–1950), and Fernando Santiván (1886–).

Around 1920 the two forces split along generic lines: in poetry a tendency toward abstraction and the employment of imagery drawn from the European vanguardist schools were introduced, but the novel and *cuento*, on the other hand, became more intensely regionalist. In the decade 1920–30, Chilean regionalism became a firmly entrenched, well-defined literary school called *criollismo*,[34] whose undisputed leader was Mariano Latorre. He and his many followers, too numerous to list here,[35] were fascinated by the landscape of their nation and set out, almost literally, to "annex" the whole country into the pages of fiction. They were, in a sense, charting the novelistic map of Chile:

> Diríase que la preocupación de los escritores chilenos de esa época es la de dar una visión detallada y concreta de los aspectos más típicos del país, sin preocuparse mayormente de la significación social o filosófica que esa realidad entraña. La novela se transforma en un extenso cuadro de costumbres. El paisaje es elemento dominante en la estructura de la obra literaria; los personajes pasan a un nivel secundario. Los novelistas compiten en el

---

34 Luis Leal has enumerated succinctly the general characteristics of literary *criollismo* which pertain not only to Chilean but also to most Spanish American literature of the period in question: "(1) interés en lo popular frente a lo culto y lo erudito de los vanguardistas; (2) uso de asuntos, escenarios, personajes y ambientes americanos; (3) uso de imágenes, motivos y símbolos americanos; (4) uso de una mitología americana que reemplaza a la europea de los modernistas, postmodernistas y vanguardistas; (5) deseo de captar la realidad americana sin estilizarla, como lo hacen los vanguardistas; (6) uso de formas orgánicas, resultado de la búsqueda de lo nativo; (7) interés en los problemas sociales y políticos de los pueblos americanos y (8) necesidad de definir lo americano y de precisar el destino del continente." Leal defines *criollismo* as "las letras que tratan de asuntos americanos, que se valen de los recursos artísticos que dan a la obra una estructura orgánica que no impone la forma desde afuera; pero, al mismo tiempo, que no rechazan los procesos de la literatura universal que puedan ser utilizados" (*Breve historia de la literatura hispanoamericana* [New York, 1971], pp. 193–94). It is clear, from this definition and the characteristics listed, that the unifying factor of *criollismo* is its fundamental emphasis on things American.

35 See Alegría, *Literatura chilena del siglo XX*, pp. 61–65.

arte de la descripción minuciosa de la naturaleza y se esfuerzan por incorporar a su idioma las idiosincrasias populares. Más que la ciudad les interesa el campo. La crítica llega a decir que la "novela de la tierra" es la expresión genuina del arte literario chileno. Un articulista, en especial, aparece como el mentor de estas tendencias: Emilo Vaïse, que usó el pseudónimo de OMER EMETH.[36]

Because of the dates of publication of Jenaro Prieto's novels in the mid-twenties, later literary developments in Chile, including the crisis of regionalism or *criollismo*, lie beyond the scope of this study. However, what immediately followed these tendencies will help to establish the context within which Prieto worked and wrote and against which he stands out because of his dissimilarities. In a sense, the narrative art of the thirties continued many of the features of *criollismo*, but it became less superficial, more socially committed, and more profound and transcendental in terms of its human and universal implications. A trend toward what Alegría has referred to as "humanismo social" or "humanismo popular" made itself felt between 1930 and 1940. This younger group of writers, followed immediately by the generation of 1938 (the year the leftist "Frente Popular" assumed political power), was committed to seeking the essence of the national spirit, defining Chilean man (and themselves), and accepting as a literary norm the social function of artistic creation. Literature was to be placed at the service of great causes, frequently those of social and political protest. The appearance in these years, elsewhere, of works like Icaza's *Huasipungo* (Ecuador, 1934), López y Fuentes' *El indio* (Mexico, 1935), Ciro Alegría's *El mundo es ancho y ajeno* (Peru, 1941), certain of the works of Rómulo Gallegos, and some of the novels of the Mexican Revolution attests to the fact that such "committed" literature was the rule in much of Spanish America during the period in question. Furthermore, the predominant tone of such writing was contentious and deadly serious; indeed, it was frequently grim. As Alegría affirms: "No es común el humorismo entre los escritores que comentamos."[37] In Chile, this new tendency was termed *neorrealismo*;[38] the abiding influence on this *nueva promo-*

---

[36] *Ibid.,* p. 61.
[37] *Ibid.,* p. 64.
[38] *Ibid.,* p. 65.

ción, and upon the subsequent generations of 1938 and 1950, was a writer who, although a member of the previous generation, was the "novelista que mayor ascendencia ha ejercido sobre las generaciones del medio siglo en Chile"[39]—Manuel Rojas (1896).

It is clear, therefore, that Jenaro Prieto's two major novels were created and published during the heyday of *criollismo* in the middle of a decade (1920–30) whose narrative art was predominantly regionalistic and *costumbrista* in character and primarily realistic in approach, theme, and technique. Both of Prieto's major novels, because of their themes, tone, spirit, and, above all, style, are anomalies within this general literary context. His prose fiction contains features which are, in many ways, very unlike the predominant characteristics of *criollismo.* Alegría has recognized Prieto's uniqueness and the exceptional nature of his work by including him among a small group of writers who "al margen de escuelas o movimientos, contribuyeron eficazmente al desarrollo de la novela realista contemporánea. . . . JENARO PRIETO (1889–1946) es uno de los contados humoristas literarios que ha producido Chile, humorista al estilo inglés, atento a las pequeñeces humanas, a las contradicciones sociales, a la relatividad de todo esfuerzo; dispuesto a caricaturizar, no a herir; más preocupado del efecto final de su sátira que de los detalles pasajeros del relato. Su obra maestra es *El socio* (1929)."[40] Hence, Prieto's novelistic art becomes a further manifestation of that tendency toward change within the traditional, that "mestizo" fusion of native and foreign elements which is so characteristic of much of Spanish American literature. Prieto's limited but significant contributions to the development of the Chilean novel place him in the vanguard of stylistic innovators of his country and of much of Spanish America. The highly imaginative and expressive qualities of his themes and style also anticipate magical realism, a much-discussed later trend in Spanish American fiction.

If Jenaro Prieto is an anomaly when seen in terms of Alegría's frame of reference, he becomes much more typical and representative of his time when viewed in the light of another eminent Chilean critic's generational presentation of his country's novel of the period

[39] *Ibid.,* pp. 65–66.
[40] *Ibid.,* p. 68.

1920–60.[41] Cedomil Goić differentiates three generations whose members possessed distinct literary tastes, aesthetic sensibilities, or what Goić terms "systems of preferences" discernible in the organic features of their writings. For purposes of convenience, we may arrange these three generations in the following manner:

NAME OF GENERATION	DATE OF BIRTH	PERIOD OF GESTATION AND PUBLICATION OF GENERATION'S EARLIEST WORKS	PERIOD OF GENERATION'S GREATEST ASCENDANCY ("vigencia")
Superrealismo	1890–1904	1920–34; that is, during predominance of the mundonovista generation	1935–50
Neorrealismo	1905–19	1935–50	1950–65
Irrealismo	1920–35	1950–65	1965–

It is readily apparent that because of the date of his birth (1889) Jenaro Prieto fits perfectly within Goić's surrealist generation. For purposes of the present study, we may, then, disregarding the two groups that follow, concentrate upon the shaping influences or "systems of preferences" of that generation and delineate some of the distinctive features of its novelistic production.

The surrealist generation (and movement) is of the utmost importance for contemporary literature because its artistic contributions ultimately produced the deepest cleavage between nineteenth-century and contemporary aesthetic traditions. Toward the middle of the generation's fifteen-year gestational period there began, in May, 1928, the polemic between imaginismo and criollismo in the pages of the Chilean journal Letras. The imagist writers who contributed to the debate were convinced that the naturalist-regionalist-costumbrista approach to the novel had become extremely restrictive and that it had exhausted its possibilities. But they felt even more intensely the creative handicap caused by Chilean intellectuals and men of letters having remained largely on the periphery of the literary experimentation and innovation taking place in Europe and elsewhere. The imaginistas advocated that Chile's literature be brought into the mainstream, set out to remedy the retarded state of national letters by disseminating the writings of the various vanguardist movements in their magazines (Letras

41 The following is based on Goić, "La novela chilena actual."

and *Indice*), and thereby universalized their cultural horizons. These literary activities contained profound significance for Chilean prose fiction. Within the short span of a generation, the whole concept of novelistic art was transformed:

> Todas las literaturas, todos los *ismos* fueron atentamente considerados, leídos y practicados por la nueva generación. El nuevo sistema de preferencias que se organizaba no aceptó limitaciones regionalistas y afirmó por encima de toda alusión a la realidad histórica inmediata, el valor universal de la obra creada, despegada de la imitación servil del propio medio y de sus manifestaciones aparentes. . . . Se trataba de un verdadero proceso de crecimiento histórico el que esta generación vivió por primera vez identificándose con las nuevas formas de vida y promoviendo los cambios más violentos y notorios en las formas hasta entonces conocidas. El nuevo universalismo hacía consonar la sensibilidad de esta generación con el momento vigente en Europa que daba la nueva estructura histórica del mundo en que vivimos. . . . Pocas veces una generación se vio abocada a una tarea creadora tan inquieta, variada y variable; solicitada por tan cambiantes formas, tan novedosas y audaces, como ofrecía la literatura europea y la norteamericana. A la experiencia histórica de esta generación pertenece la activísima moción de los *ismos*. La incitación es originalmente europea, pero—por primera vez—participaron en los momentos mismos de su gestación varios escritores hispanoamericanos, entre ellos Vicente Huidobro.
>
> La novela chilena alcanzó en esta generación una novedad acorde con las tendencias universales dominantes. Sin perder su perfil original se ciñó a las características de la nueva fantasía, penetró en los nuevos asuntos y motivos e incorporó la técnica variada de la novela moderna. Nunca presentó una faz tan compleja e inasible como la suscitada por las nuevas preferencias y pocas veces fue dado presenciar en tan corto espacio mayor número de audaces experiencias en la construcción de las formas novelísticas. El cuento, la novela corta, la novela, alcanzaron estructuras insospechadas.[42]

[42] Some of the "estructuras insospechadas" introduced into Chilean narrative art during this experimental period of exposure to international literary currents, here enumerated by Goić, correspond, in part, to the technical innovations briefly treated above: "máxima interiorización . . . el monólogo interior . . . la estratificación de la conciencia narrativa y del tiempo . . . la pluralidad de conciencias . . . los cambios de foco narrativo—el ojo cinematográfico . . . los *papiers collés* de John Dos Passos . . . nueva objetividad . . . el abandono de la continuidad narrativa . . . la multiplicidad

According to Goić, then, the aesthetic sensibility of the generation of which Jenaro Prieto formed a part was shaped by a "system of preferences" that may be regarded as generally surrealist in origin. The unreal, unharmonic, unbalanced, precarious, broken, and misshapen are keynotes of the image of reality described in the following statement, which may serve, as well as any other, as a working definition of surrealism:

> Con esta expresión pretende señalarse aquella actitud histórica que reconoce en el mundo—la verdad, tanto histórico como ficticio —una ruptura de la imagen tradicional, natural, de la realidad; de modo que estas formas del mundo que poseían antes una imagen natural y enteriza, sufren una desrealización cuando es sorprendida su anárquica, lacerada, ominosa o desintegrada condición esencial. Roto el equilibrio normal entre hombre y mundo, la imagen armónica de la realidad se desvanece. La inseguridad se proyecta hasta en las formas de la literatura y promueve en ellas una semejante desrealización de las formas estatuidas y, juntamente, la necesidad de superar las viejas formas por otras más conformes con el sentimiento actual del mundo en torno.
>
> Esta situación ha despertado en los casos más significativos una desconfianza, primero, y luego, un desplazamiento de la prioridad del sector material que la novela del mundonovismo concedió sin reservas, por una afirmación de la voluntad de crear un mundo ficticio absuelto de toda motivación en alguna realidad concreta y presunta, ajeno a la realidad histórica inmediata, incluso desprendida de la causalidad mecánica de ese mundo tal como lo habían concebido los naturalistas. Al mismo tiempo fue su ambición configurar un mundo cerrado y concluso en sí mismo, sometido a una legalidad propia y animado sin vasallaje por ninguno de los prejuicios de la generación anterior.[43]

To this "system of preferences" may be added another series of shaping forces which set the tone of the times and which functioned significantly in the intellectual and aesthetic formation of the surrealist generation. They are what another critic regards as "main

---

de planos y la búsqueda de la simultaneidad . . . la redistribución libre—*découpage*, montaje—de planos y tiempos en una secuencia insólita . . . la desrealización del mundo y de los personajes, etc." Among foreign influences, the Chilean critic highlights Proust, Dostoevski, Joyce, Virginia Woolf, Dos Passos, Faulkner, Hemingway, Gide, Aldous Huxley, Thomas Mann, Gorki, and Knut Hansum (*ibid.*, pp. 38–39).

[43] *Ibid.*, pp. 39–40.

intellectual trends of the nineteen-twenties": the interest in Freudian psychology, the subconscious, mental disorders such as *desdo-
blamiento* (splitting of the self), and the multiplicity of the
personality; attention to dreams, the marvelous, and a world above
reality; innovations made by individual writers like Rilke, Proust,
and Pirandello, and the theory and practice of the leading expo-
nents of the contemporary vanguard movements; the problem of art
and illusion versus life and reality; and the narcissistic exposing of
the inner working of art or the theatricality of the theater.[44]

It is helpful to remember, at this point, that surrealism emerged
as a well-defined artistic movement in the post–World War I period
and reached its fullest development in the 1920's and 1930's. Into
surrealism flowed many of the attitudes, aesthetic preoccupations,
Weltanschauungen, expressive techniques, and so on, of several
European and South American vanguard movements such as futurism, expressionism, cubism, dadaism, *ultraísmo, creacionismo*,
and others which already were gathering momentum before and
during World War I. Consequently, there is a certain similarity of
"strangeness" and fantasy, an almost indefinable and often undis-
tinguishable "family air," in many of the stylistic devices and much
of the imagery and general literary language of these movements
and schools of the period. As Robert Lott has cautioned, there is a
"faulty understanding of the true nature of these and other vanguard movements, especially in their individual techniques, devices,
and style features. These cannot always be considered typical of
any one movement, since some are common to several. In view of
the present state of critical confusion and a lamentable lack
of thorough studies of the literary 'isms' and of well-documented
analyses of individual works, writers, and groups of writers, these
terms should be used with extreme caution."[45] For lack of a more
sharply defined classification, then, Goić's employment of the term
surrealism (or simply *vanguardism*?) to designate Jenaro Prieto's
generation is perhaps the more useful precisely because of that
label's implicit inclusion of certain features of the other "isms."

Except for scant attention accorded him in general histories of

---

44 Robert E. Lott, "Azorín's Experimental Period and Surrealism," *PMLA*, 79
45 *Ibid.*, 320.
(1964), 306.

literature and in histories of the Spanish American novel and of
the Chilean novel, Jenaro Prieto is a writer whose work has been
almost totally neglected. Assiduous bibliographical research has
confirmed preliminary impressions concerning this lamentable
oversight of an important precursor of contemporary novelistic
tendencies. A simple indication of the widespread lack of knowledge
about the man and his writings is the confusion one encounters between the indiscriminate spelling of his first name with both *J* and
G; also indicative is the fact that prominent literary critics and historians ascribe three different dates of publication to *El socio*, none
of which are correct![46]

Obviously, Prieto's limited production of narrative fiction is the
main reason for this dearth of critical attention. Nevertheless, other
more recognized Chilean novelists, contemporaries of Prieto such
as Pedro Prado (1886–1952) and Eduardo Barrios (1884–1963) and
a younger authoress, María Luisa Bombal (1910–), were similarly
unprolific. Prado's fame rests mainly on two works (*Alsino*, 1920,
and *Un juez rural*, 1924) as does Bombal's (*La última niebla*, 1935,
and *La amortajada*, 1938); Barrios published a half-dozen good
novels in his long career but is remembered primarily for *El hermano asno* (1922).[47] On the other hand, Prieto's (and others') novelistic frugality is an anomaly and a virtue in Spanish America, where
obras completas editions frequently consist of several volumes.
Viewed even more positively, that frugality also suggests artists with
a *voluntad de estilo*, writers desirous of turning out finely wrought,
highly polished pieces of narrative prose.

Prieto's lifelong and time-consuming journalistic activity has

----

[46] Luis Alberto Sánchez, *Proceso y contenido de la novela hispanoamericana* (Madrid, 1953), p. 585 (the Peruvian critic, unsure of the year 1926, follows it with a
question mark); Enrique Anderson Imbert, *Historia de la literatura hispanoamericana*, 2d ed., rev. and enl. (Mexico City, 1957), p. 354 (the eminent Argentine critic
fixes the year of publication of *El socio* as 1920); Fernando Alegría, in both *Historia
de la novela hispanoamericana*, 3d ed. (Mexico City, 1966), p. 198, and *Literatura
chilena del siglo XX*, p. 68, suggests 1929; the American literary historians Englekirk,
Leonard, Reid and Crow, in their much used manual *An Outline History of Spanish
American Literature*, 3d ed. (New York, 1965), p. 172, list the same year as Alegría.

[47] There are other famous names accorded much attention in the history and
criticism of the Spanish American novel whose reputations rest upon only one major
work. Indeed, the phenomenon of "the one-novel genius" is a curious one in the literature of that region. Without intending to imply any comparative value judgments
whatsoever, one recalls, for example, José Mármol (*Amalia*), Jorge Isaacs (*María*),
José Eustasio Rivera (*La vorágine*), and Juan Rulfo (*Pedro Páramo*).

previously been advanced as the main reason for his failure to write more fiction. However, even in this regard the author would appear to have been typical of the surrealist generation, as Cedomil Goić asserts: "Para novelar el sector material de las luchas políticas y sociales que vivió esta generación, la forma novelística recibida se mostró al parecer insuficiente y el tratamiento de aquellos asuntos desembocó de ordinario en el *reportaje*—ninguna generación ha escrito tantos como ésta. . . ."[48] Like many intellectuals of his generation, Prieto channeled most of his ideas and feelings into newspaper and magazine articles, but his craft of fiction improved in each novel; his mastery of narrative art clearly shows change and development with each successive fictitious work. One can only speculate, unfortunately, upon how many more and what kind of novels the author would have created had he lived longer.

Prieto and the Vanguardists

Critics and scholars discern a kind of "synchronization" of Spanish American and European poetry beginning in the 1920's. Exactly how innovative trends in poetic expression, introduced through the influence of vanguard poets such as Borges and Vicente Huidobro, filtered into prose fiction remains slightly mysterious. Transferal of stylistic techniques from poetry to prose only partially explains the phenomenon. Historians and critics of the novel obsessively chant the litany of names of important European and North American novelists known and read by Spanish American writers. But these reiterations usually remain vague when it comes to answering more specific questions concerning the penetration of such influences. Several facts supply tentative answers only. The first is the widespread reading, in the original languages, of foreign books, newspapers, and literary magazines in the principal cultural centers of Spanish America. A second important consideration is the matter of translations, of which a thorough study is sorely needed. By way of example, Borges' translation of Molly Bloom's reverie in *Ulysses* (1922) a year or two after the novel's appearance provides an obvious but helpful link. Indirect acquaintance with European and North American prose writers was also made avail-

48 "La novela chilena actual," p. 39.

able throughout the continent in Spanish versions published in numerous "little magazines" and literary journals.

In Chile, such access to foreign novelistic currents was provided by the periodicals *Letras, Índice,* and others which, according to Goić, "*agrupaban lo más granado de la nueva generación* [y] *divulgaban en sus páginas los valores más significativos de la literatura extranjera*—europea, norteamericana e hispanoamericana—y paralelamente animaban con vivacidad—encuestas, polémicas, entrevistas —la hasta entonces quieta vida literaria nacional. . . ." It must be remembered, at this point, that the article by the eminent Chilean authority cited here is a study of the *novel* in Chile. The critic's ensuing statement will, therefore, furnish some notion of the magnitude and scale of the enterprise those magazines undertook to disseminate foreign prose fiction: "*Todas las literaturas, todos los ismos fueron atentamente considerados, leídos y practicados* por la nueva generación." [49]

It is, I believe, reasonable to speculate that Jenaro Prieto, as a cultured and widely read intellectual, was probably a frequent peruser of the pages of such magazines. At least there is clear evidence to support the author's acquaintance with one major figure of European fiction. A Prieto article titled "Una víctima de Proust" [50] and bearing the early date July, 1929, while evincing a playfully negative attitude toward the creator of *À la recherche du temps perdu* (1913–27) also firmly establishes the Chilean writer's familiarity with major trends in European fiction and reveals a profound awareness of the principal merits and shortcomings of Proust's masterpiece. Despite his satirical and at times severe analysis of the work of the French writer, Prieto demonstrates a perceptive, fellow-novelist's grasp of the main Proustian narrative techniques and stylistic elements: rendition of free, associative thought processes; interest in psychological, subjective time; lengthy dialogues concerning apparently trivial subjects; and minutely detailed, poetic descriptions. Interestingly enough, one finds in Prieto's *La casa vieja* a similar lyricism of the commonplace, a nostalgic, Proustian evocation of bygone days and things, and a similar use of mental associations based on sensorial impressions. The author of *El socio*

---

[49] *Ibid.,* p. 38. Italics mine.
[50] In *Con sordina,* pp. 93–101.

deplored what he considered the agonizingly protracted plot development, the lengthy, convoluted syntax, and the excessive attention to detail of the French master. Yet while Prieto faults the
French artist's lack of selectivity and synthesis, he clearly apprehends
the ultimate aesthetic effect sought by Proust: "Este resbalar constante por una pendiente interminable, acaba por producir en el
ánimo la impresión de que, en vez de adelantar, se retrocede . . .
cuanto más se lee, tanto más se acerca al principio." Notwithstanding his general aversion to Proust's style, the Chilean confesses finally that "en las últimas treinta páginas ya notaba con rubor que, de
cuando a cuando, el libro comenzaba a cogerme."

In terms of narrative structure only (considered as organization,
disposition and interrelationship of elements), the full impact of
the foreign influences that are frequently alluded to only *began* to
be felt in the Spanish American novel of the late 1930's and 1940's.
Exemplary are such "transitional" works or "precursors" of the
new Spanish American novel as Onetti's *El pozo* (1939), Mallea's
Todo verdor perecerá (1941), Asturias' *El señor presidente* (1946),
Yáñez's *Al filo del agua* (1947), and Sábato's *El túnel* (1948). The
more radical changes in form and design (shifting point of view,
fragmented temporal sequence, the use of myth, and the like) usually associated with the *nueva novela* and with its European and North
American models would appear primarily in the two decades after
mid-century. As Goić affirms: "Ninguna de nuestras novelas llegó
al extremo del sin sentido o de la anarquía estructural a que llegaron
los novelistas europeos o norteamericanos en ciertos casos."[51]

Not surprisingly, then, the novelistic contributions of Prieto's
surrealist or vanguard generation were principally in the areas of
style (considered as personal use of language) and the probing of
new zones of human experience. This exploration of unknown
territories pushed the frontiers of fiction very near those of poetry
because of the lyrical, imaginative language needed and employed
to convey the image and profile of those uncharted regions: "Si
ocasionalmente encontramos algunos psicogramas—monólogos in-
teriores de la corriente pura del inconsciente o de la corriente inor-
ganizada de la conciencia—éstos no fueron nunca sentidos
propiamente como narraciones o novelas, sino que guardaron el

[51] "La novela chilena actual," p. 40.

margen de la lírica."[52] This intensified *voluntad de estilo,* this care
for the dignity of language, and the presentation of unusual themes
and dimensions of human experience created a *novela de minorías:*
"La extrema interiorización de la substancia narrativa, en una perspectiva sostenida o cambiante; la audacia de las situaciones escogidas; la dignidad del lenguaje; la categoría intelectual y la
sensibilidad finas y elevadas; junto a la fantasía onírica y al simbolismo de variado cuño y a los rasgos exteriores de la construcción
narrativa; hicieron de la novela de esta generación, en buena
medida, un género exclusivo que la masa recién incorporada, que
acrecentaba el número de lectores considerablemente, rehuyó."[53]

Therefore, Jenaro Prieto must be considered an early innovator
not because of any radical structural advances in his narrative art
but because of his themes and, even more, his style. As we shall see,
the unique style of the artist's major work, *El socio,* is closely unified
to its striking theme; indeed, it is an outgrowth of that theme. A
"creative" theme (the creation of an imaginary, autonomous character by a fictitious personage) of necessity requires an imaginative
and creative language to express it most appropriately. Jenaro's
style fits Goić's description of the surrealist generation's attitude
and approach to the artistic idiom: "El superrealismo rechazó el
lenguaje pintoresco y caracterizador que se recogía con afán de
realismo y autenticidad. La nueva autenticidad tenía una dimensión
estrictamente artística y literaria, aquella que brotaba de la co-
herencia interna de la obra, de la entereza intrínseca de su estructura."[54]

That the author of *El socio* was keenly aware of stylistic trends
in the vanguard literature of his times is amply demonstrable in
articles he published over a number of years in *El Diario Ilustrado,*
some of which have been anthologized in *Con sordina* and *Humo
de pipa.*[55] Prieto thereby took an active part (although a rather con-

---

52 *Ibid.*
53 *Ibid.*
54 *Ibid.*
55 See especially, in *Con sordina,* "Un visitante curioso" (probably written around
1927), pp. 27–29, and "¿Seré poeta?" (2 February 1927), pp. 79–83. In *Humo de pipa*
see "Poesía de vanguardia" (30 November 1935), pp. 188–91; "Carta Vanguardista"
(4 December 1935), pp. 192–95; "¡Vengan poetas!" (31 October 1943), pp. 251–54;
"Corazón requisado" (March 1944), pp. 255–56; "Un candidato que aúlla" (12 February 1945), pp. 257–59; "Proclama lírica" (25 February 1945), pp. 260–62; and "Oda

servative position) in the debates which raged over vanguard poetry. In "¿Seré poeta?" he gently pokes fun at the style of Gabriela Mistral, the Chilean poetess and first Latin American winner of the Nobel Prize for Literature (1945). However, it is also apparent to the more discerning reader of the piece that Jenaro admired his countrywoman's work and, further, that he perceived both the new vanguardist emphasis on the daring and startling metaphor and the poetic technique of "la enumeración caótica." His article, "Un visitante curioso," a masterful and hilarious parody of vanguardist metaphorical usage, also explicitly reveals Prieto's awareness of the contemporary poets' search for enrichment and renovation of the lyrical lexicon.

Prieto generally took a very dim view, however, of some of the extreme tendencies he discerned in the writings of three other prestigious fellow countrymen—Vicente Huidobro, Pablo de Rokha, and especially Pablo Neruda. In "¡Vengan poetas!" Prieto, in verse, summons the national bards to place their pens at the service of uncovering political corruption and civic abuses of the Popular Front government (one is tempted to suspect that Jenaro disapproved more of Neruda's leftist politics than of his poetry!):

> Rimad sin palabras,
> pensad sin ideas
> pero, sobre todo,
> cantad la hermosura de las cosas feas. . . .

Aside from their obvious satirical intent, these lines clearly point to Prieto's cognizance (and implicit censure) of three well-known features of vanguardist poetic expression: (1) rejection of all former literary conventions such as rhyme; (2) what one might term the movement's "aesthetics of the ugly"; and (3) the intentional cultivation of the irrational.

In the same article Prieto suggests that Neruda and Rokha utilize

Boli-Nerudiana" (n.d.), pp. 263–64. Original dates of publication of articles in *El Diario Ilustrado* appear in parentheses after the titles; page numbers refer to pagination of *Con sordina* and *Humo de pipa*. Other relevant articles from *El Diario Ilustrado* which are not anthologized include "Música de vanguardia" (5 May 1929), "Plaga de poetas" (22 December 1929), "Divagaciones sobre el vanguardismo" (8 January 1930), "Poesía y aviación" (29 October 1934), "Con ojos de poeta" (6 February 1937), "Ofensiva lírica" (8 April 1937), "Poesía geográfica" (25 December 1937), and "Lírica electoral" (27 January 1945).

their inspiration in denouncing the lamentable state of public transportation in Santiago under the government of the Frente Popular: "¡Cuánta emoción podría poner el cantor de Stalingrado [Neruda] en esa obscura angustia urbana del tranvía en retardo!" Jenaro writes:

> Arbol inquieto, esquina viva
> florecida de esperas,
> masco la ausencia azul de tu venida
> con oídos de bruma y pies de quejas.

Beneath the surface humor lies Prieto's technical mastery of Neruda's expressive devices. (It should be emphasized that Jenaro Prieto did not compose beautiful poetry; he was a genius of humor, parody, and mimicry, not a poet.) The following techniques are shown in the above verses: (1) the attribution to one object of a quality or characteristic usually associated with another (the corner, not the tree, is seen as blooming, "*florecida*"; the corner, not the people standing there, is alive; the absence, not the trolley, is blue); (2) the attribution of abstract qualities to a concrete object or vice versa (the corner is alive with "waiting," and the abstraction "absence" is seen as blue); and (3) the complicated, triple synesthesia involving the senses of taste ("*masco*"), sight ("*azul*"), and hearing ("*oídos*").

Prieto's grasp of the "mechanical" principles of vanguardist stylistics becomes more apparent in another article, "Poesía de vanguardia" (November 30, 1935), characterized, to be sure, by the author's customary wit and satire. However, in the midst of his good-natured mockery of the difficulty of comprehending both vanguardist poetry and the even more abstruse theoretical explanations of it by Volodia Teitelboim, the author becomes momentarily serious as he declares: "Sin embargo, si se mira con más calma y, del principio abstracto, se desciende a lo que podríamos llamar 'la mecánica' de la poesía vanguardista, se ve que ella es relativamente sencilla." Although the following random selection of the writer's ensuing remarks are here presented out of context, were overly simplified in the first place, and were humorous in intent, they do reveal clearly that Prieto was well in control of the "inner workings" and certain of the broader aesthetic implications and theory behind vanguardism: "La nueva jerigonza, exige solamente, junto con el olvido total de la gramática y de la lógica más elemental, la adopción del adjetivo que menos corresponde al sujeto. . . . El lector quedará en plena libertad para imaginar lo que quiera. . . . El poema tiene una enorme fuerza descriptiva. . . . La poesía debe ponerla el lector y no el poeta. . . . Hasta hace algunos años, cuando sólo se trataba de buscar nuevas metáforas, el rompecabezas era soportable . . . pero ahora el sutil hilo de Ariadna se ha cortado. . . . No le basta, sin embargo, a los vanguardistas en su afán de oscuridad, con prescindir de la razón y adjetivar a la ventura. . . . Han descubierto el trastrueque de los cinco sentidos. . . . Se agrega una ausencia completa de sentido común. . . ."

On December 4, 1935, four days after the publication of "Poesía de vanguardia," one of Prieto's most ingenious pieces, entitled "Carta Vanguardista," appeared in his column in *El Diario Ilustrado*. In it Jenaro assumes the guise of an irate reader named Onías Pérez P.-Lota. Señor "Pelota"(!), an aesthete who is spiritually in harmony with vanguardist lyrics, takes violent exception to the offenses which the editor launched against that literature in his previous article. He informs Prieto that a panegyrist, one "Cecilio Melgar," who is, according to Onías Pérez P.-Lota, "una de las cimeras más prolíficas; de la núbil estética," has composed an "Ofertorio Lírico a Pablo Neruda." (Note the indiscriminate use of the semicolon in burlesque imitation of the vanguardist's defiance of standard punctuation.) The writer of the letter demands that Prieto publish Melgar's eulogy of the great Chilean poet in atonement for the wrongs and insults he had heaped upon Neruda in "Poesía de vanguardia." Needless to say, the "Ofertorio Lírico," like the letter to the editor, was penned by Prieto, who took special delight in parodying the style of Neruda. He thereby demonstrated, with good humor, that he could mimic, with a high degree of success, the daring, innovative imagery, figures of speech, surrealistic inspiration and vision, meter, tone, diction, rhythm, and phrasing of the language of the *ismos*. It would be difficult to find a better example of this talented, almost uncanny ability of the Chilean humorist.[56]

---

[56] González asserts that the "Ofertorio Lírico" was supposedly published previously in the imaginary (?) magazine, *ASTEROIDE*. He adds that Prieto's travesty was so successful that a group of real Central American admirers and imitators of the recent Chilean Nobel Laureate (Neruda) later picked up the poem by Melgar, Prieto's imaginary, fervent disciple of the bard of universal disintegration, took both poet

Shortly after Prieto's death a Colombian journal published a two-part article consisting of a necrology on the author with an accompanying study titled "Genaro Prieto y los Vanguardistas."[57] The necrology provides some valuable biographical information; the essay, however, reveals its author's somewhat distorted understanding of Prieto's literary contacts with the vanguard movements and a complete unawareness of the degree to which his style was influenced by them. One tends to suspect that Ballesteros used this occasion to vent his own intolerance of those innovative tendencies and simply attributed similar attitudes to the then recently deceased Chilean novelist. Ballesteros alleges, with tedious, flowery rhetoric, that Prieto found it difficult to sympathize with vanguard tendencies because of his "humanistic and classical literary formation." By implication, of course, the author of *El socio* would never have condescended to the use of such techniques. The notions presented are worth quoting, since they reveal a basic unfamiliarity with the real nature of Prieto's prose style:

> La actitud del humorista chileno ante la moderna poesía vanguardista, fue lógica; debía ser tal como fue ni más ni menos. Se sonreía él de esa frenética vanguardia que camina bizarramente a la conquista del misterio y no posee armas ni elementos de conquista. . . .
>
> La formación literaria de Prieto había sido totalmente diferente; era humanista y clásica. Había leído a los maestros bajo la tutela grávida de sus profesores que le habían señalado las bellezas, y se había entusiasmado con los románticos, como toda su generación, analizando a los que armonizaban con su espíritu volandero y soñador, en armonía con esos intangibles y simpáticos bohemios como Bécquer, Zorrilla y Espronceda y hasta había sentido fervor por Rubén, el innovador genial, que había pasado por los cursos clásicos como un rebelde, digno del anatema de los viejos maestros retóricos. . . .

---

and poem to be authentic, and published the work in a "revista tropical . . . sin comentarios en la página de honor"! According to González, Neruda apparently did not appreciate the humorous imitation. He answered Prieto "en forma airada, virulenta y hasta grosera con un soneto a base de puras letras 'pees' [the letter *P*, with which Prieto customarily signed his articles], que circuló en forma anónima y fue conocido de pocos" ("P. El humorista," p. 81).

[57] Julián de Ballesteros, "Desde Chile: Jenaro Prieto (1889–1946)," *Revista Javeriana* (Bogotá), 26 (1946), 176–83, and "Letras Chilenas: —II—Genaro [*sic*] Prieto y los Vanguardistas," *ibid.*, 197–205.

Fígaro [Larra] y el inmortal Cervantes le enseñaron la medula del idioma y le dieron la nota de sus composiciones, de su estilo, de la misma actitud, más bien optimista y bonachona que acibarada por el rencor.[58]

At this point Ballesteros hedges slightly, but then establishes what he sees as Prieto's fundamental lack of understanding of the *nuevas promociones*: "Los poetas de la vanguardia le producían un sentimiento de simpatía y curiosidad; los consideraba en un plano totalmente diferente del suyo, y puede decirse, opuesto a las inquietudes y ansias e ideales de los contemporáneos, era para él como si hubiera bajado de la luna un grupo de intelectuales y lanzaran al aire sus acentos extraños y pronunciaran palabras en otro idioma y desplegaran una sensibilidad tan distinta, en que apenas se vislumbrara el significado de los conceptos."[59]

The worst feature of the study, however, is the author's maudlin appeal to religion and Christian sanity, which would impede a writer's understanding and absorbing anything other than "classical" literary influences. Again, speaking of the vanguardists, Ballesteros maintains:

> Porque estos vates ilustres son materialistas hasta la última fibra: para ellos la soberana, la madre, *la generadora* es la materia, impalpable, ilimitada, profunda, que sin contrapeso alguno domina.
>
> El Señor de lo creado, su reino del espíritu, la *siquis* no cuentan para nada. Son por tanto fatalistas, empujados por un ciego torbellino, y ellos se arrastran por los bajos fondos y se sumergen en lo arcano del mundo: son como pulpos enceguecidos que van palpando con sus antenas hipersensibles otros cuerpos y sienten otras sensaciones inefables, que nosotros no podemos percibir.
>
> ¿Cómo podrá comprenderlos entonces esta generación actual que vive apegada a la tierra y cree en Dios y levanta la frente para buscarlo con la mirada y adorarlo y contemplar siquiera la huella de su paso?
>
> ¿Cómo podrá entenderse con ellos, esta misma generación que recibió un idioma espiritualizado que, aunque muy rico y muy hondo, no está formado para disquisiciones extrañas, idioma que posee a su haber tesoros de obras áureas y viene sirviendo para

[58] *Ibid.*, 197.
[59] *Ibid.*

que expresen su íntimo sentir gente serena y normal que vive su
vida sobre este planeta?

    La poesía debe ser un índice de la cultura, del ideal, de las in-
quietudes de una época y ¿cómo podrán tener la misma poesía, y
los mismos ideales, y las mismas inquietudes estas generaciones
actuales, desorientadas, materialistas, de un irritante sensualismo?[60]

There is no reason to doubt Prieto's probable classical, humanistic literary formation, nor need one deny that he repeatedly poked
fun at the style of the vanguard poets. What is objectionable, however, is Ballesteros' implication that the Chilean artist totally rejected innovative stylistic techniques. That the author of *El socio*
represents a clear manifestation of what we have termed at the
outset "change within the traditional" is reflected in a curious paradox: while Prieto was ridiculing and parodying the vanguardist
style, he was, perhaps unconsciously or intuitively, incorporating
features of that very style into his own artistic idiom. My main contention in opposition to Ballesteros' thesis is that Prieto clearly had
assimilated, probably between 1926 and 1928, some of the very
techniques which this critic insinuates would be beneath the dignity
of the Chilean author's supposedly lofty, purist, "classical" prose
style. A scrutiny of the language of Prieto's main work of narrative
fiction bears out this assertion.

The Imaginative Prose Style of *El socio*

Jenaro Prieto's works possess multiple literary values. Commentators stress his subtle sense of humor, his capacity for gentle satire
and irony, his modern themes, and the penetrating observations of
Chilean life evidenced in his journalistic publications. More significantly, while writing in a period dominated by *criollismo*, Prieto
constructed, in both of his completed novels, imaginative, indeed
fantastic plots which anticipated the magical realism and *literatura
fantástica* so widely cultivated and esteemed in the two or three
decades which followed. *Un muerto de mal criterio*, while not as
stylistically innovative as the artist's major work, employs the mod-

60 *Ibid.*, 199.

ern device of an apparently dead narrator; the novel's oneiric framework, revealed only in the denouement, further attests to the
author's awareness of the surrealist interest in dreams. In his best
and most well known novel, *El socio*, often compared to the writings
of Pirandello and Unamuno's *Niebla*, the artist deftly experiments
with "interior duplication" in the provocative theme of the autonomous character invented by a literary personage and with the
problem of art and illusion versus life and reality. The posthumously published *La casa vieja*, Prieto's last novelistic effort, harks
back nostalgically, in its style, to the prose poem of impressionism
and *modernismo* yet anticipates the personal intimacy and even a
slight bit of the loneliness and existentialist anguish which began
to find their way into the Spanish American novel of the late 1930's
and 1940's. In short, Prieto contributed in no small way to the
laying of the foundation and to the maturation of the contemporary
Chilean novel.

To the literary merits enumerated above may be added what is
probably the most outstanding and yet the most overlooked aesthetic value of the artist's major work—its highly imaginative and expressive language. Representative examples from the text and their
analysis will demonstrate the point that the narrative and descriptive techniques used in Prieto's masterpiece bear the unmistakable
stamp of the most current vanguard tendencies; every page of *El
socio* belies the allegation that vanguardist literature and the language of the *ismos* were alien to its author's artistic sensibility. In
the following pages, while we will mention some of the movements
in vogue in the post–World War I period, only incidentally is it
our purpose to isolate or "label" the "progenitor" (that is, the specific vanguard school or movement) or given traits of Jenaro Prieto's
style. Rather, our intention is to prove not only that the Chilean
artist understood, ridiculed, and parodied vanguardist stylistic devices, but also that he employed them consciously, creatively, and
seriously in the composition of his best work of fiction.

Excerpts chosen from various stages of the novelistic protagonist's
career and adventures consistently reveal one of the distinctive
stylistic features of literary expressionism: [61] the "objectification of

[61] Cedomil Goić establishes the presence of expressionism in Chile by including it

strong, subjective feelings."[62] The following passages manifestly attest to the writer's employment of intensely projected expression-istic imagery, which customarily externalizes a character's inner emotions and attitudes. The first three passages are taken from the moment of Julián Pardo's greatest financial and amatory triumphs. A new house, an expensive new car, and a beautiful mistress (the wife of his archrival on the stock exchange) become the outward symbols of the protagonist's newly found success. In these three images of possession, highly elaborated by the artistic vision of the writer, is externalized the feeling of euphoria felt by the fictitious personage. The first passage, which describes the new home and garden, features extensive personification and animation, devices not exclusively expressionistic in themselves but which become so when employed as frequently and as systematically as they are in

---

among the tendencies, movements, and *ismos* whose influences were brought to bear upon his surrealist Chilean generation: "Por último, *el mundo simbólico e intensa-mente proyectado de Franz Kafka y del expresionismo alemán*, y el sensualismo de D. H. Lawrence, hicieron proliferar una gama variada de manifestaciones inéditas en la nueva novela" ("La novela chilena actual," p. 39; italics mine). Enrique Anderson Imbert was probably the first to see *El socio* as an expressionistic novel: "Porque el propósito de *esta novela expresionista* es objetivar los absurdos de la imaginación (y de paso satirizar la sociedad)" (*Historia de la literatura hispanoamericana*, p. 354; italics mine). The most recent historian of the Spanish American novel has reaffirmed Anderson Imbert's earlier classification of *El socio* by referring to it as "an expres-sionistic and somewhat modernist novel . . . a kind of Chilean *Picture of Dorian Grey*" (Kessel Schwartz, *A New History of Spanish American Fiction*, vol. I [Coral Gables: University of Miami Press, 1972], p. 242).

62 See Lott, "Azorín's Experimental Period," 305. Other useful studies of literary expressionism include Ilse M. de Brugger, *El expresionismo* (Buenos Aires, 1968); Sheldon Cheney, *Expressionism in Art* (New York, 1934), especially pp. 29–43, 69–95, 373–74, 409–11; Walter Falk, *Impresionismo y expresionismo: Dolor y transformación en Rilke, Kafka y Trakl*, trans. Mario Bueno Heimerle (Madrid, 1963), especially pp. 17–35, 507–12, 529–34; and Rodolfo Enrique Modern, *El expresionismo literario* (Buenos Aires, 1958). The critical bibliography on the literary "isms" is, of course, very extensive. Two helpful works on surrealism, among others consulted in the preparation of this essay, are "Aspects of Surrealism (A Symposium)," *Books Abroad*, 43, no. 2 (Spring 1969), 165–93; and Guillermo de Torre, *¿Qué es el superrealismo?* (Buenos Aires, 1955). On impressionism, see especially Amado Alonso, et al., *El im-presionismo en el lenguaje* (Buenos Aires, 1936). Other excellent general works which include sections on the vanguard period and the *ismos* are: Richard Ellmann and Charles Feidelson, Jr., eds., *The Modern Tradition: Backgrounds of Modern Litera-ture* (New York, 1965); John Oliver Perry, ed., *Backgrounds to Modern Literature* (San Francisco, 1968); Renato Poggioli, *Teoria dell' arte d'avanguardia* (Bologna, 1962, Spanish and English translations available); Guillermo de Torre, *Historia de las literaturas de vanguardia* (Madrid, 1965); and Eugen Weber, ed., *Paths to the Present: Aspects of European Thought from Romanticism to Extistentialism* (New York, 1964), especially pp. 209–79.

El socio. Prosopopoeia becomes here a question of emphasis; it is one of Prieto's most consistent stylistic techniques for transforming and deforming reality:

> ¡Qué alegre era la nueva casa! ¡Un "cottage" del más puro estilo inglés, con sus ventanas azules que se abrían con el ingenuo asombro de unos ojos de "miss" bajo las revueltas crenchas de las enredaderas!
>
> —¡Hija de Davis al fin! —pensó Julián—, ¡ha heredado los ojos de su padre! . . .
>
> Había sol, mucho sol en el jardín. Los rayos, al filtrarse entre las hojas, dibujaban en el suelo una infinidad de discos áureos como monedas esterlinas. Oro, mucho oro. No parecía sino que el propio Davis, trepado como un mono en lo más alto del follaje, se divirtiera en lanzar libras y más libras a las plantas de su socio.[63]

The use of Anglicisms, "cottage" and "miss," is a technique used progressively more frequently throughout the work to suggest the growing reality of the imaginary, created English "partner" of the novel's title. The golden spots of sunlight on the ground seen as pounds sterling appropriately reinforce this suggestiveness, while the slightly uncanny image of the Englishman in the tree, deformed by the simile equating him with a monkey, contributes to the atmosphere of eeriness and unreality which pervades much of the story.

A second example demonstrates well the aggressive creativeness and dynamism of the expressionistic approach, which not only receives and registers sensory stimuli, as in impressionism, but projects them back completely transformed into a startlingly new and imaginative reality. The novelist, like a boxer, returns "blow for blow" the impact of reality on his sensitive retina; the artist's reworked, reconstructed vision literally superimposes itself on reality. The reader still perceives the reality depicted, but it often seems strangely out of focus to him. In the following passage, the protagonist, at the height of his good fortune and feeling very self-satisfied, leaves his home and drives to the stock exchange in his new Cadillac touring car. The imagery again bespeaks and projects the character's emotions:

---

63 Jenaro Prieto, *El socio,* 4th ed. (Buenos Aires: Espasa-Calpe, 1961), pp. 73–74. Hereafter, references to this edition of Prieto's masterpiece are incorporated into the text.

Satisfecho, jugando con el diario que traía precisamente la noticia de la salida del nuevo título aurífero al mercado, fué a tomar el automóvil. Un magnífico Cadillac de turismo que asomaba sus ojos de langosta bajo las enredaderas del garage.

¡Qué agradable la mañana fresca y risueña que se estrellaba en el parabrisas y parecía inundarle los pulmones!

En las esquinas, los chalets se volvían a mirarlo.

Las ruedas semejaban ir enrollando en sus ejes la blanca cinta del camino, y a ambos lados, los árboles, cabezudos y grotescos, con aires de burgués recién salido de la peluquería, parecían alejarse secreteándose: "Ahí va don Julián." "Ahí va don Julián Pardo." [P. 78]

But other forces besides expressionism are at work in the preceding excerpt. One of the hallmarks of vanguard literature which derives from Italian futurism, originated by Filippo Tommaso Marinetti (1876–1944) around 1910, is the use of "contemporary" images. The futurist writers were men who delighted in the modern age and its technological products, especially its streamlined machines and their speed. The whole apparatus of the twentieth century's capitalistic, mechanized, and industrialized civilization, and its new artistic forms as well—automobiles, airplanes, engines of war, the telephone, the stock exchange, radio, movies, jazz, and so on—were sources of inspiration in which the futurists reveled. Prieto, a writer who knew Italy, her language, and her literature,[64] bedecks his entire novel with precisely this type of "contemporary trappings." We have singled out the image of the car, but most of the others enumerated above are also present in the work.

Noteworthy here is the evident pleasure taken in the description of the automobile, revealed in the adjective *magnífico*; further attention is focused upon details of the luxurious machine: its shiny headlights ("ojos de langosta"), the windshield, which receives joyously the impact of the fresh, clear morning, the wheels, and the axle. The sensation of speed, distance covered, and mechanical efficiency is conveyed through the vivid, futuristic image of the painted line on the road being rolled up on the axle, much as a

[64] See, for example, his article titled "Algo sobre Pirandello," which appeared the year the author of *Sei personaggi* won the Nobel Prize for Literature, in *El Diario Ilustrado*, 27 November 1934. Also published in *Italia Nuova*, November 1934, 10–12.

typewriter's ribbon is wound onto its reel. This impression of velocity is intensified by the highly elaborated personification of the trees (humorously depicted as large-headed, naïve bourgeois types emerging, closely cropped, from the barbershop) seen swiftly receding into the distance with scarcely enough time to whisper: "There goes Don Julián." These futuristic images are intensified by the more expressionistic device of intense animatism,[65] which also abounds in the above passage and in the work in general (for example, "ojos de langosta," which implies a perceiving creature; "mañana *risueña*"; gawking chalets; and gossiping trees).

A new note, the exotic, oriental, and the decadent, is struck in the description of the love nest where Julián clandestinely meets his mistress, Anita. Persian rugs, a softly-cushioned divan, an ottoman, a statue of a paunchy Buddha, a Chinese lamp, and the final touch, a narghile (a hookah or Eastern tobacco pipe, in which the smoke is filtered through water), make up the furnishings and accouterments of the apartment. Such typically *modernista* trappings continued to delight the fancies of the vanguard generation. The novelist describes the narghile with characteristic personification: "Parecía un pequeño jarrón despanzurrado que alargara el cuello con horror para no ver sus propios intestinos. Hasta esa boquilla negra y larga en que terminaba la sonda de caucho era de un prosaísmo insoportable. Un irrigador pensativo. Eso era aquello" (p. 71). Upon her arrival, his mistress kisses Julián, and all of his passion is objectified in a kinetic presentation of the objects previously enumerated. Most noteworthy, however, is the presence of the word *cubista* in the following description. As a painter, Prieto was intensely aware of currents in contemporary art and found it easy to create the verbal *equivalents* (not *parallels*) for the techniques of his other artistic medium. He deftly creates a cubistic vision of reality, the elements of which are intensely altered and rearranged in the consciousness of the protagonist and then projected forth: "La lámpara chinesca, los cojines, el narguilé bailaron una danza cubista. Todo el trabajo de arreglo del diván desapareció en pocos instantes y Julián no vió ya sino los ojos entornados de Anita, sus

---

[65] Animatism is a form of personification; it is the attribution of *consciousness* to inanimate objects and natural phenomena.

labios entreabiertos y las alas de su nariz que palpitaban con un latir de corazón" (p. 73). The entire description is, of course, one prolonged metaphor symbolic of the sexual act.

As the main character's financial fortunes begin to decline, his outlook on reality becomes more intensely distorted by feelings of suspicion and panic. The Frankenstein monster he has created in his nonexistent English partner, Mr. Walter Davis, is gradually undermining his sanity. Earlier, the clever Anita had created an equally imaginary character in the person of Madame Duprés, a *modiste*; a sign hung in the window of the apartment where the lovers meet announces a nonexistent dress designer's shop which serves as a front concealing the presence of the love nest. The protagonist, terrified that his Mr. Davis has engendered a son with Anita's Madame Duprés, goes in search of a friend, Luis Alvear, for help. He finds the latter in a typical roaring twenties cabaret, where a dance is in progress:

> Bailaba con una niña a quien Julián no conocía, y durante algunos minutos permaneció de pie, atontado, perdido en el tumulto de notas y colores estridentes. . . . Todo oscilaba, todo se sacudía en torno suyo con movimientos de muñecos de cartón. Piernas, brazos, acordes y actitudes se quebraban en ángulos agudos. Los codos de los bailarines tiranteaban con hilos invisibles la cabeza de los negros del "jazz," imprimiéndoles el mismo bamboleo. Sus rostros se partían horizontalmente en una risa de tajada de melón, o se inflaban en grotescas protuberancias de gaita en la embocadura del saxofón o del clarinete. Los platillos aplaudían a rabiar, entre los alaridos del serrucho y las carcajadas de vieja de las castañuelas.
>
> Era imposible precisar dónde terminaba un color y comenzaba un sonido. . . .
>
> El "jazz-band" volvió a convertirse en una fragua chispeante de notas y colores. Julián sentía que esos relámpagos chillones le atravesaban el cerebro y el estómago, comunicándole una extraña vibración. El negro de la batería, tomándole sin duda por el bombo, parecía golpearle sin piedad los ojos, los oídos, la cabeza. . . . [P. 84]

The above passage is a "melting pot" of various vanguardist literary techniques. The "contemporary," futuristic images of the jazz band and the dance succeed well in capturing the carefree tone of the novel's temporal setting in the 1920's. The composite image of arms, legs, and choreographic postures "broken off at sharp angles" and the black musicians' faces "split horizontally in the laughter of a slice of watermelon" imposes upon the entire scene a certain cubistic quality involving an intellectualization of space, the displacement and rearrangement of visual elements and planes. Prieto's reference to the "movimientos de muñecos de cartón" and the "hilos invisibles" which connect the dancers' elbows to the bobbing heads of the musicians and tug at them, "imprimiéndoles el mismo bamboleo," recalls the surrealists' fascination with puppets, clowns, and the like because of their surprising, unexpected behavior and the comical view of human existence they symbolize (*homo ludens*).

However, it is the expressionistic vision of reality which presides over the passage as a whole. The fictitious character's highly agitated state of mind is projected, expressionistically, in the garish colors, the grotesque, twisted postures of the dancers, and the loud auditory images he perceives. The intense type of personification often associated with expressionistic style is present in the auditory images of the "wildly *applauding* cymbals," the "*howling* bow of the bass fiddle," and the castanets' laughter, which is likened to "the guffaws of an old lady." Julián's general confusion and dazed state of mind are summarized and projected in the synesthetic statement, "Era imposible precisar dónde terminaba un color y comenzaba un sonido."

The second paragraph is an interesting example to illustrate the difference between literary impressionism and expressionism. It begins with a more impressionistic (that is, a more objective, a more faithful) registering of auditory impressions which become tactile: "El 'jazz-band' volvió a convertirse en una fragua chispeante de notas y colores. Julián sentía que esos relámpagos chillones le atravesaban el cerebro y el estómago, comunicándole una extraña vibración."

Then the expressionist in Prieto takes over with the more subjective identification of self and external reality, or better, the projection of the *yo*'s feelings onto reality. Julián's head, eyes, and ears literally become the drums unmercifully pounded by the Negro drummer.

Finally, the phrase "todo oscilaba, todo se sacudía en torno suyo" calls to mind a critic's isolation of another important expressionistic device which frequently recurs in *El socio*: "the correlation between the protagonist's psyche and whirling or enlarged and multiple images." [66] In the above passage, Julián features himself at the center of a swirling vortex of human bodies, sounds, and sights.

As the central character's sanity continues to disintegrate, the whirling, spherical images (round cushions, planets, orbits, eyes, concentric circles, a full moon, and a carrousel) increase in a passage such as the following, in which Julián imagines Davis making love to Madame Duprés. The center of the spiral motion is seen first as Julián's imaginary offspring, Mr. Davis, and then himself as the axis of a gigantic, dizzying merry-go-round:

> Se cubrió los ojos con las manos. Ahora veía patente a Davis, con ademanes de camello, abrazando desaforadamente a la francesa sobre un diván lleno de cojines. . . .
>
> Los almohadones redondos y brillantes volaban por el aire como planetas multicolores, describiendo extrañas órbitas. Se entrecruzaban, parpadeaban, y al entrar en conjunción parecían incorporarse unos en otros como círculos concéntricos. Sólo el cojín de lama de plata de la cabecera permanecía inmóvil, en actitud de luna llena, y se reía con unos dientes largos y amarillos.
>
> La sonrisa de Davis.
>
> Julián se sentía el eje de un inmenso carrousel y se apoyaba en el muro para no caerse. [P. 88]

In addition to the whirling, enlarged, and multiple images of expressionism, one notes here also the shifting, superimposing, and intersecting planes of visual elements usually asociated with cubism.

Expressionism is the art of tortured and twisted forms, of grotesque distortion and deformation. The use of enlarged, spherical, superimposed, and intersecting imagery is intensified now as the protagonist finds himself in danger of losing the immense wealth gained through the creation of his imaginary English *socio*. At the outset of a crucial day's session at the stock exchange pit (significantly called the *rueda* in Spanish), Julián is in a state of mind approaching terror, objectified by a distorted vision of reality in danger of total collapse and disintegration, symbolic, of course, of his tottering

---

[66] Lott, "Azorin's Experimental Period," 305.

mind. The following passages are quoted without comment; significant elements are italicized to call attention to the stylistic features we have been discussing and to the intensity and frequency with which Jenaro Prieto has recourse to them:

> El *timbre eléctrico*, estridente, monótono como un dolor de oídos, anunciaba el comienzo de la *"rueda"*.
>
> Empujó con violencia la mampara, abriéndose paso entre la multitud, se aferró con desesperación a la *baranda* que *circundaba* el recinto de los corredores. . . .
>
> Algunas filas más adelante, casi en el *centro del redondel*, se destacaba la calva apergaminada de Urioste.
>
> Frente al pupitre del director de turno, un muchacho gordo, moreno, vestido de negro, iba anotando en una *enorme pizarra* las operaciones. Cuando escribía, *el traje, el pizarrón y la cabeza se confundían, y sólo de divisaba el puño blanco*. Parecía que escribiera con el puño. [P. 89]

Julián's head, void of sound and thought, experiences the maddening sensation of a *huge* horse fly zooming *round about* inside (the technique of the enlarged and whirling image). Then, one recalls Prieto's personal attachment to the sea as he brings into play the maritime image of a gigantic wave, the projection of the protagonist's fears, which seems almost to engulf him (again the technique of the enlarged image):

> Entonces experimentaba una especie de *vértigo*. Le parecía que estaba al borde de un mar agitado y resonante. . . . A impulsos del oleaje, las acciones subían y bajaban como ingenuos buquecitos de papel de diario. . . . Veía sus nombres escritos en toscos caracteres de imprenta. Llallagua, La Fortuna, Tuca-Tuca, El Delirio. . . . Una *ola inmensa* se formaba; era verde y arrebatadora como la esperanza; subía, subía mucho, más alto que la baranda, más que el pupitre del director de turno; llegaba hasta la pizarra, y su cresta de espuma dejaba como un rastro de tiza las cotizaciones. Luego se oía un ruido sordo; la ola caía con estrépito. . . . Sólo dos o tres buquecitos de papel se mantenían aún a flote. . . . [P. 90]

All of the character's surroundings are now expressionistically distorted, enlarged, and grotesquely animated as a succession of architectural images become kinetic (see above, pp. 165–66), thereby projecting the financial worries and obsessions of the individual:

"Julián no distinguía las voces y las palabras, que se fundían en un solo barullo; pero miraba las cotizaciones, y le parecía que la sala entera se columpiaba, oscilaba a compás de las 'Auríferas.' . . . Subían, y las columnas se alargaban, los muros retrocedían y el "plafond" se hacía más alto y más ancho hasta confundirse con el cielo. . . . Bajaban y las columnas se retorcían, las murallas se acercaban y la cúpula, como una chata cripta funeraria, le oprimía la cabeza hasta estrecharlo con el pavimento . . ." (p. 92). Finally, the architectural and the nautical images are fused in a crescendo of motion and enlargement: "El edificio de la Bolsa se estremecía como una caja de cartón con el vocerío de los compradores. La ola inmensa iba creciendo más y más, con la augusta majestad de la marea. Apenas se distinguían las manos amarillentas y crispadas de Urioste —manos de ahogado—, que por momentos se asomaban y desaparecían . . ." (p. 93).

Unsatisfied with the mythical Madame Duprés, the invented *socio* now takes the beloved mistress away from his master. The Frankenstein monster utterly destroys his maker. The night he loses Anita to the creature of his imagination, Julián Pardo experiences a terrifying nightmare. This oneiric experience is reproduced below to demonstrate that the author of *El socio* also exploited the intensified surrealistic probing of previously unexplored levels of the human mind's activity—including the unconscious, delirium, insanity, and, above all, the dream world:

> ¡Qué noche aquella! La cama parecía hundirse y las ropas le cubrían la cara, el pecho, los brazos, sin permitirle el más leve movimiento. Se ahogaba, sentía que el corazón iba a estallar. Era una angustia horrible, una angustia tan sólo comparable a aquella que sintiera cuando Anita le dejó. . . .
> Un sudor frío le entumecía.
> El lecho se iba hundiendo más y más; estaba al fondo de un abismo, cubierto por esas ropas blancas y pesadas como un inmenso cúmulo de nieve. En lo alto presentía el cielo oscuro, moteado de una infinidad de copos blancos.
> Ahora estaban muy arriba. Altos, enormemente altos. Se movían al menor soplo de viento, como si fueran a desprenderse.
> Desde su sepultura de hielo Julián alcanzaba a oír la voz de Davis, que sentado en la blanca llanura, justamente encima de su

pecho, miraba las albas plumillas y comentaba con indiferencia:
—Están altas: sí, ahora están altas. . . . Hay alza en el mercado,
pero luego caerán: no se preocupe. . . . En la Bolsa sucede esto con
frecuencia. Las acciones son así. Yo las haré bajar cuando quiera.

La nieve se sacudía y una lluvia de besos estallaba arriba.

—¡Walter, mi querido Walter! ¡qué bueno eres!

La voz de Anita sonaba arrulladora con un trino, y Davis la
atraía hacia su pecho. Confundidos en un estrecho abrazo, sus
cuerpos se hundían en la nieve como un edredón. ¡Qué infamia!
Julián, presa de un verdadero frenesí, se agitaba en el fondo de su
sepulcro. No podía levantarse, pero sus manos, violáceas como dos
jaivas gigantescas, arañaban sin cesar. . . . ¡Quería salir de allí,
coger a Davis por el cuello, estrangularlo! Luchaba, ahogado por
la nieve. Sus algodones se le introducían por las narices, la boca y
los oídos.

Por fin, sus dedos crispados lograron asir un brazo. ¡No, no era
eso! Una garganta, una garganta tibia, que se retorcía entre roncos
estertores. Sonaba como un fuelle roto. Ya apenas se la sentía, y
¡Dios mío!, ¡qué blanda y qué suave era!

Ahora quería abrir las manos; pero éstas no le obedecían. Los
dedos, rígidos como dos garfios de hierro, se fundían en una sola
argolla. El cuello inerte pasaba a través de ella como un cable suelto.
También Julián sentía que las fuerzas le abandonaban.

Encima de él resonó una carcajada.

—¡Se ha equivocado, míster Pardo! Esa garganta no es la mía.

Julián dió un salto y despertó. [Pp. 102–3]

The Chilean author's versatile talents and multifaceted personality led him to cultivate many professional, human and aesthetic
interests. His imaginative language in *El socio*, a stylistic anomaly
when viewed against a background of *criollista* literary hegemony,
his intense awareness of contemporary artistic tendencies coupled
with demonstrated ability to imitate seriously as well as facetiously
the vanguardists' poetic idiom, and a probing of unrealistic innovative themes amidst the supremacy of novelistic regionalism are but
a few of this remarkable writer's achievements. These factors combine to make of Jenaro Prieto Letelier an exceptional figure of his
times, an outstanding example of that characteristically Latin American cultural phenomenon we have termed "change within the
traditional."

From *Criollismo* to the Grotesque:
Approaches to José Donoso

Kirsten F. Nigro

In 1842 José Victorino Lastarria urged Chilean writers to forget about Europe and to look to their own country for inspiration. He insisted: "Nuestra literatura debe sernos exclusivamente propia, debe ser enteramente nacional. Fuerza es que seamos originales; tenemos en nuestra sociedad todos los elementos para serlo, para convertir nuestra literatura en la expresión auténtica de nuestra nacionalidad."[1] At that time few people questioned what he had to say. Nationalistic fervor was high. Chile was a new and independent country, and it was time that she also defined her spiritual and cultural autonomy. What better way to do this than to define those things which are uniquely Chilean? So when Lastarria and other writers of that period set out to discover the meaning of *chilenidad*, critics called them *costumbristas* and thought it a good thing that Chileans should write about Chile.

Alberto Blest Gana most successfully executed the literary program outlined by Lastarria. His documentation of nineteenth-century Chilean society was nearly encyclopedic, and his novels are like an enormous fresco, depicting Chileans in almost every walk of life: "el chileno rico, viajero y adaptado a otras atmósferas. . . . El arribista, el rico surgido de la prosperidad minera . . . el chileno típico de la clase media, el señorón engolado, el aprendiz de cons-

---

[1] Quoted by Milton Rossel in "Significación y contenido del criollismo," *Atenea*, 121 (no. 358, April 1955), 11.

pirador pipiolo, el aprovechado y el mestizo."[2] Blest Gana was hailed as "el padre de la novela chilena," as Chile's first master of narrative realism. His novels set the example which many writers were to follow, and no one really objected. It still seemed a good thing for Chileans to write about Chile.

Years later Mariano Latorre called Chile "un país de rincones" and insisted that not every nook and cranny of her geography had yet been discovered. Blest Gana had managed to cover a fair amount of territory, but mostly urban and not rural. Latorre felt that a true expression of *chilenidad* was to be found not so much in the larger metropolitan areas, with their cosmopolitan ways, but rather in the country, in small towns and seaports, in the *huaso*, and in the Chilean *campesino*. From 1912 until his death in 1955, Latorre wrote innumerable novels and short stories which charted Chile's varied topography, extending from "la pampa salitrera, la cordillera de la costa, la selva del sur, Chiloé y sus canales, [hasta] Magallanes y las estepas erizadas con la maravilla del Coirón."[3]

Latorre also had his followers, yet critics did not call them *costumbristas* or *realistas* but rather *criollistas*. If Blest Gana had been "el padre de la novela chilena," Latorre was indisputably "el padre del criollismo." But this time many people *were* complaining, and Latorre lived to see not only himself but also the entire *criollista* movement become the target of violent attacks. It seemed that it was no longer acceptable to write about Chile, or at least not in the way that Latorre did.

As early as 1920 critics began to grumble. Hernán Díaz Arrieta (Alone), for example, found *criollismo* prosaic, if not utterly boring, and said of Latorre's *Zurzulita* that "el campo es monótono; él [Latorre] es monótono; el campo es simple y pesado; los campesinos hablan y piensan tonterías bajas, vulgares, pequeñas; él se encierra en un círculo asfixiante de estupideces capaces de matar a cualquiera."[4] More than a few people shared Díaz Arrieta's sentiments,

---

[2] Ricardo Latcham, "Balzac en la novela hispanoamericana," in *Páginas escogidas* (Santiago: Andrés Bello, 1959), pp. 47–48.

[3] Quoted by Homero Castillo in *El criollismo en la novelística chilena* (Mexico City: Andrea, 1962), p. 36.

[4] Quoted by Mario Ferrero in "La prosa chilena del medio siglo: Introducción," *Atenea*, 135 (no. 385, July–September 1959), 118.

and in 1928 one group of writers, the *imaginistas*, declared war on the *criollistas*.

Fernando Alegría has referred to this confrontation as the first between defenders of "lo regional y lo universal . . . el realismo y el imaginismo" in Chilean literature.[5] It may very well have been the first, but it most certainly was not the last. The debate erupted again in 1954 during a "Foro público sobre el criollismo" held at the University of Chile. It was renewed in 1958 at the "Primer encuentro de escritores chilenos" at the University of Concepción. And in 1959 it was a major issue in the polemic waged over the generation of 1950.

Each time, the *criollistas* have been denounced for failing to recognize that Chile is no longer "un país de rincones," for being excessively regional, and for not dealing with pressing political and social issues. They have been assailed for turning their backs on the city and for preferring the *huaso* to the *roto*, or to anybody else for that matter. They also have been accused of rejecting categorically all foreign influences, of refusing to accept change, and of allowing the novel to fossilize in their hands. The general consensus among its opponents has been that *criollismo* outlived itself, that it began to die sometime around 1938 and was finally buried in 1959.

As for the *criollistas*, they have dismissed Díaz Arrieta as a city snob and an intellectual highbrow and have further retaliated by stating: "Las acusaciones más generalizadas acerca del criollismo son vulgares perogrulladas, cuando no pecan de superficialidad o ausencia casi absoluta de criterio histórico."[6] Although most *criollistas* admit being partial to rural Chile, they deny that they are exclusively so. Even Latorre himself wrote "criollismo del medio urbano" in novels like *La paquera* (1958). And José Santos González Vera, for example, described in his *Vidas mínimas* (1923) the poverty of the urban proletariat, destined to live and die in the misery of the "conventillo chileno." Their chaotic existence, far from being presented with photographic precision, was reflected in the disjointed structure of the novel, itself a series of juxtaposed episodes often lacking continuity and logic. Therefore, how could

---

[5] *La literatura chilena contemporánea* (Buenos Aires: Centro Editor de América Latina, 1968), p. 23.
[6] Ferrero, "La prosa chilena," 120.

they be accused of snubbing the city and of holding fast to the obsolete dictums of realism and naturalism? They point to González Vera, among others, as proof that "las sucesivas facetas que determinan la evolución de la literatura europea se encuentran en el criollismo chileno: el naturalismo, el realismo, el expresionismo y sus proyecciones en la gama de la creación subjetiva."[7] By their calculations, *criollismo* is not only alive and well, but still at the helm of Chilean literature.

La querella del criollismo: A Post-Mortem

So then, who is right? Who has won the "querella del criollismo"? No one really. The debate has reached a stalemate because neither side could really win. The *criollistas* were not going to lay down their pens just because they were under constant attack, nor were their opponents going to quietly retire because the *criollistas* wanted them to. Nevertheless, for too many years the debate was waged as if it were a fight to the death. The *anticriollistas* perhaps have been most guilty of this; they are the ones who have reached "un acuerdo tácito para enterrar las cenizas de un costumbrismo caduco";[8] they have demanded "la muerte del criollismo." It is this hostility which often makes the recent history of Chilean literature read something like the rise and fall of one literary generation after another, each claiming to have dealt *criollismo* its final deathblow only to discover that in fact it had not.

By confronting each other as bitter enemies, many lost sight of the fact that during this time native and foreign elements in Chilean literature have developed along parallel lines. Granted, at differing periods one may have dominated the other, and undeniably there has been friction between them. However, there have been, from the very beginning, those authors who have earnestly attempted to fuse the two. Even early *criollistas*, members of the "generación del Centenario," were aware that Chilean literature could not afford to be overly regional. Many of them were influenced by the great

[7] Lautaro Yankas, "Dilucidación del criollismo," *Atenea*, 121 (no. 360, June 1955), 400.
[8] Fernando Alegría, "Sobre el encuentro de escritores en Concepción," *Atenea*, 130 (no. 379, February–March 1958), 174.

masters of psychological realism—Gogol, Dostoevski, Gorki, and Turgenev. Eduardo Barrios, for example, emulated Dostoevski by exploring the hidden depths of man's abnormal psychology in novels like *El niño que enloqueció de amor* (1915) and *El hermano asno* (1922). Pedro Prado, in particular, sought to combine many of the conflicting tendencies current at that time; few can deny that his *Alsino* (1924) is one of the most accomplished efforts at making Chilean realism universal.

Obviously then, foreign and native elements need not be incompatible. But often participants in the "querella del criollismo" have tended to see Chilean literature as a house divided, so to speak. As a consequence, they have expected that novelists be either *criollistas*, *neorrealistas*, *vanguardistas*, or such. They have looked for the stereotype and missed the individual cases which do not fit into any of their categories. Therefore, critics have pigeonholed novelists into neat classifications and generations. Some, like Lautaro Yankas, would go to the opposite extreme and do away with all literary tags, that is, all except one—*criollismo*; in his opinion "no es concebible la realidad de una obra nacida en este u otro rincón del mundo, sea ella o no de tipo subjetivo, que deje de ser substancialmente criolla."[9] He also solves the problem by not allowing for those particular novelists who, in the best sense of the word, are original.

Of course there always have been serious critics who have avoided such a facile schematization of Chilean novelists. Although they have not totally discarded literary labels, those who use them recognize them for what they are, a necessary evil, "un artificio ordenador," and nothing more. Cedomil Goić has spoken of "literary preferences," which is perhaps more to the point and allows for exceptions within general tendencies.[10] There are and always will be differences among Chilean writers; some will be vernacular, others more universal. There are many, however, who have managed to neutralize the tensions between these two tendencies by

---

[9] Yankas, "Dilucidación del criollismo," 399.

[10] See Cedomil Goić's "La novela chilena actual: Tendencias y generaciones," *Anales de la Universidad de Chile*, 118 (no. 119, 3d semester, 1960), 250–58. Goić's study shows to what extent foreign influences have operated in the development of the twentieth-century Chilean novel. For a detailed, unbiased, and cogent analysis of the development and changes within *criollismo*, its significance in Chilean literature, and a general bibliography dealing with it, see Ricardo Latcham, "Historia del criollismo," *Atenea*, 113 (no. 94, February–March 1954), 5–22.

combining them, thus paving the way for most contemporary Chilean novelists.

When speaking of the latter, Julio Durán Cerda has said, "La posición de estos jóvenes obedecía . . . a un impulso perfectamente coherente y oportuno, y la ansiada superación se abrió paso hacia anchas posibilidades de desenvolvimiento. Pero no debe olvidarse que esa conquista es la culminación de un proceso inaugurado, con los primeros intentos de 'cerrar el timón,' allá en la órbita de los imaginistas del 28."[11] On the other hand, Mario Ferrero has said that they are characterized by "su actitud crítica ante la sociedad y esa búsqueda de los valores universales, partiendo de lo propio, de lo estrictamente nacional. Ambos son elementos esenciales para un [sic] superación definitiva del criollismo sin dejar de conocer que fue el criollismo, precisamente, el que abrió el camino a esta posibilidad."[12] To a certain extent, each of these statements is correct, but if we combine them we get closest to the truth. The contemporary Chilean novel represents a final synchronization of both tendencies, one which culminated in the generation of 1950. With these writers old formulas soon lost prestige and were replaced by new ones which help to define the Chilean novel today.

The Generation of 1950

In 1959 Jorge Iván Hübner launched a major attack against a group of young writers known as "the generation of 1950." While referring specifically to Claudio Giaconi, Enrique Lafourcade, and José Donoso, Hübner said that in general, "En todos ellos, por encima de sus diversas características personales, hay una serie de marcados elementos comunes: filosofía subyacente o manifiesta de la desesperanza . . . predilección por las miserias humanas (ebrios, delincuentes, meretrices, afeminados), y afán realista que se solaza en las escenas chocantes y las palabras procaces. Esta joven literatura chilena, pese a su indudable valor, ha sufrido el contagio del 'existencialismo' que envilece y rebaja las creaciones artísticas."[13]

11 "El cuento chileno contemporáneo," *Studies in Short Fiction*, 8 (Winter 1971), 57.
12 Mario Ferrero, "La prosa chilena del medio siglo: Continuación," *Atenea*, 135 (no. 386, December 1959), 153.
13 Quoted by Enrique Lafourcade in "La nueva literatura chilena," *Cuadernos Americanos*, 123 (no. 4, 1962), 236.

As far as Hübner was concerned, "la filosofía del desastre" should stay in Europe, where it belonged, where civilization was supposedly at its nadir. It had no place in Chile, "país en crecimiento, lleno de vitalidad y el optimismo de los pueblos jóvenes, [donde] no se concibe—sino como un morbo imitativo y decadente—una literatura materialista, sombría y desesperanzada."[14] Hübner's statements were explosive and set off another polemic, but the outcome of this one proved to be somewhat different and, as a result, brought "la querella del criollismo," such as it was, to an end.

When Hübner accused these writers of being existentialists, they in turn refused to be catalogued in that or any other literary school. They insisted that the only common denominator which united them was that they were "una generación vocacionalmente comprometida," one wholly dedicated to the craft of fiction. They defended their right to be different, to write as they pleased, without bowing to a set of rules imposed on them by critics and literary theorists. Perhaps as a group they did not conform to scholarly definitions of the term *generation*; this was not their main concern. Lafourcade, who himself had baptized them "the generation of 1950," quickly silenced their critics on this account by admitting that "las razones que [tuve] para esta denominación son perfectamente irracionales. Ninguna en particular. [Me] pareció que el medio siglo era una buena frontera. Además, alrededor de esta fecha se habían publicado algunas de las obras más significativas de nuestra literatura."[15] Perhaps many of their novels were unconventional, unorthodox, exceeding the limits of traditional classifications; this *was* the point, this is what they were all about. They considered themselves eclectic and defied their critics to see them as anything else. As Lafourcade emphasized, "Hay un cambio fundamental. Se advierte en la literatura chilena la presencia de un movimiento rico y diferenciado, exógono, que tiene el valor de escapar de las clausuras de escuelas, doctrinas o ideologías paralizantes."[16]

The generation of 1950, Hübner to the contrary, was not determined to subvert the accomplishments of previous Chilean writ-

---

14 *Ibid.*
15 *Ibid.*, 242.
16 *Ibid.*, 237.

ers. As they saw it, "no habría un rompimiento violento con la tradición literaria chilena. Más bien una exaltada continuación de la misma."[17] They were quick to recognize their debt to their predecessors, to writers like Benjamín Subercaseaux, María Luisa Bombal, Vicente Huidobro, and Manuel Rojas. Nevertheless, by *continuación* they also meant reform and change; they, too, wanted to make the Chilean novel universal. When asked which writers outside of Chile had influenced them the most, they mentioned those who by then were standard on lists of "foreign influences": Joyce, Faulkner, Gide, Hemingway, Dos Passos, Woolf. But they also added new and significant Spanish American names: Agustín Yáñez, Juan Rulfo, Alejo Carpentier, Miguel Angel Asturias, writers for whom "la literatura es . . . una forma de conocimiento antes que una simple efusión afectiva o sensible. Pero un conocimiento que se busca 'a través de valores estéticos,' y que proviene de la preocupación común . . . por escalar no ya tan sólo los grandes problemas de la ontología y la metafísica . . . sino aquella familia de relaciones sutiles entre hombre y circunstancia."[18] Writers, in short, who were not only discovering America, but also giving it a new expression.

Benjamín Subercaseaux once said that the writers of the generation of 1950 "nos han liberado del criollismo y eso ya es meretorio."[19] This is not really true; *criollismo* is not dead. Yet they have put an end to any "querella del criollismo" which would reduce the Chilean novel to clear-cut and exclusive schools. The generation of 1950 was a product of many influences, Chilean and foreign alike; so were many of its predecessors. Yet their primary concern was to adapt these influences to make the novel an expression of the historical, as well as the inner, psychological determinants which make the Chilean both singular and universal. It is no longer a question of native versus foreign elements, but one of native and foreign influences and how well each novelist manages to deal with them.

Since the 1950's, the Chilean novel has undergone considerable

17 *Ibid.*, 254.
18 *Ibid.*, 249.
19 Quoted by Enrique Lafourcade in *Cuentos de la generación del 50* (Santiago: Nuevo Extremo, 1959), p. 10.

change, and according to Fernando Alegría, "ya en la década de 1960 a 1970 da frutos definidos de lo que pudiera considerarse un nuevo estilo," one in which novelists "intentaron una nueva narrativa de alusiones, no de planteamientos; de mitificación, no de análisis."[20] Like Lafourcade, he believes that this new style "marca el cambio de un lenguaje literario por otro, de una concepción historicista del mundo chileno por una concepción estética, de una perspectiva totalizadora por otra fragmentaria y abierta que, como consecuencia directa, acaba con el inveterado respeto local por la medida de los géneros literarios."[21]

It would seem logical then, that this "nuevo estilo" would call for a "nueva crítica." Both Alegría and Lafourcade have understood the meaning of the contemporary Chilean novel; so have other critics. Unfortunately, there are still those who are using yesterday's formulas for criticism; the novel has progressed, but many critics have not managed to keep pace with it. We have said that the generation of 1950 brought an end to the "querella del criollismo," and this is true, insofar as critics can no longer justifiably disregard the fact that many contemporary Chilean novels are a hybrid form and for that very reason all the more complex. But this does not mean that they all are prepared to deal with the novel such as it is today. Many are lagging behind their novelists, and in one particular case, that of José Donoso, although critics have showered him with praise, some have done so for all the wrong reasons.

The Grotesque World of José Donoso

José Donoso (1924–) has emerged from the generation of 1950 as Chile's most widely acclaimed contemporary novelist.[22] He began

[20] "La narrativa chilena (1960–1970)," *Nueva Narrativa Hispanoamericana*, 2 (no. 1, January 1972), 59.

[21] *Ibid.*

[22] Although the generation of 1950 imposed a "new style," critics are at variance about just how well that generation and subsequent novelists have in fact mastered it. That is, they question the quality of today's novelists. However much they may disagree, they agree unanimously that Donoso, along with Carlos Droguett and Antonio Skármeta, is one of Chile's most accomplished novelists. See Ariel Dorfman, "Perspectivas y limitaciones de la novela chilena actual," *Anales de la Universidad de Chile*, 124 (no. 140, October–December 1966), 110–67; and especially "Temas y problemas de la narrativa chilena actual," in *Chile, hoy* (Mexico City: Siglo XXI, 1970), pp. 385–407. Also see Cristián Huneeus, "¿Existe la novela chilena?" *Mundo Nuevo*, no. 11

by writing short stories, and in 1955 he published *Veraneo y otros cuentos*, which was awarded the Premio Municipal de Cuentos. Another volume of his stories, *El charleston*, appeared in 1960, and in 1966 an edition of *Los mejores cuentos de José Donoso*. In 1971 the collection *Cuentos* was published by Seix Barral. His first novel, *Coronación* (1957), was selected in 1962 by the Faulkner Foundation as the best Chilean novel written since World War II. He began to dedicate more time to the novel, and in 1966 he published two more, *El lugar sin límites* and *Este domingo*. His last novel, *El obsceno pájaro de la noche* (1970), received the Premio Pedro de Oña for the most outstanding Chilean novel of 1969–70. His work has been or is currently being translated into English, French, Italian, and Polish. Donoso is now considered a major figure in the great "boom" of the Latin American novel along with others like Fuentes, García Márquez, Vargas Llosa, and Cabrera Infante.

What is peculiar about "el fenómeno José Donoso" is the scarcity of critics who have really studied him in great depth.[23] Those who have done so have focused attention mainly on what is most obvious in his novels: the continued development of a single theme—the decay of a rigidly structured Chilean society. Old and crumbling ancestral mansions, aging servants, families who spiritually and physically crucify each other, congenital insanity, insinuations of incest, the rank odor of things gone old and sour—these are the ele-

(May 1967), 88–89, as well as Alegría, "La narrativa chilena (1960–1970)."

[23] See John J. Hassett, Charles M. Tatum, and Kirsten Nigro, "Biobibliography: José Donoso," *Chasqui*, 2 (no. 1, November 1972), 15–30. Our bibliography shows that there is by no means a dearth of material written about Donoso, but it also shows that the majority of that material consists of book reviews and brief articles. Of those articles which are in-depth studies of Donoso's work, in addition to Dorfman's "Temas y problemas de la narrativa chilena actual," we recommend the following: George R. McMurray, "La temática en los cuentos de José Donoso," *Nueva Narrativa Hispanoamericana*, 1 (no. 2, September 1971), 133–38; Anita Muller, "La dialéctica de la realidad en *El obsceno pájaro de la noche*," *Nueva Narrativa Hispanoamericana*, 2 (no. 2, September 1972), 93–100; Emir Rodríguez Monegal, "El mundo de José Donoso," *Mundo Nuevo*, no. 12 (June 1967), 77–85; Severo Sarduy, "Escritura/Travestismo," *Mundo Nuevo*, no. 20 (February 1968), 72–74; and "El arte narrativo de Donoso: regalo japonés, crónica goyesca, lugar sin límites," *Siempre*, no. 965, supp. II (22 December 1971). Donoso has recently received much critical attention, due in large part to the success of *El obsceno pájaro de la noche* and to the publication of another work, *Tres novelitas burguesas* (Barcelona: Seix Barral, 1973). See George R. McMurray, "José Donoso: Bibliography—Addendum," *Chasqui*, 3 (no. 2, February 1974), 23–44, for an exhaustive bibliography on Donoso's narrative to date.

ments in Donoso's novels which lead some critics to believe that he is "un recio novelista y cuentista preocupado por la decadencia del clan familiar" or of specific social classes.[24]

It is true that Donoso's novels can be read as chronicles of domestic and class disintegration. *Coronación* and *El obsceno pájaro de la noche* depict the final stages of moral and economic ruin in once-aristocratic families. *Este domingo* paints a similar picture, only this time within the framework of dehumanizing middle-class values. In *El lugar sin límites* a symbolic family, housed in a brothel, represents disease and corruption at its worst, especially among Chilean landowners. For this reason some critics consider Donoso a naturalist obsessed with death and decay. They have called him a writer with a message, bent on exposing a society in decadence, although Donoso himself has insisted, "No tengo visión social. Es un ejercicio interior. No hay ninguna actitud o propósito mío respecto a la sociedad."[25]

Since Chile is very much present in Donoso's novels, and since he often devotes long passages to the accumulation of descriptive detail, other critics call him a realist, a master painter of Chilean customs and language. Raúl Silva Castro, for example, has said of *Coronación* that "algún día se podrá estudiar esta obra como testimonio del lenguaje usado por el chileno en 1957, transportado al libro con el mínimum de sacrificio de la espontaneidad."[26] One critic has gone so far as to call *Coronación* a "novela costumbrista chilena" and to compare Donoso to Blest Gana.[27] Even outside Chile Donoso has been the object of such traditional interpretations. The Uruguayan critic Mario Benedetti has praised Donoso for describing with realistic precision the different types in Chilean society and has spoken of his novel as "una novela de ciudad."[28]

Other critics have applauded Donoso for depicting skillfully the upper and lower strata of Chilean society, for placing them in direct contraposition to underscore their differences as well as the ties,

[24] Alegría, *La literatura chilena contemporánea*, p. 41.

[25] Quoted by Guillermo I. Castillo in "José Donoso y su última novela," *Hispania*, 54, no. 4 (1971), 958.

[26] "Coronación," *Anales de la Universidad de Chile*, nos. 109–10 (1958), 507.

[27] See L. A. M., "Coronación," *Atenea*, 129 (no. 378, October–December 1957), 285.

[28] See Mario Benedetti, "José Donoso: Mundo chileno en varios planos," in *Letras del continente mestizo* (Montevideo: Arca, 1967), pp. 118–23.

mostly sexual, which bind them together. They have commented that structurally his novels are perfectly balanced and reflect the "oposición de clases" which is their major theme. Donoso has been called "traditional," perhaps mainly because his first three novels are not overly experimental and because they "unquestionably give every evidence of a modest and perfectly calculated kind of realistic literary practice."[29]

But Donoso is deceptive, and his so-called realism is a mask, a disguise which has fooled many of his critics, who are still equating realism with nativism and universalism with all extremes of experimentation. Of course, *El obsceno pájaro de la noche*, a totally schizophrenic and chaotic novel, can by no stretch of the imagination be called "traditional" or "realistic." For those who have seen Donoso as a rather conservative writer, that work would represent an abrupt about-face. But nothing is farther from the truth. Donoso's novels present a clear line of progression in chaos, a creative trajectory which begins in the crumbling mansion of Misiá Elisita Abalos in *Coronación* and terminates in the disconnected and labyrinthine nightmare of *El obsceno pájaro de la noche*. The chaos has always been there, but behind a false façade of realism which many critics have not penetrated.

The chaos in Donoso's novels can best be described as grotesque. Alfonso Calderón has said, "El aporte capital de esta generación [del 50] radica en la configuración de lo grotesco, que consiste en una mirada de espejo deformante de la realidad inmediata. Culminaciones de este 'modo de mirar' se hallarán en obras como *Coronación* de Donoso."[30] What Calderón says is true—*Coronación* is grotesque. The grotesque, however, is not a distorted reflection of reality in a concave mirror; the grotesque reflects a reality which is already distorted and fragmented.

Although critics are still far from agreeing on a definition of the grotesque, Wolfgang Kayser, in his study of *The Grotesque in Art*

---

[29] Alexander Coleman, "Some Thoughts on José Donoso's Traditionalism," *Studies in Short Fiction*, 8 (Winter 1971), 155. Coleman is also perplexed by the fact that critics have seen Donoso as a traditionalist. He adds that to see Donoso as nothing more than a realist is to ignore the "insidious and quite beautifully disguised thematics" in his work.

[30] Quoted by Rosa Larraín Cox in "La generación del 50: ¿Mito o realidad?" *memoria de prueba* for selection for the title of Pedagogo en Castellano, Catholic University, Santiago, 1969, p. 33.

and Literature, reaches various conclusions with which I agree for the most part.[31] Kayser tells us that the grotesque is an estranged world. It is not merely a strange or alien world, like that in a fairy tale. It is our world which is transformed, and we react with terror or surprise because we no longer feel it to be reliable: "The grotesque world is—and is not—our world. The ambiguous way in which we are affected by it results from our awareness that the familiar and apparently harmonious world is alienated under the impact of abysmal forces which break it up and shatter its coherence."[32] Kayser adds that structurally this estrangement "presupposes that the categories which apply to our world view become inapplicable. We have observed the progressive dissolution which has occurred since the ornamental art of the Renaissance: the fusion of realms which we know to be separated, the abolition of the laws of statics, the loss of identity, the distortion of 'natural' size and shape, the suspension of the category of objects, the destruction of personality, and the fragmentation of historical order."[33]

In other words, the grotesque depicts a world without all the comfortable illusions of structured reality. Kayser insists that the process of disintegration must be experienced on a physical level and that the grotesque does not concern itself with man's individual actions or with the destruction of moral order. But Kayser has dedicated very little of his study to the more recent manifestations

---

[31] Malcolm Griffith has stated that "the basic disagreement about the nature of the grotesque seriously calls into question the possibility of arriving at a real (true) definition of the term. And such a doubt is reinforced when we realize how remote are the resemblances between some of the works of art which have responsibly been called grotesque. Perhaps the effort to define 'grotesque' has been a misdirected one" ("Theories of the Grotesque," in *Ramón del Valle-Inclán; An Appraisal of his Life and Works,* ed. Anthony N. Zahareas [New York: Las Américas, 1968], pp. 483–92). Griffith feels that things which are grotesque share not so much common traits as, rather, family resemblances and that there can never be a *real, true* definition of the grotesque. My study of the grotesque leads me to a similar conclusion. I offer my definition not as one which purports to be all-inclusive and to cover all works which have been called grotesque but as one which defines the grotesque as it is seen in Donoso's work. In formulating it, I have followed Griffith's criteria for determining those properties which may allow one to speak of the grotesque in a specific work of art: (1) the paradigm case rule—decision whether a specific work is grotesque by seeing how similar it is to works that commonly are called grotesque, and (2) the paradigm properties rule—decision whether a specific work is grotesque by seeing how many traditional defining properties of the term it has (*ibid.,* pp. 490–91).

[32] *The Grotesque in Art and Literature,* trans. Ulrich Weisstein (New York: McGraw-Hill, 1966), p. 37.

[33] *Ibid.,* p. 185.

of the grotesque, where it is man, with his moral and psychic aberrations, who is an active participant in, if not the creator of, a world of grotesque dimensions. Consequently, the grotesque in contemporary fiction tends to depict a corrosive process which encompasses not only physical but psychic reality as well. The psychic grotesque or spiritual cripple is symbolic of "l'homme traqué," who, lacking a sense of identity and order within himself, can bring chaos and destruction to others. The chaos depicted can still make us lose the ground under our feet, to use Kayser's telling phrase, not only because protective natural order has collapsed before our eyes, but also because we do not relate psychologically or spiritually to the drama we are witnessing.

Kayser also insists that grotesque chaos must be brought about by demonic forces which remain beyond human comprehension, a theory with which I cannot agree. There is in fact an outside force, beyond man's control, which also directs this disintegrative process, but it is not totally incomprehensible. What helps to undermine order in the grotesque, at least in Donoso's novels, is an "irresistible process implacably grinding down whatever sense of structure has been raised as an ordering principle against it,"[34] a process known as entropy, a law of physics which determines that in man and his universe there is "a tendency to sink back into that original chaos from which [they] may have emerged."[35] Entropy takes chaos one step beyond into formlessness and stasis, to a total leveling of all material distinctions and ordering principles.

The grotesque has many ways of projecting or symbolizing this entropic process, all of them employed by Donoso in his novels: psychological fragmentation, spiritual or physical atrophy and hypertrophy, ambiguity or inversion of sexual roles, symbolical substitution, insanity, and human travesty. Donoso makes use of these to depict the agonizing obliteration of man's personal identity, a spiritual dismembering which throws his world into chaos. He himself has stated: "Uno de los grandes terrores míos . . . es el terror de la destrucción, de la abyección, de la no existencia, de la reducción a la nada, del ser que se elimina, de la explotación del ser humano

[34] Alvin Greenberg, "The Novel of Disintegration: Paradoxical Impossibility in Contemporary Fiction," *Wisconsin Studies in Contemporary Fiction*, 7 (1966), 109.

[35] Wylie Sypher, "Existence and Entropy," in *Loss of the Self in Modern Art and Literature* (New York: Random House, 1962), p. 73.

por el ser humano, en todos los planos de la destrucción. El tema no me interesa en el sentido social; me interesa el ser humano explotado, destructor y destruido."[36] For Donoso, the principal aim of his novels is "deshacer la unidad psicológica, ese mito terrible que nos hemos inventado."[37] The undermining of this myth jerks Donoso's narrative world off its axis and leads to its grotesque disorder and ultimate destruction.

His four novels, therefore, are more than commentaries on Chilean society in progressive stages of decay; they are monstrous visions of diseased and withered souls. His characters are victims of frustrated sexuality and morbid obsessions which erupt into violence to shatter the monotony and rigidity of their individual lives. They are engaged in an endless and futile battle against the encroachments of chaos from without and within. Although bound for sure destruction, they do their best "para no presenciar ese desmoronamiento del orden natural mediante la intrusión del absurdo."[38] In the end, they are defeated. The following analysis of *El lugar sin límites* will show how and to what extent the grotesque functions as an inexorable force in Donoso's narrative world.

El lugar sin límites

El lugar sin límites, as Donoso tells us, is hell on earth; in this case the author has limited that hell geographically to the town of Estación El Olivo in central Chile. The events which take place there in one day's time represent the violent culmination of the collective decay of this small community, which Severo Sarduy has aptly described as "un mundo al revés" in which social and sexual roles are so inverted that no one person can be defined by common norms.[39] The novel spins an intricate web of interpersonal relationships in which each character reacts violently in order to combat the forces of chaos. Eventually, their world collapses and we, as readers, feel estranged from this world because nothing with which we normally

36 Quoted by Emir Rodríguez Monegal in "José Donoso: La novela como 'Happening,'" *Revista Iberoamericana,* 38 (nos. 76–77, July–December 1971), 521.

37 *Ibid.,* 522.

38 José Donoso, "Paseo," in *Los mejores cuentos de José Donoso,* ed. Luis Domínguez (Santiago: Zig-Zag, 1966), p. 148.

39 "Escritura/Travestismo," 72.

measure or define reality can make sense of it. As Donoso has stated, "Es un mundo en que los seres comienzan a deformarse, a perder sus dimensiones llamadas normal; se transforman en algo casi irreconocible, en que las pautas de la normalidad moral, sexual, pasional, etc., pierden su significado y empiezan a trizarse."[40]

The novel depicts one day in the life of four main characters: La Manuela, his daughter La Japonesita, Pancho Vega, and Don Alejandro Cruz. A fifth character, La Japonesa Grande, does not participate directly in the action, but her importance is revealed through a flashback to a day eighteen years before. La Manuela, an aging and pathetic transvestite, is the owner of a whorehouse, which is managed and maintained by La Japonesita, "una puta frígida." The immediate action of the novel is sparked by Pancho Vega's return to Estación El Olivo. The year before, Pancho had visited the house, an event which La Manuela fears will repeat itself. In a drunken rage, Pancho had torn the place apart and had tried to abuse both La Manuela and his daughter. But at that moment, "llegó don Alejo, como por milagro, como si lo hubieran invocado."[41] Yet Pancho has sworn to get his revenge, that "a las dos me las voy a montar bien montadas, a la Japonesita y al maricón del papá" (p. 10). This is, in fact, what happens. Pancho returns with his brother-in-law Octavio, and they relive the scene of the previous year. But this time La Manuela is brutally beaten, and although the author does not make it absolutely clear, we are led to believe that at the end he dies.

From the very beginning each of the four characters is qualified by specific traits or symbolical meanings. La Manuela and La Japonesita are feminine beings, sex objects used and destroyed by the aggressive male, "estos hombrones de cejas gruesas y voces ásperas," represented by Pancho. Don Alejo, described in Godlike terms, is a father figure, the embodiment of order. For La Japonesita and especially for La Manuela, he represents paternal protection. In the case of Pancho, Don Alejo is the domineering patriarch who thwarts his every effort at exerting his own masculine superiority.

---

[40] Quoted by Guillermo I. Castillo in "José Donoso y su última novela," 958.

[41] José Donoso, *El lugar sin límites* (Mexico City: Joaquín Mortiz, 1966), p. 11. Hereafter, citations from this edition are incorporated in the text. Unless otherwise noted, any italics in these passages is my emphasis and not Donoso's.

These are the most obvious links among the four, but the way in which they are further related within the novel makes clear that they are all extensions of one another and that Don Alejo is the umbilical cord which feeds them and eventually chokes them to death.

The saddest victim of this parasitical world is La Manuela. If we were to accept the more standard definitions of the grotesque, (that is, its dictionary definitions, or the way the term is employed in colloquial speech) we would have to say that his being a transvestite in itself makes him grotesque. The grotesque is generally, and erroneously, identified with that which is simply dehumanized, deformed, and abnormal. Although Donoso does describe La Manuela in dehumanizing terms, with "su pequeña cara arrugada como una pasa, sus fosas nasales negras y pelosas de yegua vieja" (p. 12), this alone does not make that character grotesque. He is a man who dresses, thinks, and behaves like a woman, who assumes the feminine (passive) role in homosexual relationships, but who at the same time has fathered a child, a situation perhaps not so unusual in itself, but one which is devastating for the characters in the novel.

It is the awareness that somewhere behind that masquerade of pastiche sexuality there is a man as potent as he that is particularly threatening to Pancho Vega. That La Manuela has chosen to deny his masculinity is the greatest threat he presents to La Japonesita. For La Manuela the realization that he is not impotent and not incapable of engaging in heterosexual lovemaking cracks the once integral identity he had assumed as a transvestite. Before La Manuela went to Estación El Olivo he never doubted his feminine role. He lived to be "la reina de la fiesta," to put on "su famoso vestido de española colorado con lunares blancos," and to dance to the applause of excited whores and drunken men. That these same men later mocked and beat him and forced him to quit one town after another was the only tragedy in his life. But as long as he could go on to another brothel and again be the center of attention, life afforded him a certain measure of happiness. All this changed once La Manuela slept with La Japonesa Grande and fathered her child. His outward existence was not altered; he continued to dance and to carry on "como una loca." Yet he was also aware that inwardly he was a paradox, and he spends the rest of his life trying to define his sexual identity. He turns to Pancho as a means of asserting what is feminine in him and disclaims La Japonesita for exactly the same reason.

La Japonesita is the constant reminder of his heterosexuality. He resents her presence and even more her calling him father. She refuses to call him La Manuela; to do so would be to admit that she is the perverse product of an even more perverted sexual encounter. La Japonesita is a grotesque oxymoron, as critics have been quick to point out. She is a virgin who runs a whorehouse; she is frigid, yet she wants to be a *puta*. The irony is that no man wants to sleep with her. La Japonesita reflects her father's sexual inversion, only to a greater degree. He is a man who *wants* to be a woman, whereas biologically she is *not* a woman. At age eighteen she has no breasts, no pubic hair, and has not begun to menstruate. Her biological constitution, plus her businesslike behavior, make her a male figure, another grotesque inversion, one whose total characteristics are defined ambiguously. She will not accept her father in his feminine role, but she never allows him to assume male authority. She only serves to remind him of his own equivocal nature. Whenever he feels secure in his role, "de pronto la Japonesita le decía esa palabra [padre] y su propia imagen se borroneaba como si le hubiera caído encima una gota de agua y él entonces, se perdía de vista a sí misma, mismo, yo misma no sé, él no sabe, ni ve a la Manuela y no quedaba nada, esta pena, esta incapacidad, nada más, este gran borrón de agua en que naufraga" (p. 52).

This ambiguity in turn explains La Manuela's, as well as La Japonesita's, masochistic fixation on Pancho. She wants him to seduce her, to prove that she is a woman, "para saber quién eres Japonesita, ahora lo sabrás y esa mano y ese calor de su cuerpo pesado y entonces, aunque él se vaya, quedará algo siquiera de esta noche" (p. 121). La Japonesita needs Pancho, in a perverse way, so that she can assert her identity, define her sexual integrity by paradoxically violating it. Pancho denies her this opportunity, and she remains an amorphous being. By the same token, La Manuela knows that what "ese macho bruto . . . prepotente" wants is to kill him; yet he identifies what is violent in Pancho with feminine submission. Pancho's "ñato camión colorado con doble llanta en las ruedas traseras" is an obvious sexual symbol which appears throughout the novel. He drives through town, honking its horn as if its piercing noise could "atravesar la noche de parte en parte para no quedar nada" (p. 94). When La Manuela hears its "bocinazo caliente como una llama, insistente, colorada, que venía acercándose" (p. 62), he smiles in anticipation. To submit to Pancho will once again put him in the passive (feminine) role of the homosexual, a regression to his initial sexual inversion. He uses Pancho to blot out the memory of his experience with La Japonesa Grande when he assumed the identity "de hombre pasivo que engendra a su pesar."[42]

What further complicates this inversion of roles is the fact that both La Japonesa Grande and Pancho react to what is masculine and not feminine in La Manuela. La Japonesa's most obvious reason for sleeping with him is that she has bet Don Alejo that she can excite La Manuela. If she wins, Don Alejo will give her the "casa de putas" that she rents from him. The one condition is that Don Alejo and his friends be able to watch them copulate. La Japonesa knows that she will not lose the wager, since she has sensed something others have not—that La Manuela, despite all his superficial feminine trappings, is very much a man underneath: "Si no fuera así jamás se hubiera fijado en él para nada" (p. 89).

Pancho, on the other hand, feels threatened by that residue of masculinity in La Manuela. La Manuela himself is used to the violent way in which other men react to him: "Estoy acostumbrada. No sé por qué siempre me hacen esto o algo parecido cuando bailo, es como si me tuvieran miedo, no sé por qué, siendo que saben que una es loca" (p. 84). Not even Pancho is aware of why he feels this fear. Yet when he returns to the whorehouse and sees La Manuela whirling and contorting his body, dancing in his torn and muddy flamenco dress, Pancho stops laughing at this circus spectacle. It is deadly serious now, because he suddenly realizes that "eso increíblemente asqueroso y que increíblemente es fiesta, eso está bailando para él, él sabe que desea tocarlo y acariciarlo, desea que ese retorcerse no sea sólo allá . . . el viejo maricón que baila para él y él se deja bailar y que . . . es como si él, también, estuviera anhelando" (p. 126). Pancho at first tries to justify his reactions by thinking that a man is entitled to experience all emotions. But he knows that this is not true, just as he knows that it is he, a "macho" with strong

---

[42] Sarduy, "Escritura/Travestismo," 72.

homosexual tendencies, who is reacting to a "vieja verde" who is both a man and a woman.

The nature of that fear which La Manuela had not understood becomes painfully clear when he recognizes that it is as a man, and not as a woman, that he is a threat to others: "Parada en el barro de la calzada mientras Octavio la paralizaba retorciéndole el brazo, la Manuela despertó. No era la Manuela. Era él Manuel González Astica. El. Y porque era él iban a hacerle daño y Manuel González Astica sintió terror" (p. 130). This realization signals La Manuela's spiritual and physical death. The only other time that he refers to himself by his true name is when he envisions his funeral, "y la enterraron en un nicho en el cementerio de San Alfonso bajo una piedra que dijera 'Manuel González Astica' " (p. 61). On the other hand, La Manuela, by forcing Pancho to this confrontation, also destroys him; he wounds Pancho's masculinity and leaves him a shattered being.

These characters all lead back to Don Alejandro Cruz, and it really does not matter what they do or what they are, because "don Alejo los va a borrar a todos estos huevones porque le dio la real gana" (p. 125). Don Alejo is very fond of practical jokes, and the funniest of all was to build this town next to his Fundo El Olivo and then let it slowly die. He is all-powerful, "no hay nadie como don Alejo, es único. Aquí en el pueblo es como un Dios. Hace lo que quiere. Todos le tienen miedo" (p. 74). He is treated with reverence and addressed as "el señor." According to La Manuela, he has the visage of "Tatita Dios . . . con sus ojos como loza azulina y sus bigotes y cejas de nieve" (p. 11). Yet Don Alejo's white eyebrows and clear eyes stand in bold contrast to his black soul.

Don Alejandro represents a powerful but human force which controls and destroys the individual and collective *yo* which inhabits his world. And it *is* Don Alejo's world, for with the exception of La Manuela's place and a few other run-down shacks, he owns all of Estación El Olivo. He has complete control over everyone's economic security and spiritual integrity as well. La Japonesita, as her mother also once did, looks to Don Alejo as the man who literally will bring light to Estación El Olivo, for the town has no electricity. He had always promised to convince the local politicians to install electricity there and "con la electricidad todo esto iba a

cambiar. Esta intemperie" (p. 43). The electricity is symbolic; Don
Alejo is the man who will deliver them from the darkness of hell.
But in this world where everything is upside down and nothing is
what it seems, Don Alejo, the incarnation of order, condemns them
to eternal chaos and decay. He never had any intention of getting
electricity for them. In fact, he purposely avoided the issue so that
the people would gradually abandon the town and he could buy
their land and extend his vineyards.

Don Alejo will be the cause of La Japonesita's death just as surely
as he was of her mother's, who did not die of a liver ailment, as everyone says, but "de pena porque la Estación El Olivo se iba para abajo,
porque ya no era lo que fue" (p. 44). La Japonesita rebels and refuses to sell her property; she will stay there and rot, like everything
else. La Japonesita is tied to Don Alejo in another way. Symbol-
ically, she owes her perverse existence to him. The "cuadro plás-
tico," that pornographic peep-show in which she was conceived,
was in reality staged and directed by Don Alejo. Again, Don Alejo
is a grotesque paradox; he is both the maker and the slayer of his
children.

Pancho also rebels against Don Alejo, but in this case the question
of paternity may not be just symbolic, a possibility that Pancho at
first denies: "Hijo, decían, de don Alejo. Pero lo decían de todos, de
la señorita Lila y de la Japonesita y de qué sé yo quién más, tanto
peón de ojo azul por estos lados, pero yo no. Meto la mano al fuego
por mi vieja, y los ojos, los tengo negros y las cejas, a veces me creen
turco" (p. 38). Toward the end of the novel Pancho tells La Japonesita that "Don Alejo es tu papá. Y el mío. . . . No es cierto. La Manuela es tu papá" (p. 123). Yet he does not deny that Don Alejo is his.
Whatever the true origin of their relationship, Pancho reacts to
Don Alejo as he would toward a father he hates and wants to defy.
The latter has told Pancho to leave La Manuela alone, and seen in
this context, Pancho's encounter with the "viejo maricón" takes on
a second significance: La Manuela also symbolizes the forbidden
fruit, denied to him by an authoritarian, Godlike figure. Pancho
assaults La Manuela not only to preserve order (within himself), but
also to destroy order and authority (externally in the person of Don
Alejo). So again it is Don Alejo who has "los hilos de todo el mundo
en sus dedos" (p. 98).

Don Alejo's power of death over others is symbolized in his four dogs, Negus, Sultán, Otelo, and Moro, "sus cuatro perros negros como la sombra de los lobos [que] tienen los colmillos sanguinarios, las pesadas patas feroces de la raza más pura" (p. 39). The dogs follow behind him; they obey his every order and imitate his every move: "Don Alejo se sacudió el agua de la manta y del sombrero. Los perros también se sacudieron" (p. 33). They are their master's shadow, a symbolic extension of his black soul. Thus, it is significant that the sound of their barking is associated with the shrill honking of Pancho's little red car. The dogs barking in the vineyard and the noise of Pancho's car had kept La Manuela up the night Pancho returned. The same dogs and the same car disturb the still quiet of Estación El Olivo the night that he is beaten, even though "los perros . . . no tenían por qué andar sueltos en la viña en este tiempo, cuando ya no quedaba ni un racimo que robarse" (p. 18). But Don Alejo is old, and his doctors have told him that he will soon die. He lets his dogs loose as a last revenge against the town and the people to whom he had, ironically, promised life. La Manuela, if he has managed to survive the wrath of Pancho, will not be so lucky as to escape the dogs. They will devour him physically, as Don Alejo had spiritually violated him eighteen years before. Death (the four black dogs) and sacrificial blood (Pancho's red car) fuse into a single image of chaos and destruction.

The internal anarchy of these characters is also reflected in the spatial configuration of the novel, which is divided between two parallel and seemingly well defined geographical units: to the one side there stands the town, forgotten by those who matter, abandoned by its former inhabitants, and on the verge of collapsing; to the other side and separated from it by a canal looms "la ordenación de las viñas" of Don Alejo's property, which seems to extend into eternity.

Estación El Olivo was not always a ghost town. At one time it had been a thriving little community, bustling with activity, especially for the local prostitutes. But this all came to an abrupt end when the main highway bypassed the town. Its connection with the outside world was cut off, and Don Alejo, by denying it electricity, condemned it and its few inhabitants to a slow but sure death: "Ahora no era más que un potrero cruzado por la línea, un semáforo *in-*

válido, un andén de concreto *resquebrajado,* y *tumbada* entre los hinojos debajo del par de eucaliptos *estrafalarios,* una máquina trilladora *antidiluviana* entre cuyos fierros anaranjados por el *orín* jugaban los niños como en un *saurio* domesticado" (p. 20). The town is an anachronism in its time; it is old, useless, and ridiculous. The author makes this clear by the words he uses to describe it: *inválido, orín, resquebrajado,* and *tumbada* refer to its decomposition; *antidiluviana, saurio,* and *estrafalarios* underscore the fact that it has outlived its usefulness.

In contrast to this heap of refuge are the vineyards: "Más allá, detrás del galpón de madera encanecida, más zarzas y un canal separaban el pueblo de las viñas de don Alejo. . . . Viñas y viñas y más viñas por todos lados hasta donde alcanzaba la vista, hasta la cordillera" (p. 20).

Ironically, this is "el lugar sin límites," a grotesque subversion of order. One passage in the novel makes amply clear the paradox involved in any order which defines this world: "El Olivo no es más que un *desorden* de casas *ruinosas sitiado* por la geometría de las viñas que parece que van a *tragárselo*" (p. 46). Order here is aggressive and devours those who enter it. When La Manuela flees his assailants, he runs towards "las viñas donde don Alejo espera benevolente" (p. 133), towards order and safety. But Don Alejo has let his dogs loose as a prelude to his final destruction of Estación El Olivo. He senses that he will die before he can buy those few shacks which do not belong to him. The angry God takes revenge on his children—he will let the vineyards overrun the town and engulf it all, "El achurado regular, el ordenamiento que situaba al caserío de murallones derruidos, la tendalera de este lugar que las viñas iban a borrar" (p. 125).

Yet Don Alejo is also the victim of a corrosion which not even he can escape; the entropic process runs its full course towards inertia, homogeneity, and, finally, death. His blue eyes lose their luster; his face becomes a shadow: "Se puso el sombrero y apagó su rostro" (p. 58). Just as he gave life to Estación El Olivo, he will erase the town from the face of the earth: "Echaría abajo todas las casas, borraría las calles ásperas de barro y boñigas, volvería a unir los adobes de los perendones a la tierra de donde surgieron y araría esa tierra" (pp. 59–60). The irony is that not a trace of Don Alejo will be left either. Everything and everybody in *El lugar sin límites* will fade away, leaving no signs that they ever existed. La Manuela is beaten to a pulp, "hasta que ya no queda nada y la Manuela apenas ve, apenas oye, apenas siente" (p. 133); Pancho disappears into the night, "No iba a volver nunca más" (p. 137); Don Alejo will die and "no quedará nada después de él porque todos sus proyectos le fracasaron" (p. 115); and La Japonesita will wither and dry up, "hasta que le pasaran el arado por encima a todo el pueblo" (p. 137).

Estación El Olivo was doomed to die because of the very nature of the people who lived there—chaotic beings, all trapped in the same painful process of disintegration. Estación El Olivo was marginal not simply because the main highway bypassed it but because its inhabitants were on the periphery of normalcy; everything there was inverted, ambiguous, parasitic. La Manuela, Pancho, Don Alejo, and La Japonesita destroyed each other in a futile attempt to escape their final disintegration, to make order out of chaos. But with each move they made, their world collapsed a little more, until all that remained was the lonely echo of Don Alejo's dogs barking in the vineyards.

Conclusion

The chaos in *El lugar sin límites* is the same inexorable force which leads to death and insanity in *Coronación* and *Este domingo*; it also explains El Mudito's mysterious metamorphosis into a pile of ashes at the end of *El obsceno pájaro de la noche*. This grotesque chaos does not operate to expose the decadence of a rigid and hierarchical society, as some critics believe. In Donoso's novels all order falls to pieces because it is a reflection of a false myth, of the mistaken concept that man possesses an internal symmetry. When seen in this light it seems ludicrous to consider Donoso a *costumbrista*, or a realist, or to read his novels in search of some social message. His novels do have a central thesis indeed, one that he develops obsessively and which he summarizes by stating, "No creo—es decir, no puedo decir que no creo porque no creo es una afirmación y no me atrevo a afirmar nada—pero en fin, *creo que no creo* que exista una unidad psicológica en el ser humano."[43] It is in this context that

43 Monegal, "José Donoso: La novela como 'Happening,' " 221.

his work is best understood and that it is a reflection of what Alvin Greenberg has called the "modern novel of disintegration."[44] Consequently, the critic who would analyze Donoso's novels on the basis of time-worn critical approaches in vogue when the novel was a structured reflection of a seemingly structured reality is denying the true meaning of that writer's work.

[44] "The Novel of Disintegration," 45.

Contributors

ANOAR AIEX, born in Brazil and educated there and in France, has been at the University of Illinois since 1968 and is now associate professor of Portuguese. His current research interests include the development of Latin American culture and the history of ideas in Europe and Latin America. His edition and translation into Portuguese of David Hume's *An Enquiry Concerning Human Understanding* appeared in 1972.

GERARD H. BÉHAGUE is professor of music at the University of Texas. He was born in France and educated in Brazil, France, and the United States, and was at the University of Illinois until 1974. He is interested in Latin American musicology, especially Brazilian art, folk, and popular music. He serves as music editor for the *Handbook of Latin American Studies*, is the new editor of *Ethnomusicology*, and has recently published a monograph entitled *The Beginnings of Musical Nationalism in Brazil* (1971).

MERLIN H. FORSTER is professor of Spanish and Portuguese and director of the Center for Latin American and Caribbean Studies at the University of Illinois, where he has been since 1962. His research interests are twentieth-century Latin American poetry and drama and the history of Latin American literature in the decades between the two world wars. Recent publications include a book on death in Mexican poetry, an anotated index to the Mexican journal *Letras de México*, and several articles on contemporary poets and dramatists. His book *Fire and Ice: The Poetry of Xavier Villaurrutia* is scheduled for publication in 1975.

LUIS LEAL is professor of Spanish at the University of Illinois. He was born in Mexico, was educated in the United States, and has been at the university since 1959. His research interest is the development of prose fiction in Spanish America, with special emphasis on the twentieth century and the history of the short story, and his publications in this area are extensive. Recent books include *Historia del cuento hispanoamericano* (second edition, 1971), *Mariano Azuela* (1971), and *Breve historia de la literatura hispanoamericana* (1971). He is also a contributing editor of *Handbook of Latin American Studies* for Mexican prose fiction.

THOMAS C. MEEHAN is associate professor of Spanish at the University of Illinois, where he has been since 1967. His research interest is contemporary Spanish American prose fiction, and his recent publications include articles on such important writers as Ernesto Sábato and Adolfo Bioy Casares. He is currently working on a longer study of Bioy's prose fiction and a translation of *El sueño de los héroes*.

KIRSTEN F. NIGRO is assistant professor of Spanish at the University of Arizona, having completed her doctorate at the University of Illinois. Her research interest is the contemporary Spanish American novel, particularly that of southern South America, and her dissertation was on the Chilean novelist José Donoso.

DAGOBERTO ORRANTIA is instructor in Spanish at John Jay College, City University of New York, and is completing his doctorate at the University of Illinois. He was born in Mexico and educated there and in this country, and he is writing his dissertation on recent Spanish American prose fiction.

RICHARD A. PRETO-RODAS has been associate professor of Portuguese and Spanish at the University of Illinois since 1970. His research has ranged broadly across Luso-Brazilian literature, and his recent publications include *Negritude As a Theme in the Poetry of the Portuguese-Speaking World* (1970), *Francisco Rodrigues Lobo: Dialogue and Courtly Lore in Renaissance Portugal* (1971), and several articles on major modern writers. He is currently doing research on the use of irony in Portuguese and Brazilian literature, particularly in the works of Raul Leoni.

Index

Acevedo, Jesús T., 111
Actual, 48
Acuña, Manuel, 139
Adán, Martín, 17
Afro-Brazilian cults, 69–72, 79, 80; music, 9, 72–80
Agoristas, 43
Aguilar Mora, Jorge, 121
Aguirre, Manuel Agustín, 22
Aguirre, Raúl Gustavo, 37
Agustín, José, 112, 118, 120, 122, 124
Alarcón, Pedro Antonio de, 104
Alegría, Ciro, 180
Alegría, Fernando, 177, 178, 180, 181, 210, 216
Alencar, José de, 82
Alerano, Sofia, 168
Alessandri, Arturo, 172–74
Allende, Salvador, 4
Altamirano, Ignacio Manuel, 106
Alvaro, Corrado, 168
Amado, Jorge, 6
Amauta, 16
Americanismo literario, 7
Andrade, Mário de, 16, 20, 37, 38, 49, 50, 52, 69
Andrade, Oswald de, 20, 37, 39, 41, 49
Andreyer, Leonid, 115
Apollinaire, Guillaume, 140
Aragon, Louis, 25
Araya, Alfredo, 164
Aridjis, Homero, 10, 152–56
Arlt, Roberto, 161
Arreola, Juan José, 112, 116, 127

Arzubide, Germán List, 23
Asturias, Miguel Angel, 6, 189, 215
Ateneo de la Juventud, 108
Ataíde, Tristão de, *see* Lima, Alceu Amoroso
Avilés Fabila, René, 124–26
Azuela, Mariano, 6, 103, 104, 106, 110, 112, 115, 125

Baciu, Stefan, 26, 48
Balbuena, Bernardo de, 139
Ballesteros, Julián de, 194–96
Balzac, Honoré de, 177
Barrés, Maurice, 57, 58
Barreto, Tobias, 56, 57
Barrios, Eduardo, 6, 179, 186, 212
Beauduin, Nicolas, 46
Bécquer, Adolfo, 194
Benedetti, Mario, 218
Bergson, Henri, 57, 108
Bernhardt, Sarah, 38
Bevilaqua, Clóvis, 56
Bjørnson, Bjørnstjerne, 115
Blest Gana, Alberto, 177, 208, 209, 218
Bombal, María Luisa, 186, 215
Bontempelli, Massimo, 168
Borges, Jorge Luis, 6, 28, 49, 127, 161, 187
Boutroux, Émile, 108
Breton, André, 25
Brushwood, John S., 103, 104
Buchwald, Art, 172

Cabrera Infante, Guillermo, 6, 217
Calderón, Alfonso, 219

Campo, Angel de, 105
Campo, Xorge del, 121
Campos, Haroldo de, 6
Campos Alatorre, Cipriano, 115
Camus, Albert, 3
Candela, Félix, 5
Cansinos-Asséns, Rafael, 28, 34, 35
Carballo, Emmanuel, 115, 116
Cardenal, Ernesto, 6
Cardoso, Fausto, 55
Carlota Amalia, Empress of Mexico, 108
Carpentier, Alejo, 6, 129, 130, 158, 215
Carpio, Manuel, 106
Carter, Boyd G., 13
Caso, Antonio, 108
Castello, Aderaldo, 96
Castillo Infante, Fernando, 172
Castro Alves, Antônio, 82, 91
Cervantes y Saavedra, Miguel de, 39, 195
Chávez, Carlos, 5
Claridad, 31
Cocteau, Jean, 25
Coleman, Alexander, 219
Contemporáneos, 16
Correio Paulistano, 38
Cortázar, Julio, 6, 18, 128, 161
Corvalán, Octavio, 13, 158
Cosmópolis, 28
Costumbrismo, 178, 182, 208, 209, 211, 231
Cousin, Victor, 56
Creationism, 8, 20, 23, 32-37, 44, 49, 185
Criollismo, 7, 11, 12, 178, 182, 196, 207-12, 214-16
Cross, Elsa, 121
Cruchaga, Angel, 34, 35, 46
Cruz, Sor Juana Inés de la, 139
Cruz Costa, João, 52, 53
Cubism, 20, 36, 160, 185, 201, 204
Cúellar, José Tomás de, 102-4
Cuevas, José Luis, 5

Dadaism, 19, 23, 25, 185
Dallal, Alberto, 123
Dalton, Margarita, 121
Dante, Alighieri, 39, 168
Darío, Rubén, 1, 6, 36, 157, 178, 194
Darwin, Charles, 2
Daudet, Alphonse, 105, 107

Del Paso, Fernando, 10, 112, 124, 125, 129-38
D'Halmar, Augusto, 177, 179
Díaz, Don Porfirio, 105, 107, 108
Díaz Arrieta, Hernán [Alone], 178, 209, 210
Díaz Garcés, Joaquín, 164
Díaz Mirón, Salvador, 139
Dickens, Charles, 1, 104, 105
Diego, Gerardo, 36
Donoso, José, 6, 11, 208-32
Dos Passos, John, 112, 114, 115, 117, 160, 215
Dostoevski, Fedor Mijailovich, 31, 212
Drummond de Andrade, Carlos, 6, 17, 37, 41, 49, 51, 52
Dumas, Alexandre (pére), 104
Durán Cerda, Julio, 213
Dutra, Waltensir, 92

Edwards, Alberto, 164
Edwards Bello, Joaquín, 172
Eguren, José María, 15
Einstein, Albert, 2
El Diario Ilustrado, 162-64, 166-69, 173, 175, 190, 193
Eliot, T. S., 3
Elizondo, Salvador, 112, 120, 124
Ellison, Fred, 13
El Mercurio, 34, 46, 175
El Movimiento, 126, 127
El Siglo XIX, 105
Eluard, Paul, 25
Espronceda, José de, 194
Estridentismo, 23, 24, 36, 48, 49, 111
Existentialism, 26
Expressionism, 20, 160, 185, 198, 203-5, 211

Faguet, Émile, 57
Farill, Manuel, 121
Faulkner, William, 3, 112, 113, 115, 160, 215
Fernández de Lizardi, José Joaquín, 10, 102, 110
Fernández Moreno, Baldomero, 29
Ferrero, Mario, 213
Festa, 41
Figueroa Larrain, Emiliano, 173

Flaubert, Gustave, 107
Florit, Eugenio, 15
Franco, Jean, 4
Frazier, Franklin, 67
Freud, Sigmund, 2, 25, 185
Freyre, Gilberto, 83–85, 88, 94, 99, 100
Fuentes, Carlos, 6, 110, 112, 116–19, 125, 127–29, 217
Futurism, 8, 12, 19–24, 44, 160, 185, 200, 201

Gallardo, Salvador, 23
Gallegos, Rómulo, 6, 180
Gálvez, Manuel, 45
Gama, Luis, 82
Gamboa, Federico, 104, 105
García, Lautaro, 169–71, 175
García Games, Julia, 165, 166
García Márquez, Gabriel, 6, 135, 217
García Saldaña, Parménides, 121, 123
Garrido, Luis, 109
Generation of 1950, 11, 213–16
Gentile, Giovanni, 167
Gerchunoff, Alberto, 166
Giaconi, Claudio, 213
Gide, André, 215
Ginastera, Alberto, 5
Gironella, Alberto, 5
Gogol, Nicolas, 212
Goić, Cedomil, 18, 27, 182–85, 187–90, 212
Gómez de la Serna, Ramón, 21, 31
Gonçalves Dias, Antônio, 82
Goncourt, Edmond de, 107
Goncourt, Jules de, 107
González, Manuel Pedro, 104, 117
González de Eslava, Fernán, 139
González de la Garza, Mauricio, 124
González Martínez, Enrique, 140
González Vera, José Santos, 210, 211
Gorki, Alexis Maximovich, 212
Gorostiza, José, 17, 18, 140
Graça Aranha, José Pereira, 9, 51–67
Grecia, 28
Greenberg, Alvin, 232
Guarnieri, Camargo, 5
Guayasamín, Oswaldo, 5
Guillén, Nicolás, 49
Guimarães Rosa, João, 6, 18, 115
Güiraldes, Ricardo, 6, 158, 159, 161, 178

Gullón, Ricardo, 15
Gutiérrez Nájera, Manuel, 105, 106, 139, 157
Guzmán, Humberto, 121
Guzmán, Martín Luis, 110, 112, 127

Hamsun, Knut, 115
Harss, Luis, 3
Hemingway, Ernest, 112, 115, 160, 215
Henríquez Ureña, Max, 157
Henríquez Ureña, Pedro, 108, 109, 110
Hernández, Efrén, 115
Herskovits, Melville, 67, 71, 73, 77, 78
Hidalgo, Alberto, 36, 42
Hinojosa, Armando, 175
Hiriart, Luis, 175
Hübner, Jorge Iván, 213, 214
Hugo, Victor, 107
Huidobro, Vicente, 6, 14, 17, 21, 27, 32–37, 49, 142, 183, 187, 191, 215
Huxley, Aldous, 112

Ibáñez del Campo, Carlos, 166, 167, 170, 173, 174
Icaza, Jorge, 180
Imaginismo, 177–79, 182, 210, 213
Impressionism, 175, 197, 199, 203
Inclán, Luis G., 102–4
Índice, 178, 183, 188

James, Henry, 108
Jiménez, José Olivio, 15
Jiménez, Juan Ramón, 15
Jitanjáfora, 13
Jornal do Comércio, 38
Joyce, James, 3, 112, 117, 123, 130, 133, 160, 187, 215
Juárez, Benito, 108
Júnior, Peregrino, 48

Kafka, Franz, 3, 160
Kayser, Wolfgang, 219–21
Klaxon, 16, 38, 39
Korolenko, Vladimir, 115

Lafourcade, Enrique, 213, 214, 216
Lagerlöf, Selma, 115
La Información, 162
La Nación, 166

La Onda, 123
Larra, Mariano José de, 195
Larrea, Juan, 36
Larreta, Enrique, 157, 158
Lastarria, José Victorino, 208
Latorre, Mariano, 178, 179, 209, 210
Lawrence, D. H., 115
Laxness, Halldor Kiljan, 115
Le Figaro, 20
Leo XIII, 57
León, Miguel Angel, 19
Le Parc, Julio, 5
Le Roy, Grégoire, 57
Lesage, Alain René, 103
Letelier, María, 161
Letras, 178, 182, 188
Lezama Lima, José, 6, 18, 129, 130, 133
Lillo, Baldomero, 179
Lima, Alceu Amoroso, 14, 52
Lima, Jorge de, 6, 9, 40, 49, 81–94, 97, 99–101
Lins do Rêgo, José, 6, 9, 81–83, 94–101
Lispector, Clarice, 49
Lobato, Monteiro, 82
López Albújar, Enrique, 44
López Portillo y Rojas, José, 104, 105
López Velarde, Ramón, 140, 155
López y Fuentes, Gregorio, 112, 180
Lomax, Alan, 79
Los Contemporáneos, 111, 140, 155
Los Diez, 164
Lott, Robert E., 185
Lowry, Malcolm, 115
Lugones, Leopoldo, 30, 157

Magallanes Moure, Manuel, 164, 165
Magical Realism, 181, 196
Mallea, Eduardo, 6, 189
Manjarrez, Héctor, 121
Maples Arce, Manuel, 23, 48, 49
Marechal, Leopoldo, 129
Mariani, Roberto, 31
Mariátegui, José Carlos, 17, 49
Marinetti, Filippo Tommaso, 20–23, 58, 200
Marín, Juan, 22
Martí, José, 157
Martínez Zuviría, Gustavo [Hugo Wast], 30
Martín Fierro, 16, 22, 29–32, 48

Martins, Wilson, 13
Maupassant, Guy de, 107
Mayo, Hugo, 36, 37
Maximilian, Emperor of Mexico, 108
Meireles, Cecília, 41
Melo Neto, João Cabral de, 6, 18
Mendes, Murilo, 41
Méndez, Evar, 29
Miró Quesada S., Aurelio, 46
Mistral, Gabriela, 6, 191
Modernism: Brazilian, 8, 20, 21, 37–41, 44, 48, 49, 51, 52, 101; Spanish American, 12, 14, 18, 41, 108, 155, 157, 158, 197–201
Monguió, Luis, 13
Montes de Oca, Marco Antonio, 10, 128, 141–45, 155
Moretti, Marino, 168
Moro, César, 26
Mundonovismo, 7, 178

Naturalism, 211
Neimeyer, Oscar, 5
Neorealism, 180, 212
Neruda, Pablo, 6, 17, 49, 174, 191–93
Nervo, Amado, 105, 106, 139
"New novel," 10, 119–25, 129
Nezahualcóyotl, 139
Nietzsche, Friedrich Wilhelm, 61
Nist, John, 13
Nord-Sud, 33

O Estado de São Paulo, 20
O'Gorman, Juan, 5
Onetti, Juan Carlos, 6, 189
Orozco, José Clemente, 5
Ortiz, Orlando, 121
Ortiz de Montellano, Bernardo, 111
Orwell, George, 151
Otero, Alejandro, 5
Ovalle, Pedro, 164

Pacheco, José Emilio, 10, 112, 119, 148–52, 155, 156
Pacífico Magazine, 164, 165
Palma, Clemente, 25
Papini, Giovanni, 168
Parnassianism, 157
Parra, Nicanor, 6, 18
Payno, Manuel, 102

Paz, Octavio, 6, 18, 113, 115, 125, 127, 128, 131, 139–41, 155, 156
Pellicer, Carlos, 140, 141, 155, 156
Pereda, José María de, 104, 107
Peret, Benjamin, 26
Pérez Galdós, Benito, 107
Perón, Juan Domingo, 4
Petorutti, Emilio, 5
Picasso, Pablo, 3
Pichia, Menotti de, 40
Picón Salas, Manuel, 15
Pimentel, Francisco, 106
Pirandello, Luigi, 168, 185, 197
Pollak, Louis, 165
Portinari, Cândido, 5
Postmodernism, 15, 17, 43, 157, 158, 160, 178
Postvanguardism, 17, 18
Pound, Ezra, 120
Prado, Bento, Jr., 53
Prado, Pedro, 164, 177, 179, 186, 212
Premodernism (Brazilian), 14
Prieto, José Joaquín, 161
Prieto Hurtado, Jenaro, 161
Prieto Letelier, Jenaro, 11, 157–207
Prisma, 29
Proa, 16, 29, 31
Prometeo, 21
Proust, Marcel, 3, 160, 174, 185, 188, 189

Que, 27
Quintilla, Luis, 23
Quiroga, Horacio, 6

Ramos, Artur, 67
Rangel Bendeira, Antônio, 90, 91, 96, 100
Realism, 107, 177, 209–12
Reverdy, Pierre, 33
Revista de Antropofagia, 16
Revista de Avance, 16
Revista Oral, 42
Revueltas, José, 112, 113
Revueltas, Silvestre, 5
Reyes, Alfonso, 108, 127
Reyes, Bernardo, 109
Rhode, Jorge Max, 30
Ribeiro, René, 67, 73
Ricardo, Cassiano, 40
Rilke, Rainer Maria, 185
Rivera, Diego, 5

Rivera, José Eustasio, 6
Robbe-Grillet, Alain, 112
Rodó, José Enrique, 157
Rodrigues, Nina, 67
Rodríguez Monegal, 129
Rojas, Manuel, 181, 215
Rojas González, Francisco, 115
Rojas Pinilla, Gustavo, 4
Rokha, Pablo de, 191, 192
Rolling Stones, 121
Rulfo, Juan, 6, 112, 114–16, 215
Rumazo González, Alfonso, 47
Runrunismo, 43

Sábato, Ernesto, 6, 189
Sainz, Gustavo, 112, 121, 122
Salgado, Plínio, 40
Sand, George, 107
Santiván, Fernando, 177, 179
Sardou, Victorien, 175
Sarduy, Severo, 222
Sarraute, Nathalie, 112
Sartre, Jean-Paul, 3
Savia Moderna, 108
Schmidt, Augusto Frederico, 40, 49
Schneider, Luis Mario, 23
Schulman, Ivan, 15
Seeger, Charles, 80
Semana de Arte Moderna, 19–22, 25, 38, 41, 52, 54
Shakespeare, William, 39
Sierra, Justo, 105, 108
Sillanpää, Frans Eemil, 115
Silva, Luis A., 169
Silva Brito, Mário da, 24
Silva Castro, Raúl, 218
Silva Vildósola, C., 173, 174
Simplismo, 42
Siqueiros, David Alfaro, 5
Sommers, Joseph, 117
Sotomayor, José Martínez, 111
Spota, Luis, 127
Stimson, Frederick S., 13
Stravinsky, Igor, 3
Strozzi, Luis, 165
Subercaseaux, Benjamín, 215
Subercaseaux, Pedro, 165
Sue, Eugéne, 107
Surrealism, 8, 12, 19, 20, 25–27, 43, 49, 160, 182–90, 197, 203, 206

Swift, Jonathan, 173
Symbolism, 12, 14, 157

Tablada, José Juan, 105, 140, 155
Tamayo, Rufino, 5
Teitelboim, Volodia, 192
Tolstoy, Leo, 177
Torre, Guillermo de, 12, 28
Torres Bodet, Jaime, 111
Tovar, Juan, 124, 126
Trujillo, Rafael, 4
Turgenev, Ivan, 212

Ultra, 28
Ultraísmo, 8, 20, 23, 28–32, 36, 44, 49, 185
Unamuno, Miguel de, 197

Vaise, Emilio, 180
Valdés, Rafael, 164
Valera, Juan, 107
Valle-Arizpe, Artemio de, 111
Vallejo, César, 6, 26, 47, 49
Vanguardism, 7, 11, 17, 18, 23, 31, 43, 44,
    46–49, 111, 158, 174, 182, 183, 185–207,
    212
Varas, Fernando, 169

Vargas, Getúlio, 4, 52
Vargas Llosa, Mario, 6, 135–38, 217
Vasconcelos, José, 108
Vega, Daniel de la, 175
Vega, Manuel, 166
Vela, Arqueles, 23
Verde, 48
Vial, Doña Elvira, 163, 170, 171
Villa-Lobos, Heitor, 5
Villaurrutia, Xavier, 27, 49, 111, 140
Vitalism, 57

Weber, Eugen, 1
Westphalen, Emilio, 26
Whitman, Walt, 88
Woolf, Thomas, 112
Woolf, Virginia, 160, 215

Yáñez, Agustín, 6, 112, 113, 115, 189, 215
Yankas, Lautaro, 212

Zaid, Gabriel, 10, 145–48, 155, 156
Zamora, Diego, 165
Zola, Émile, 104, 107
Zorrilla y del Moral, José, 194